Lauer Series in Rhetoric and Composition
Series Editors, Catherine Hobbs and Patricia Sullivan

LAUER SERIES IN RHETORIC AND COMPOSITION
Series Editors, Catherine Hobbs and Patricia Sullivan

The Lauer Series in Rhetoric and Composition honors the contributions Janice Lauer Hutton has made to the emergence of Rhetoric and Composition as a disciplinary study. It publishes scholarship that carries on Professor Lauer's varied work in the history of written rhetoric, disciplinarity in composition studies, contemporary pedagogical theory, and written literacy theory and research.

Books in the Series

Rhetorics, Poetics, and Cultures: Refiguring College English Studies (Expanded Edition) by James A. Berlin (2003)

Historical Studies of Writing Program Administration

Historical Studies of Writing Program Administration

Individuals, Communities, and the Formation of a Discipline

Editors
Barbara L'Eplattenier
Lisa Mastrangelo

Parlor Press
West Lafayette, Indiana
www.parlorpress.com

Parlor Press LLC, West Lafayette, Indiana 47906

© 2004 by Parlor Press
All rights reserved.
Printed in the United States of America
Acknowledgments are listed on page 283.

SAN: 254-8879

Library of Congress Control Number: 2004103502

Historical Studies of Writing Program Administration : Individuals, Communities, and the Formation of a Discipline / edited by Barbara L'Eplattenier and Lisa Mastrangelo

    p.   cm.   – (Lauer series in rhetoric and composition)

Includes introduction, notes, illustrations, bibliographical references, and index.

1. English language – Rhetoric –Study and teaching. 2. English language – Rhetoric – Study and teaching – History. 3. English language – Rhetoric – Study and teaching – 19th century. 4. English language – Rhetoric – Study and teaching – 20th century. 5. Report writing – Study and teaching (Higher)
I. Title. II. Series.

ISBN 1-932559-22-1   (Paper)
ISBN 1-932559-23-X   (Cloth)
ISBN 1-932559-24-8   (Adobe eBook)
ISBN 1-932559-25-6   (TK3)

Printed on acid-free paper.

Cover photographs key (starting top right, moving left to right and down): Laura J. Wylie, Gertrude Buck and Laura J. Wylie, Edwin Hopkins, Regina Crandall, Clara Frances Stevens, Rose Colby.

Parlor Press, LLC is an independent publisher of scholarly and trade titles in print and multimedia formats. This book is also available in printed cloth, as well as in Adobe eBook and Night Kitchen (TK3) formats, from Parlor Press on the WWW at http://www.parlorpress.com. For submission information or to find out about Parlor Press publications, write to Parlor Press, 816 Robinson St., West Lafayette, Indiana, 47906, or e-mail editor@parlorpress.com.

We would like to dedicate this book to all of those administrators whose stories remain untold; those who supported us in this endeavor; and Betty and Janet, who were there when we weren't.

—Barbara L'Eplattenier and Lisa Mastrangelo

Contents

List of Figures and Tables	xi
Preface	xiii
Edward M. White	
Acknowledgments	xv
Why Administrative Histories?	xvii
Barbara L'Eplattenier and Lisa Mastrangelo	

Part I: Individuals   3

1 The WPA as Publishing Scholar: Edwin Hopkins   5
and The Labor and Cost of the Teaching of English
Randall Popken

2 "Replacing Nice, Thin Bryn Mawr Miss Crandall   23
with Fat, Harvard Savage": WPAs at Bryn Mawr
College, 1902 to 1923
D'Ann George

3 Cooperative Writing 'Program' Administration at   37
Illinois State Normal University: The Committee
on English of 1904-05 and the Influence of
Professor J. Rose Colby
Kenneth Lindblom and Patricia A. Dunn

4 Building a Career by Directing Composition: 71
Harvard, Professionalism, and Stith Thompson
at Indiana University
Jill Terry Rudy

Part II: Communities — 89

5 The "Advance" Toward Democratic Administration: Laura Johnson Wylie and Gertrude Buck of Vassar College — 91
Suzanne Bordelon

6 "Is It the Pleasure of this Conference to Have Another?" Women's Colleges Meeting and Talking about Writing in the Progressive Era — 117
Lisa Mastrangelo and Barbara L'Eplattenier

7 Sifting Through Fifty Years of Change: Writing Program Administration at an Historically Black University — 145
Deany M. Cheramie

Part III: Discipline — 167

8 A Genesis of Writing Program Administration: George Jardine at the University of Glasgow — 169
Lynée Lewis Gaillet

9 Moving Toward a Group Identity: WPA Professionalization from the 1940s to the 1970s — 191
Amy Heckathorn

10 Representing the Intellectual Work of Writing Program Administration: Professional Narratives of George Wykoff at Purdue, 1933-1967 — 221
Shirley K Rose

11 Industrial-Strength Composition and the Impact of Load on Teaching — 241
John Heyda

12 Doomed to Repeat It?: A Needed Space for Critique in Historical Recovery — 263
Jeanne Gunner

Contributing Authors — 279
Acknowledgments and Illustration Credits — 283
Index — 285

List of Figures and Tables

Table 1: List of 1919 Conference Participants	122
Figure 1. Wykoff's c.v. card page 1	230
Figure 2. Wykoff's c.v. card page 2	230
Figure 3. Wykoff's c.v. card page 3	231
Figure 4. Wykoff's Personnel Record page 1	232
Figure 5. Wykoff's Personnel Record page 2	233
Figure 6. Wykoff's Personnel Record page 3	234–35

Preface

Edward M. White

Jorge Luis Borges, in his essay "The Tradition of Kafka," argues that a tradition can be a kind of back-formation: Kafka, he asserts, created his own tradition. That is, a series of forebears of Kafka have written throughout the ages in ways anticipating Kafka's style, but nobody actually thought of linking them until scholars began to study the work of Kafka and look for antecedents. At that point, the tradition gained shape and numbers of writers from the past seemed to fit together in a group: now, centuries after they first wrote, we can speak of the Kafka tradition.

And so it is here. Most of the beleaguered professionals we meet in this unusual work of history would be astonished to find themselves in the same book, or even considered as Writing Program Administrators. The modern concept of the WPA—with wide-ranging responsibilities for writing assessment, the writing curriculum, course staffing and standards, writing across the curriculum, and in some cases the literacy standard for graduates—is barely three generations old. Edward P. J. Corbett dates the first American WPA at 1946. The National Council of WPAs was formed in 1970, followed shortly afterwards by the journal *WPA: Writing Program Administration*. The first book on the subject was Albert Kitzhaber's *Themes, Theories, and Therapy: The Teaching of Writing in College* (1963). And yet, WPA work needed to be done as writing programs developed at least 200 years ago and a number of heroic individuals wound up doing it, with little reward or compensation. The essays collected here represent the first effort to document and shape the WPA tradition, to provide a professional genealogy for present-day WPAs, often struggling with the same problems that beset those doing the same job without the name many years earlier.

The accounts of early faculty serving the WPA function before the title was even thought of are oddly familiar. My favorite is Professor Edwin Hopkins, desperately trying to find time and clerical help for his major work on the teaching loads of writing teachers. Randall Popken's essay on Hopkins includes a letter to a key administrator of the University of Kansas in 1917 in which Hopkins asserts that he has spent ten percent of his yearly salary of $3,000 on providing his own (and the department's) clerical help. His pleas for enough funds to do his job well and for enough assigned time to get his book completed will remind many modern WPAs of their own memos—assuming they can find the time to read this ample volume.

Many university and college writing programs remain rudimentary even now, with little sense of the history of the field or of those who have led it through the centuries. Although 65 doctoral programs in rhetoric and composition are in place at the turn of the twenty-first century, professional leadership of writing programs remains relatively unusual in American colleges and universities and almost unknown in other countries. But modern programs are slowly gaining the kind of history that leads to status. By combining rhetoric with composition, the field gained the prestige of an ancient study whose power dominated the curriculum for over a thousand years. Historians of writing programs, such as James Berlin and Thomas Miller, have provided grounds for an elaborated tradition of teaching and scholarship. Now Barbara L'Eplattenier and Lisa Mastrangelo come forward with this rich compilation of essays, detailing the evolution of the modern WPA in a remarkable book with unforgettable characters. They have now created the tradition of the WPA in the university and the history of English studies will never again be quite the same.

—Edward M. White
Flagstaff, Arizona
December, 2003

Acknowledgments

We would like to thank those who helped make this book possible: the people at Parlor Press—David Blakesley for his encouragement, editorial assistance and willingness to work with novice editors; Patricia A. Sullivan, Catherine Hobbs, and Ed White for their editorial help. We also wish to acknowledge and thank Janice M. Lauer for her continual support of the project. As director of the Rhetoric and Composition program at Purdue, Janice served as an inspiration for both us and the collection. This collection exists, in great part, because we wondered where *her* story—and others like it—were told in the history of our field. Amy Heckathorn graciously (and quickly) proofread the manuscript for us at the last minute.

Additionally, this collection would not have been possible without any of the archivists, some of whom are thanked by name in the collection. As every historian knows, a good archivist is essential to the success of any historical project. Knowledge of the archives—and the ability to locate materials—is a special gift and we acknowledge this, and them, gratefully.

Barb L'Eplattenier: I would like to thank my colleagues at the University of Arkansas—Little Rock, who consistently encouraged me in this endeavor. Chuck Anderson was incredibly generous with invaluable advice on the proposal and editing process; his excitement when we signed our contract was as great as ours. Rich Raymond, a wonderful chair and colleague, supported this project from its inception and encouraged me to proceed with it. Karen Palmer was, as always, gracious about my frantic inquiries regarding faxed permissions. Finally, this project has been made all the richer and exciting because of Lisa's laughter, hard work, editorial skills, and raccoon/squirrel/dog stories. Working with her is a joy and a pleasure.

Lisa Mastrangelo: I would like to thank my colleagues at the College of Saint Elizabeth. In particular, my department chair, Kathleen Hunter, has been excited and supportive about the project from the beginning. Anthony has been consistently patient with my disappearances and a more-than-willing reader. Barb has been a wonderful co-conspirator. Her presence made me realize yet again why writing is not—and should not be—a solitary activity.

Why Administrative Histories?

Barbara L'Eplattenier
Lisa Mastrangelo

> How is it that thought detaches itself from the squares it inhabited before—general grammar, natural history, wealth—and allows what less than twenty years before had been posited and affirmed in the luminous space of understanding to topple down into error, into the realm of fantasy, into non-knowledge? What event, what law do they obey, these mutations that suddenly decide that things are no longer perceived, described, expressed, characterized, classified, and known in the same way, and that it is no longer wealth, living beings, and discourse that are presented to knowledge in the interstices of words or through their transparencies, but beings radically different from them?
>
> —*Michel Foucault*

Historical Studies of Writing Program Administration: Individuals, Communities, and the Formation of a Discipline presents a rich, previously unknown history focusing on the existence and work of people who performed what we today call writing program administration prior to the formation of the Council of Writing Program Administrators in 1976. The stories told in this collection are the result of digging for archival records in different places, viewing historical documents through different lenses, and looking beyond the surface appearance of academic careers and departmental histories. These unearthed stories reveal WPA work that occurred in different countries, took place in non-research-oriented universities, involved females instead of males, and/or addressed issues such as workload and professional development. These histories reveal what happened within universities that allowed various programs to exist; they tell about the internal ideological, fiscal, and political arguments used in relation to introductory composition programs and WPA work. These stories tell us how WPAs worked to professionalize and intellectualize their programmatic work, often in the face of unsupportive, unreflective, and/or uninterested higher administration personnel. Finally, these histories remind us of the larger political issues at stake, not just in the administration of programs, but also in the writing of such histories.

Traditionally, histories that focused on introductory composition could be divided into roughly two groups: 1) inquiries into the ideological/pedagogical theories and practices of composition; and 2) more localized inquiries into the classroom practices of individual teachers. Perhaps the most famous and influential of the sweeping histories are James Berlin's *Writing Instruction in Nineteenth Century American Colleges* and *Rhetoric and Reality*.[1] Of the pedagogical histories, many famous teachers have been studied, such as Fred Newton Scott and Gertrude Buck.[2,3]

These histories provided the ideological and pedagogical history of the composition classroom needed to legitimize our discipline. However, they do not reflect the fact that these programs and teachers required an administrative space within which to function. Contrary to the popular thought that such needs are new, Warner Taylor's comprehensive 1929 survey, *A National Survey of Conditions in Freshman English,* indicates that freshman composition in the late 1920s was nearly ubiquitous on college campuses. Taylor distributed surveys asking about the freshman composition programs to 300 colleges or universities with enrollments of 500 students or more, located in all parts of the country and representative of all types of institutions. An astonishing 232 (77.3 percent) of the schools returned the survey; there was an average of 400 freshmen per school. About 65 percent of the schools indicated that they classified or ranked their students in some way (Brereton 545-46). The question at issue here becomes the tasks inherent in such classification work, not the actual job title of the person doing the classification. Recognized or ignored, titled or untitled, appreciated or unappreciated, paid or unpaid—someone classified students, assigned teachers, worried about standards, and did all the other

Why Administrative Histories?

administrative tasks inherent to writing programs. Someone, much earlier than 1976, functioned as a WPA.

While some of the stories told in this collection may sound familiar, using an administrative lens to examine the past changes the history being told. It locates the writing program within the larger institutional context that so often explains their formation. As any WPA knows, local politics are an important component in the creation and shape of the composition program; as the chapters in this collection demonstrate, such politics usually involve interactions with deans, presidents, chancellors, boards of trustees, alumni, and the like. This collection argues that in ignoring such interactions we miss an opportunity to explore a significant factor in the existence and formation of the composition program. As such, an administrative history asks questions such as these: How was the introductory composition program viewed by the rest of the university? What kind of political sway did the administrator have with the university president or other higher-level administrators? What do the fiscal reports and the other types of documentation that invariably accompany the running of a department reveal? Can they be located? What other documents might tell us about the negotiating and hidden influences that affect political decisions? How did these people represent their work? Was there a community of like-minded people? What was the impact of their work? How do external political issues become institutionalized both administratively and departmentally? These types of questions are quite different from those that drive a history focused on the lives of the students and/or teachers.

It is not surprising, however, that we have been blinded to the need for administrative histories. There is, of course, Edward P. J. Corbett's famous 1993 statement quoted in several of the manuscripts in this collection:

> I have been unable to discover from my readings whether early in this century any college English departments in America had such a position as the now familiar director of freshman English. I suspect that in the 1920's, 1930's and the first half of the 1940's the composition program was such a relatively small operation in our colleges and universities that [. . .] some factotum [sic] in the department could run the

programs out of his or her back pocket. ("A History of Writing Program Administration" 63)

Corbett's statement has been accepted at face value for a long time, and it is easy to understand why. Published research on administrative work often did not describe that work in administrative terms (see Heckathorn, Heyda, and Gaillet) or the administrative aspect of people's work was seen by others as a tangential component in their career and not worthy of notice or reward (see Popken, George, Rudy, and Rose). In a world where the important work of administration rarely had (and still rarely has) a valued position within the university system of rewards, it is not surprising that few early administrators published explicitly on their administrative work. More astonishingly, however, is that some did publish on precisely these issues (see Heckathorn and Heyda). Both university administrators and writing program administrators need to rethink the classification of such work (see Gunner). Aside from their publications, much of the work in administering writing programs is not even recognized as reflecting larger social issues, but rather is seen as wholly apolitical and pragmatic (see Gunner and Cheramie).

In part, these stories have remained untold because of their very nature. Administrative work is not always easy to find within archival documents; its traces are often destroyed or hidden in a multitude of files within the archives or a professor's files—unlike the more easily accessible and recognizable students' papers and textbooks. Administrative documents end up in the president's files or the faculty minutes or in letters to members of the board of trustees or the annual reports of the department; these are not always available or even considered when researching programs (see Bordelon, Mastrangelo and L'Eplattenier, Cheramie, George, and Lindblom and Dunn).

Another reason for the lack of previous attention to administrative histories is that, as contemporary WPAs know, administrative decision-making often occurs in ways that are never recorded; informal decision-making, trade-offs, and unexplained accommodations are common. Spur-of-the-moment administrative decisions can have a great deal of impact on the life of a program or department but are not always significantly explained within documents. Administrators are also not likely to save their annual reports because they believe in their intrinsic value to future audiences—or take such pride in their work that they believe it should be saved for posterity, as are students' records and papers. Memos on teacher-student ratios, salaries, working conditions, professional development and the like are rarely seen as important historical documents: rather, they are the ephemeral, disposable documents of everyday administrative work.

Despite the difficulties in doing administrative histories, our call for papers brought us a much richer, varied, and exciting collection of work than we had anticipated. Once we had gathered the manuscripts, however, we were left with the difficult task of organizing them into a cohesive whole because of their richness and variety. Rather than present the work chronologically, as was our first impulse, we have organized it into three sections: Individuals, Communities, and Discipline. A chronological order suggests a neat and steady historical progression, implying an idealized—although not necessarily ideal—past, something with which we were quite uncomfortable. Grouping the chapters thematically reflects our belief that the "picture" is not quite so neat. This presents a more complicated notion of WPA histories, a concrete recognition of the multiplicity of ways in which histories function. For example, does an institution struggling to design a legitimate, scholarly composition program (Cheramie) constitute an essay on community or discipline? Does the work of George Jardine (Gaillet) in the eighteenth century constitute the work of an individual or disciplinary formation? Does Stith Thompson's academic career (Rudy) represent an individual's story or a disciplinary grand narrative? Our organization of the essays into these three groups still raises issues for us, but it reflects the complexity that exists within this history, which is not simply a series of apolitical events placed on a timeline.

Individuals

Much work in the history of rhetoric and composition as it currently exists focuses on teachers such as Gertrude Buck and Fred Newton Scott. The first chapters in the collection present figures who also served as administrators. Hopkins, Colby, and Crandall all worked in positions such as "writing director," "director of the writing program," or "head of the essay department" (See Popken, Lindblom and Dunn, and George). Similarly, Stith Thompson (see Rudy) worked within composition as an administrator while attempting to create his professional identity in other subject areas (in Thompson's case, folklore). All of their stories reflect the early confusion (still present today) about the legitimacy and professional nature of the writing program administrator position. It becomes clear in this group of chapters that writing program administrators, regardless of their time period, have struggled with professional identity and job descriptions, fighting a number of battles: writing administrator vs. the department, writing administrator vs. the university, and writing administrator vs. university administration. These chapters add depth and breadth to current conversations about composition and rhetoric's history: what were people doing about writing program administration, when were they doing it, and how did they do it?

Communities

The individuals noted above fought difficult and solitary battles with colleagues, departments, and higher administration. Others, however, did not have to work alone. The chapters in this section reflect the different types of communities formed in the struggle to develop and administer writing programs. Some clearly devoted planning and significant resources to their programs (see Bordelon and Mastrangelo and L'Eplattenier). Others worked diligently, although without much support or resources, until the renewal of interest in composition in the 1970s (see Cheramie). Often, community was the driving force behind such programs. Regardless of the investment into the program, all focused on how best to help students succeed, however that might be defined. The chapters in this section reveal that these communities struggled with issues that sound familiar to most administrators today: entrance examinations, placement into writing sections, use of standardized English, and a unified curriculum. Their efforts to improve the quality and quantity of their writing offerings are remarkable.

Discipline

The essays in the third section reflect the many facets of disciplinary formation. Ranging in time from the eighteenth century to modern day, these chapters trace the development of an active, intellectual, professionalized WPA community. At the heart of these chapters are the questions of professionalization that a community must wrestle with as it becomes a discipline—issues such as representation (Rose), naming (Heckathorn and Rose), institutional standing (Heyda), disciplinary identity (Heckathorn), and standards (Heyda). All of these re-

Why Administrative Histories? xxiii

flections on our past, however, must be accompanied by some critique of the current WPA positions and a vision of the future (see Heyda and Gunner).

This collection is really just the first telling of a previously uncharted story. As with any "first" history, we know that it has gaps, faults, and cracks in it, which now can be recast, retold, and reformulated for a different and continued reading and understanding. In the spirit of Foucault, we hope that the histories presented here will not remain stable but will continue to be explored, challenged, and built upon by successive generations of curious researchers and historians.

Notes

1. Other ideological/pedagogical histories that trace the pedagogical trends, through textbooks, classroom material, or student and teacher responses, of the nineteenth and twentieth century include Johnson's *Nineteenth-Century Rhetoric in North America*; Crowley's *The Methodical Memory*; Wozniak's *English Composition in Eastern Colleges, 1850-1940*; Connors's *Composition-Rhetoric: Backgrounds, Theory, and Pedagogy*, Halloran's "From Rhetoric to Composition: The Teaching of Writing in America to 1900;" Schultz's *The Young Composers;* Adams's *A Group of Their Own;* Varnum's *Fencing with Words*; Miller's *The Formation of College English;* and Russell's *Writing in the Academic Disciplines*. Areas related to composition and rhetoric, such as professional writing, have followed the same trend of ideological/pedagogical issues. Katherine Adams presents the mostly male world of professional writing pedagogy in *A History of Professional Writing Pedagogy Instruction in American Colleges*. Michael G. Moran has examined Frank Aydelotte's pedagogical approach at MIT. Bibliographies on the subject of the history of professional writing include William Rivers's "Studies in the History of Business and Technical Writing" and W. Tracy Dillon's "The New Historicism and Studies in the History of Business and Technical Writing."

2. Gertrude Buck and her theory of organic rhetoric, for example, have been explored in great detail (Abordonado; Vivian; Koch; Conway "Buck;" Mulderig "Buck;" Campbell, *Toward a Feminist Rhetoric* and "Gertrude Buck"). Other studied notables include Clara Stevens who taught at Mount Holyoke during the Progressive Era (Smith; Mastrangelo) and Mary Augusta Jordan, a contemporary of Buck's, who taught at Smith (Wagner; Kates). Donald Stewart focused on Fred Newton Scott and his program at Ann Arbor and by default, Child and Kittredge at Harvard ("The Barnyard Goose;" "Rediscovering Fred Newton Scott;" "Two Model Teachers;" "A Model for Our Times;" "Harvard's Influence on English Studies;" "The Status of Composition;" *The Life and Legacy of Fred Newton Scott*). In addition to his

archival work (*The Origins of Composition Studies in the American College, 1875-1925*), John Brereton has explored the pedagogy and textbooks of John Matthews Manly, who taught at Brown and the University of Chicago, and Norman Foerster, who taught at North Carolina and Iowa ("Composition and English Departments").

3. Another area of rhetorical histories focuses on alternative sites of rhetoric or the activities of "nontraditional" rhetors. Examples of these texts include Brody's *Manly Writing*; Ritchie and Ronald's *Available Means*; Kates's *Activist Rhetorics and American Higher Education*; Logan's *We Are Coming*; Royster's *Traces in a Stream*; Johnson's *Gender and Rhetorical Space in American Life, 1866-1920*; Mattingly's *Well-Tempered Women*; and Pfaelzer's *Parlor Radical*.

Works Cited

Abordonado, Valentina M. "Gertrude Buck's Theory of Discourse: A New Historical Perspective." Conference on College Composition and Communication. San Diego, Mar. 31–April 3, 1993.

Adams, Katherine. *A Group of Their Own: College Writing Courses and American Women Writers, 1880-1940.* Albany: SUNY P, 2001.

—. *A History of Professional Writing Instruction in American Colleges: Years of Acceptance, Growth, and Doubt.* Dallas: Southern Methodist UP, 1993.

Ballif, Michelle. "Re/Dressing Histories; or, On Re/Covering Figures Who Have Been Laid Bare By Our Gaze." *Rhetoric Society Quarterly* 22 (1992): 91-97.

Berlin, James. *Rhetoric and Reality: Writing Instruction in American Colleges, 1900-1985.* Carbondale: Southern Illinois UP, 1987.

—. *Writing Instruction in Nineteenth-Century American Colleges.* Carbondale: Southern Illinois UP, 1984.

Brereton, John C., ed. *The Origins of Composition Studies in the American College, 1875-1925: A Documentary History.* Pittsburgh: U of Pittsburgh P, 1995.

—. "Composition and English Departments, 1900-1925." *Audits of Meaning: A Festschrift in Honor of Anne Berthoff.* Ed. Louis Z. Smith. Portsmouth, NH: Boynton Cook, 1988. 41-54.

Brody, Miriam. *Manly Writing: Gender, Rhetoric, and the Rise of Composition.* Carbondale: Southern Illinois UP, 1993.

Campbell, JoAnn. "Gertrude Buck and the Celebration of Community: A History of Writing Instruction at Vassar College, 1897-1922." Diss. U of Texas, Austin, 1989.

—, ed. *Toward a Feminist Rhetoric: The Writing of Gertrude Buck.* Pittsburgh; U of Pittsburgh P, 1996.

Connors, Robert. *Composition-Rhetoric: Backgrounds, Theory, and Pedagogy.* Pittsburgh: U of Pittsburgh P, 1997.

Conway, Kathryn M. "Gertrude Buck, Rhetorician." Conference on College Composition and Communication. St. Louis, March 17-19, 1988.

Corbett, Edward. "A History of Writing Program Administration." *Learning from the Histories of Rhetoric.* Ed. Theresa Enos. Carbondale: Southern Illinois UP, 1993. 60-74.

Crowley, Sharon. *The Methodological Memory: Invention in Current-Traditional Rhetoric.* Carbondale: Southern Illinois UP, 1990.

Dillon, W. Tracey. "The New Historicism and Studies in the History of Business and Technical Writing." *Journal of Business and Technical Communication* 11.1 (1997): 60-73.

Foucault, Michel. *The Order of Things.* New York: Vintage Books, 1994.

Halloran, Michael S. "From Rhetoric to Composition: The Teaching of Writing in America to 1900." *A Short History of Writing Instruction: From Ancient Greece to Twentieth-Century America.* Ed. James J. Murphy. Davis, CA: Hermagoras P, 1990. 151-82.

Johnson, Nan. *Gender and Rhetorical Space in American Life, 1866-1910.* Carbondale: Southern Illinois UP, 2002.

—. *Nineteenth-Century Rhetoric in North America.* Carbondale: Southern Illinois UP, 1991.

Kates, Susan. *Activist Rhetorics and American Higher Education, 1885-1937.* Carbondale: Southern Illinois UP, 2001.

Koch, Kevin James. "Gertrude Buck and the Emergence of a Transactional Theory of Language." Diss. U of Iowa, 1992.

Logan, Shirley Wilson. *"We Are Coming": The Persuasive Discourse of Nineteenth-Century Black Women.* Carbondale: Southern Illinois UP, 1999.

Mastrangelo, Lisa. "Learning from the Past: Composition, Rhetoric, and Debate at Mount Holyoke College." *Rhetoric Review* 18 (Fall 1999): 46-64.

Mattingly, Carol. *Well-Tempered Women: Nineteenth-Century Temperance Rhetoric.* Carbondale: Southern Illinois UP, 1998.

Miller, Thomas. *The Formation of College English.* Pittsburgh: U of Pittsburgh P, 1997.

Moran, Michael G. "The Road Not Taken: Frank Aydelotte and the Thought Approach to Engineering Writing." *Technical Communication Quarterly* 2.2 (1993): 161-75.

Mulderig, Gerald. "Gertrude Buck's Rhetorical Theory and Modern Composition Teaching." *Rhetoric Society Quarterly* 14 (1984): 95-104.

Pfaelzer, Jean. *Parlor Radical: Rebecca Harding Davis and the Origins of American Social Realism.* Pittsburgh: U of Pittsburgh P, 1997.

Rivers, William E. "Studies in the History of Business and Technical Writing: A Bibliographical Essay." *Journal of Business and Technical Communication* 8.1 (1994): 5-67.

Ritchie, Joy, and Kate Ronald. *Available Means: An Anthology of Women's Rhetoric(s)*. Pittsburgh: U of Pittsburgh P, 2001.
Royster, Jacqueline Jones. *Traces of a Stream: Literacy and Social Change among African-American Women*. Pittsburgh: U of Pittsburgh P, 2000.
Russell, David R. *Writing in the Academic Disciplines, 1870-1990: A Curricular History*. Carbondale: Southern Illinois UP, 1991.
Schultz, Lucille M. *The Young Composers: Composition's Beginnings in Nineteenth-Century Schools*. Carbondale: Southern Illinois UP, 1999.
Smith, Carolyn H. "Narratives of Discourse Beyond Academic Boundaries: Mount Holyoke, 1897-1904." Conference on College Composition and Communication. Milwaukee, March 27-30, 1996.
Stewart, Donald C. "A Model for Our Times: Fred Newton Scott's Rhetoric Program at Michigan." *Learning from the Histories of Rhetoric*. Ed. Theresa Enos. Carbondale: Southern Illinois UP, 1993. 42-59.
—. "Rediscovering Fred Newton Scott." *College English* 40 (1979): 539-47.
—. "The Barnyard Goose, History, and Fred Newton Scott." *English Journal* 67 (1978): 14-17.
—. "Two Model Teachers and the Harvardization of English Departments." *The Rhetorical Tradition and Modern Writing*. Ed. James J. Murphy. New York: MLA, 1982. 118-29.
—. "Harvard's Influence on English Studies: Perceptions from Three Universities in the Early 20th Century." *College Composition and Communication* 43 (1992): 455-71.
—. "The Status of Composition and Rhetoric in American Colleges, 1880-1902: An MLA Perspective." *College English* 47 (1985): 734-45.
Stewart, Donald, and Patricia L. Stewart. *The Life and Legacy of Fred Newton Scott*. Pittsburgh: U of Pittsburgh P, 1997.
Taylor, Warner. "A National Survey of Conditions in Freshman English." *The Origins of Composition Studies in the American College, 1875-1925*. Ed. John Brereton. Pittsburgh: U of Pittsburgh P, 1995. 545-62.
Vivian, Barbara G. "Gertrude Buck on Metaphor: Twentieth Century Concepts in a Late Nineteenth-Century Dissertation." Conference on College Composition and Communication. Cincinnati, March 19-21, 1992.
Varnum, Robin. *Fencing with Words*. Urbana, IL: NCTE, 1996.
Wagner, Joanne. "'Intelligent Members or Restless Disturbers': Women's Rhetorical Styles, 1880-1920." *Reclaiming Rhetorica: Women in the Rhetorical Tradition*. Ed. Andrea Lunsford. Pittsburgh: U of Pittsburgh P, 1995. 185-202.
Wozniak, John Michael. *English Composition in Eastern Colleges, 1850-1940*. Washington: UP of America, 1978.

Historical Studies of Writing Program Administration

Part I: Individuals

1

The WPA as Publishing Scholar: Edwin Hopkins and *The Labor and Cost of the Teaching of English*

Randall Popken

In the introduction to their book, *The Writing Program Administrator as Researcher*, Shirley K Rose and Irwin Weiser lobby for an enlarged understanding of the intellectual work done by writing program administrators. They go on to argue that, because of the critical role played by research in the "rewards system of higher education," understanding more about the research carried out by WPAs is a critical part of professionalizing the field (vi). As a supplement to Rose and Weiser's work, I want to suggest that understanding the present intellectual work of WPAs also involves understanding the history of the participation by writing program administrators in research. In this chapter, as an opening gambit, I look at work by one of the earliest publishing WPAs, Edwin M. Hopkins (1862-1946), who taught at the University of Kansas his entire career (1889 to 1937). Practically from the date of his first arrival in Lawrence, in November 1889, through at least 1923, Hopkins used his experiences as a composition teacher and program administrator as the basis for his research.[1] Furthermore, throughout his career, Hopkins used his scholarship in an attempt to advance the interests of the composition community.

Hopkins was an important national figure in English teaching throughout his career. Robert Connors places him in the category of Harvard English faculty members A.S. Hill, Barrett Wendell,

LeBaron Briggs, and Charles Copeland, all of whom tried to "create a new rhetoric of written communication during the period 1880 to 1910" ("Rhetoric" 64). As a founding member of the National Council of Teachers of English, Hopkins attended the founders' meeting in Chicago on December 1 and 2, 1911, where he joined Fred Newton Scott and four others as the only college and university members of the ten-member board of directors. Later, Hopkins served as the fifth president of NCTE (1915-16), and he was an associate editor of *English Journal* from 1911 to 1926. For several years, he crisscrossed the U.S. giving presentations and generally trying to organize teachers of writing (Hopkins, Letter to Frank Strong, 8 June 1903; Hopkins Scrapbook 18; 15; 27). Furthermore, as a result of his abiding interest in secondary and elementary school teaching of English, Hopkins also founded the Kansas Association of Teachers of English and the *Kansas English Bulletin* (1915) ("Hopkins" 1), which he edited from 1915 to 1919 ("E. M. Hopkins" 1). He chaired a statewide Kansas committee on the organization of a state course of study in secondary schools (1917) and served on a state committee on survey and revision of English in the state's elementary schools ("E. M. Hopkins (Personal Record)").

Hopkins also published work on the teaching of literature and, in particular, composition. In 1904, he published his *Handbook on the Teaching of English*, a summary review of a series of pedagogical practices in new composition, literature, and English language textbooks. But Hopkins is best known for his publications associated with his crusade to improve the plight of the labor of composition teachers at college, secondary, and elementary levels (Berlin, 53-54; Connors, *Composition-Rhetoric* 192; Russell 140-42). His first major article, "Can Good Teaching Be Done Under Current Conditions?" which appeared in 1912, was the lead entry in the initial edition of the *English Journal*; in this article, Hopkins argued that composition teaching at all levels in the U.S. had failed because faculty members had too many students and too many teaching responsibilities. Over the years, in a number of shorter articles ("English in Grammar Schools"; "The Forthcoming"; "Forty Years"; "Cost and Labor"; "The Cost and Labor"; "The Need of Improvement"; "Present Status"; "Should English Teachers"; "Wanted") Hopkins pounded away on the theme of the insurmountable workload of writing teachers.

Even more than in these articles, Hopkins addressed the overwork issue in a long empirical research project—one of the first of its kind in composition history: *The Labor and Cost of the Teaching of English in Colleges and Secondary Schools with Especial Reference to English Composition*. This monograph was published by NCTE through the special assistance of the U.S. Department of Education in 1923; it went through sixteen editions that sold 130,000 copies throughout the U.S. ("E. M. Hopkins"), including sales to a number of state education departments ("A Recognition"; "Big Colleges"). In this chapter, I investigate the story of Edwin Hopkins's publication of this famous piece of scholarship. In particular, I look at his personal relationship to the subject matter of *The Labor and Cost,* the difficulties he had getting time enough to complete the project, and his struggle dealing with administrative disdain for the project. What I offer is a historical case study that gives a glimpse of how it was to be both a WPA and a publishing scholar nearly a hundred years ago.

The Labor and Cost Project

The Labor and Cost is a report on and interpretation of the results of a survey of 624 secondary-level and 265 college-level teachers, nearly 900 English teachers in all. At an MLA division meeting in Iowa City in 1909, Hopkins spoke for the first time about the poor working conditions of English faculty. He also persuaded the organization to sponsor a committee to study the matter and to appoint him as chair. Over the years, the project grew in magnitude, and Hopkins eventually got other organizations involved: the newly-formed National Council of Teachers of English, the National Education Association, and the U.S. Bureau of Education. Through the years, at least fifteen English faculty members from secondary to university levels took part in the project, but ultimately it was Hopkins who was in charge of mailing out questionnaires, collecting responses, tabulating results, writing the text, and raising money for support. The title page of *The Labor and Cost* bears Hopkins's name and no other on it.

James Berlin considers *The Labor and Cost* to be part of the "efficiency movement"—an educational development which swept through American professional circles in the early twentieth century (53). The sacred text for the efficiency movement was Frederick Taylor's *The Principles of Scientific Management,* published in 1911. In this widely read book, Taylor, a past president of the American Society of Mechanical Engineers, criticized American business for failing to get workers to maximize their time spent on the job. Taylor's stated goal was that all American industry should increase productivity—having each worker reach "his highest state of efficiency [. . .] that is, when he is turning out his largest daily output" (11). Taylor believed that, through the application of scientific principles and "accurate, minute, motion and time study" (25), managers could improve American industrial output by great numbers. Furthermore, beyond its use in industry, Taylor believed that his model could be "applied with equal force" to other agencies, including government and education (8). In fact, the efficiency movement did influence public education, particularly in elementary and high schools. It became fashionable, for instance, right before and after World War I to regard school superintendents as "general managers," whose function it was to try to squeeze the most out of teachers (Callahan 199-200). A major theme in the efficiency movement in education was the notion that class sizes and teacher loads could be increased, as they were in many school districts around the country in the 1920s (Callahan 222-23). Efficiency movement-inspired empirical research such as a 1922 study by Paul Stevenson and Calvin Davis "proved" that student performance wasn't at all affected by increasing class size (qtd. in Callahan 234).

Indeed, Berlin is correct in thinking that Hopkins was influenced by the efficiency movement for the project. Earlier in "Can Good Composition Be Taught?" Hopkins admitted that the public was in an uproar about the fact that "the investment in English teaching yields but a small fraction of the desired returns" (1). However, in *The Labor and Cost*, "efficiency" meant something very different for Hopkins than for Taylor. In fact, the interesting part of *The Labor and Cost* is that, rather than using empirical results to show how teaching English at the college level could be made more efficient, Hopkins used data to demonstrate the deplorable conditions endured by writing faculty. Rather than studying student performance to determine its relationship to faculty member time spent, Hopkins centered on the experiences of beleaguered faculty members. He attempted to get inside the experiences of those faculty members—in particular, the time spent in class preparation, contact with students, and, of course, reading and evaluating writing. The survey in *The Labor and Cost* asked faculty members a series of questions about their opinions of time demands on their work: for instance, what ought to be done with the amount of required manuscript reading, and how many hours a day a human can read student writing. Thus, though *The Labor and Cost* gives the surface-level guise of objective, scientific discourse, it is a document fashioned by a program administrator fighting for composition teaching.

Even before he began the project, Hopkins was of the opinion that writing teachers had too many classes and too many students, and he set out to prove it by searching for evidence of the negative effects of this overload. In fact, the survey asked teachers about what happened to their students' work when they had too many students. Faculty members overwhelmingly agreed that if they did not "give attention to all the written work that a pupil has done," it would destroy the student's interest in the subject (*The Labor and Cost* 24). Hopkins also asked faculty members what their ideal teaching load was, especially in contrast to their current load. Faculty members in the survey had an average of 104.1 students per semester, with one faculty member reporting a student load of 200 students (26). Many respondents in the study commented that they often slighted their work because of the student load; they "endeavor[ed] to read all manuscript[s], but with extreme haste and consequent 'skimming' and 'slighting'" (25). Still others—thirty-nine teachers surveyed—found it "totally impossible to read all the freshman manuscript" (25).

Hopkins also set out to prove that there were serious physical and emotional ramifications for faculty members when they had too many students. Through the survey, he tried to quantify the upper threshold of student writing that a teacher could read in an hour, a day, and a week. Survey respondents estimated that, under maximum conditions, they could read about 2,600 words an hour of student work, though a more normal amount was 2,000 words per hour (25). Teachers in the survey also reported that their students produced about 630 words per week, which meant that faculty with 100 students had over 60,000 words to read per assignment. Using this calculation, Hopkins argued, if these faculty members were to read all of an assignment in a week, they would be reading more than thirty hours. In fact, respondents in Hopkins's survey reported reading student manuscripts for an average of 20.6 hours per week. However, these respondents also believed that the maximum number of hours they actually could read student writing a day was 2.07 hours (25). Putting these numbers together, Hopkins estimated that, in order to do their jobs effectively, writing faculty members could at best read 2,200 words an hour for ten hours per week, with students writing 500 words per week.

Hopkins then used the results of his survey to argue that a reasonable student load for each English faculty member would be thirty-six students. If the faculty members were to stretch their paper reading to twelve hours per week, the number would increase to forty-three. At its absolute maximum, according to Hopkins's calculations, faculty members could handle sixty-two students each. Hopkins also factored student conferences into the load. His survey showed that writing faculty should hold individual conferences "at least as often as every two or three weeks with pupils that need them, and average 15 minutes in length, ranging from one minute to one hour" (27); faculty reported that a reasonable office schedule time was from six to seven hours weekly (28).

Hopkins's Experiences as Administrator and Teacher

The arguments that Hopkins made in *The Labor and Cost* about the workload problem were rooted deeply in his own—and sometimes painful—experiences teaching writing and administering the program at Kansas. As a faculty member, Hopkins had a large teaching load, especially early in his career. For instance, in his first complete fall term at Kansas (1890), he taught Chaucer at 9:00 a.m., Middle English at 10:00 a.m., and American literature at 2:00 p.m., each of which met every day. Furthermore, he taught all the writing courses in the Department of English Literature, Rhetoric, and *Belles Lettres*. His section of Rhetoric (a first-year composition course) met daily at 11:00 a.m. and included eighty-one students.[2] He also taught the only section of Essentials of English Composition, a "sub-freshman" course offered in the University's preparatory school; in Fall 1890, this course contained approximately thirty-eight students (*Annual Catalogue 1890-1891*). Thus, adding the first-year and the sub-freshman rhetoric classes, Hopkins had five courses for Fall 1890—five preparations, including about 120 writing students.

As program administrator for the Department of Rhetoric and English Language, Hopkins scheduled courses and assigned faculty (Hopkins, Letter to Strong, 5 June 1909); hired faculty (Hopkins, Letter to Strong, 8 June 1903); worked with the departmental budget (Hopkins, "Salary List"); served as composition course spokesperson regarding teaching loads (Hopkins, Letter to Strong, 5 July 1909); and lined up paid manuscript readers to support composition faculty reading (Hopkins, "Salary List"; Hopkins, Letter to Templin, 28 Oct. 1909). Hopkins also reported that from 1889 to 1919 he authored virtually "all departmental monographs [. . .] having to do with departmental administration" ("E. M. Hopkins (Personal Record)" 2). For instance, in 1897, he published a twenty-eight page monograph called *Suggestions for the Teaching of English Classics in the High Schools*, which circulated to secondary school teachers in the Lawrence area. The document includes detailed suggestions about the types of readings students would need to do in order to succeed in their college work at Kansas. Looking back over thirty years of administrative experiences, Hopkins reported that the "time required for administrative duty and the correspondence resulting from that and from other activities that have grown out of it [. . .] is from four to sometimes twelve hours daily exclusive of teaching duty" ("E. M. Hopkins (Personal Record)" 1).

Even serving as program director for the Department of Rhetoric and English Language appears to have had no bearing on Hopkins's teaching load. In Fall 1906, for instance, he had Exposition and Argument (MWF, 8:00 a.m.), American Literature (MWF, 9:00 a.m.), Old English (MWF, 10:15 a.m.), Transitional English (TTH, at 9:00 a.m.), Literary Criticism (TTH, at 10:15 a.m.), and Versification (W, 11:15 a.m.) (*Annual Catalog, 1906-1907*). As late as Spring 1918, Hopkins still taught four courses: Argumentation, Advanced Argument, Prose Invention, and American Literature (*Annual Catalog, 1917-1918*). Hopkins also taught several years in the university's extension division (referred to officially as a "correspondence school"). During 1893-94, for instance, he lectured in Lawrence and Ottawa, Kansas, on a variety of subjects: American literature; New England and Colonial Literature; English Literature; Puritan literature; and Emerson (Hopkins Scrapbook 5; 8).[3]

The Process of Producing *The Labor and Cost*

Hopkins worked on *The Labor and Cost* for at least fifteen years, during which time he struggled to coordinate his own workload with his research goals. Moreover, during this time he was frequently at odds with administrators over the legitimacy of his project.

A letter he wrote in early 1908 to his chancellor, Frank Strong, indicates that Hopkins was probably already planning the project. Despite his desire to embark on such a project, Hopkins shows concern in this letter that his own workload would mean that his research—or as he refers to it, "productive work, the highest duty of a man in my position"—would not be possible. Feeling the crunch of his administrative responsibilities, Hopkins tells Strong that "I have had almost no time in these years for reading or authorship beyond that demanded by regular department duties, teaching and executive." Then, Hopkins, who was forty-five at the time, asks permission to "lighten my teaching a little before I am entirely past the age of production" in order to carry on some research. Hopkins then repeats the point later in the letter: "reasonable relief" at least from his teaching load would give him "some chance [for scholarship] before my years of usefulness are ended" (Letter to Strong, 21 Mar. 1908). Strong does not respond to Hopkins's request in writing, though he may have orally. However, Strong appears to have rejected it: Hopkins's teaching load remained as it was.

Two years later Hopkins again writes to Strong, this time in a letter that indirectly requests leave time to work on and complete *The Labor and Cost* project. In this letter Hopkins alludes to the fact that he would like to have a meeting with Strong to discuss his request. Hopkins reports that his progress on the study "is now so far advanced that results can be formulated." However, repeating the theme of age from the earlier letter, Hopkins (who is now nearly forty-eight) says that he is concerned that "at my age, certain things must be determined if I am not to waste such energy as remains to me" (Letter to Strong, 13 June 1910). The "certain things [that] must be determined" again involve what administrative support there would be for his research efforts. As previously, though, there seems to have been none.

Hopkins returns to the subject of released time in a letter to the chancellor five years later; by this time *The Labor and Cost* project had fallen seriously behind schedule, and in fact Hopkins was still just collecting data. He begins his letter by referring to an earlier meeting with the chair of the Kansas Board of Administration, Edward T. Hackney, who had "told me to let him know if I found myself in need of more help" regarding the project. Again Hopkins reports on the progress of the project, including the fact of his juggling of funds from the U.S. Bureau of Education and from the National Education

Association. In his appeal to Strong, Hopkins asks for both financial support for clerical help and for a leave for himself. He repeats his assertion of how administrative responsibilities are preventing him from making progress on the project: "the details of departmental and miscellaneous business that have to be attended to whether important or otherwise [. . . can] wear a man out faster than anything else" (Letter to Strong, 18 Dec. 1915).

Strong responds to this letter in two different installments over a six-month period. In his first response, he reports that the Board has decided to increase the budget for clerical help to Hopkins from $200 to $250 for the year (Strong, Letter to Hopkins, 18 Feb. 1916). In the second letter, however, Strong informs Hopkins that the Board has rejected his request for a leave, in part because Strong himself "could not recommend it." Strong goes on to explain that the university "is not in position to set aside one of its teachers for outside work of this kind." He further tells Hopkins that he ought to work with his dean to find ways to alleviate some of his administrative and professional responsibilities. In particular, Strong wants Hopkins to "limit membership in outside organizations" (Letter to Hopkins, 3 July 1916).

By the next year (1917), Hopkins again writes to Strong to get clerical help for *The Labor and Cost* project, which he had been working on for nearly ten years. Hopkins reports to Strong that he has "a stenographer and secretary in my office on full time, eight hours a day"; these two workers split their time between work on the project and work on university administrative matters, "class and departmental work and state and general correspondence." Half of these workers' salaries came from Hopkins's NEA grant while the other half was budgeted university money. Because he wants to complete his research, Hopkins needs the two workers to spend more time on *The Labor and Cost* project, but there is too much "purely departmental and University business." In fact, Hopkins even finds himself having to do more of the clerical duties himself: "I give all my own spare time to correspondence, day and night, [though I] am now two months behind with parts of my work [on the project]." He tells Strong that the administrative burden is so great that without help "I could not carry on my office duties and correspondence for a single day, even if I gave all my time to it without any teaching duty. [. . .]" To alleviate the strain somewhat, Hopkins has had to use some of his own money to pay for office help; in fact, at the current pace he tells Strong that he will have spent about ten percent of his $3,000 yearly salary on administrative help (Letter to Strong, 30 Oct 1917).

Three weeks later, acting on a suggestion from English Department Chair Charles Dunlap, Hopkins requests that he be permitted to shift $150 that wasn't being used from the English Department budget to his own use and, further, that he have access to additional money from the university's general fund. Strong passes the letter on to Olin Templin, Dean of the College of Liberal Arts, who advises him to reject Hopkins's proposal (Templin, Letter to Strong, 13 Nov. 1917). In his letter to Hopkins, Strong cites the declining enrollment and shrinking university budget due to the U.S. involvement in World War I. Strong indicates that it is "practically impossible to set aside for special funds anything not already in the budget and that does not directly concern the war and war conditions." Strong ends his letter by telling Hopkins to put an end to his research, at least until the war ends (Letter to Hopkins, 13 Nov. 1917). In a follow-up letter to Hopkins four days later, Strong repeats his suggestion of curtailing his research, telling Hopkins that he ought to "reduce your outside work until the University is more adequately supplied with funds." Ironically (and somewhat inconsistently), however, Strong also tells Hopkins that he might try to apply for a research leave (Letter to Hopkins, 17 Nov. 1917). Strong seems to have forgotten that he rejected Hopkins's request for a leave two years earlier.

Hopkins appears to have been deeply disappointed at Strong's letter, and he responds to it immediately. He says that Strong's rejection of the proposal "was not unexpected, since I realized that it might have to be based on absolute necessity, waiving its justice altogether." He says that he will have to go on using his own money to fund clerical help "for carrying on my part of the departmental business" (Letter to Strong, 19 Nov. 1917).

A year later, in the fall of 1918, Hopkins again writes to Strong for funding help. Though none of it is documented in official letters to Strong, it is clear in his September 25, 1918, letter that Hopkins did an end-around on both Chancellor Strong and Dean Templin in 1917-18 by receiving money for clerical help from Frederick Kelly, Dean of the School of Education.[4] The issue in the September 25, 1918, letter continues to be the fact that Hopkins has to use some of his own money to pay for clerical staff to do the double duty of research work and administrative functions. Specifically, Hopkins asks for a $200 budget increase.

There is no record of a response from Strong to this request, and, in fact, Hopkins asks for the same amount in his letter about six months later, by which time the War has ended. In this letter, Hopkins's reasons "are the same as they have been for the past six years"—for clerical help both for research and office functions. Research for *The Labor and Cost* project, which is now in its second decade, is not yet finished; the "survey work and general preliminaries are now practically completed," though Hopkins envisions about five more years of work in preparing the project for publication (Letter to Strong, 1 Apr. 1919). Two months later, having received no written response from Strong, Hopkins makes the same request. That letter is returned to Hopkins with Strong's handwritten note on the bottom: "Wait until fall. No promise" (Letter to Strong, 11 June 1919).

However, Hopkins writes again just three months later—right before the beginning of the Fall 1919 semester—this time changing his request. Perhaps acting on Strong's reference to leave time mentioned in November of 1917, Hopkins now requests a leave, but it is not for research purposes. Instead, he asks for a semester's "sick leave." Hopkins had spent four weeks in summer 1919 hospitalized for "increasing nervous exhaustion with dental infection added" (Letter to Strong, 9 Sept. 1919). Ultimately, Strong grants Hopkins first a semester's leave of absence—and then an entire year's—from his teaching duties, during which time Hopkins convalesces in Asheville, North Carolina (Letter to Hopkins, 24 Sept. 1919).

While recuperating in North Carolina, Hopkins tries one last time to get both funding and release time to complete *The Labor and Cost* project. This time Hopkins's appeal isn't to the chancellor but to the university's Board of Administrator secretary, Dr. Wilbur M. Mason, a clergyman and former college president (Griffin 369). Hopkins tells Mason that he isn't certain at this point whether he ever will teach again because his "recent illness may mean that I have come to the end of my usefulness as a teacher and writer." Summarizing for Mason the three areas of his university responsibilities for the last thirty years (teaching, administration, and research), Hopkins blames the administrative load for being the one thing "which has done most to break my health." He also regrets deeply the fact that, of the three responsibility areas, research has always had to come last. Thus, if he is able to return to Kansas in Fall 1920, Hopkins asks Mason to take legislative action to reduce his teaching load and increase his funding for office assistance (Letter to Mason, 5 Jan. 1920). Hopkins receives a letter just four days later in which Mason responds by speaking about Hopkins's condition. But he dodges Hopkins's request for release time and clerical help with his research, indicating that it "involves matters calling for careful consideration and will doubtless require conference before a proper reply can be sent" (Mason, Letter to Hopkins, 9 Jan. 1920).

There is no record of a response by Mason to Hopkins's requests. Strong, who undoubtedly knew about Hopkins's final request, writes to Hopkins in February of 1920, but the letter avoids reference to the request for help with research. Instead, Strong writes about the mild winter in Kansas, the recent outbreak of influenza, and his own plans to retire and build a new home (Letter to Hopkins, 13 Feb. 1920).

Though it may be the case, there is no evidence in any of this correspondence involving Hopkins, Strong, and Templin that the relatively low status of composition had anything to do with Strong's disregard for *The Labor and Cost* project. However, there must have been something in the nature of the project that Strong just didn't like. It wasn't that Strong was opposed to faculty research as a general principle, and the climate for research at Kansas had been quite good for some time. In fact, as early as 1890, the administration tried, at least nominally, to create a culture in which research might flourish; seeing the growing importance of research and publication to the status of aspiring major universities, Strong's predecessor, Francis Snow, declared that professors "with superior research abilities should be released from much of their classroom teaching, which should be given to less competent researchers" (Griffin 80). A particularly strong commitment toward research existed in the college of liberal arts (Griffin 312); even as early as 1889, when Hopkins first arrived on campus, in the college a "strength of the faculty was that it continued the tradition of scholarly research established in an earlier day" (Griffin 312). In fact, the Kansas faculty was often the target of "raids" by other institutions looking to hire publishing scholars (Griffin 312-13). It is true that much of the research at Kansas during Hopkins's early years was produced by scientists, although historians such as Carl Becker were also publishing often. Moreover, at least two of Hopkins's English colleagues enjoyed active careers as publishing scholars. Selden Lincoln Whitcomb published several critical volumes (*Outlines for the Study of English Drama;*

Chronological Outlines of American Literature; Outlines for the Study of Modern Prose Fiction; and *A Study of the Novel*). In addition to articles, Frank Egbert Bryant published a monograph called *On the Limits of Descriptive Writing, Apropos of Lessing's Laocoon,* and he was at work on *A History of English Balladry Through Elizabeth* when he died prematurely in 1911.

It may be the potentially polemical nature of *The Labor and Cost* project that made Strong most uncomfortable. Even early in the project, Hopkins used his ideas to argue for improved work conditions for writing faculty on his own campus. Just months before debuting his idea at MLA, Hopkins had proposed that Dean Templin carry out a similar survey on the Kansas campus, this one a study of the work load of faculty members in all disciplines to find out how much time they spent on planning lectures and evaluating student work (Letter to Strong, 5 June 1909). Hopkins fully expected that such a survey would reveal how many more hours per week the composition faculty worked than did faculty in other disciplines. In fact, he had already done a pilot study of one department and found out that "instructors [. . .] teaching seventeen and eighteen hours a week have two or three hours a day less of labor than does the English instructor of corresponding grade" (Letter to Strong, 5 June 1909). Hopkins even went so far as to suggest a formula for determining faculty load that counts "theme and exercise correcting" on the same level as "conducting recitations." His proposed formula would have counted each clock hour of teaching as a single unit. In addition, two hours of laboratory time, conference time, paper reading, and exercise correcting also were to be counted as one unit. His guess is that "the teaching average of my instructors is now, not fifteen hours a week, but as I think somewhere above thirty; and the number of actual working hours exclusive of preparation for classes is in some cases fifty or more" (Letter to Strong, 5 June 1909).

It may have been that Strong feared what Hopkins was going to do with his findings, even on his own campus. After all, Hopkins used the results of his pilot study to request that the chancellor grant him a "free hand in making up and distributing sections" of composition courses (Letter to Strong, 5 June 1909) so that he could "equalize the work of instructors and lessen the demand for manuscript reading" (Letter to Strong, 5 July 1909). Strong was not convinced by this proposal, nor was Templin, who ended up making fun of the proposal itself. The proposal even got Hopkins in conflict with other faculty members who believed he was trying to get special favors for his program (Hopkins, Letter to Strong, 5 July 1909). From the standpoint of Strong and Templin, it seems more likely that they felt that Hopkins was doing dangerous work.

But Hopkins prevailed. Though by no means entirely healed from his physical and emotional problems, he returned to his work at Kansas after his sick leave year in North Carolina. Hopkins also returned to complete *The Labor and Cost of the Teaching of English*, which he presented to the National Education Association in Des Moines, Iowa in July 1921 and to the U.S. Bureau of Education, also in 1921. He taught at Kansas until 1937, though his campaign for workload reform diminished after the publication of *The Labor and Cost*.

Conclusion

The immediate impact of Hopkins's research efforts can't be documented very accurately. A study by Walter Miller five years after the publication of *The Labor and Cost* gives no indication that composition teaching loads were anywhere close to the 36 student load that Hopkins recommended—or even the 62 maximum. Taylor's study, published in 1929, indicated that the national average student load per composition faculty member was still 93, although the situation seems to have been better in private colleges in the East than in state universities (Brereton 557-58). On the other hand, in spite of the conflicts Hopkins had with his chancellor and dean, there was a clear trend at Kansas in the aftermath of Hopkins's work. The student load per composition faculty member dropped from 177 in 1901 to 89 in 1913 to 55.2 in 1920 and 49 in 1925 (*Annual Catalogue* 1901-02; 1906-07; 1917-18; 1920-21; 1925-26).

For nearly twenty years, Edwin Hopkins fought for time and respect for his research project. What sustained him was his belief that the evidence from his research would ultimately help create policy changes in writing programs across the country (Letter to Strong, 5 June 1909). By looking at WPA research in this way, Hopkins was far ahead of his time. Today, one of the "qualities of good WPA research," according to Rose and Weiser, is that it should "enable WPAs to justify strategic plans to implement program change where appropriate or to justify decisions to preserve program practices where appropriate" (viii). In other words, Hopkins recognized the special nature of WPA scholarship: the WPA "must acknowledge that the outcome of [an] inquiry may have an immediate, obvious impact on many teachers and students" (Rose and Weiser viii). Furthermore, another special characteristic of good WPA research was anticipated by Hopkins's work: that the "WPA finds it disingenuous to narrate the story of the research project as though she were a disinterested inquirer" (Rose and Weiser viii). Indeed, at no time was Edwin Hopkins ever a disinterested inquirer; his research was always close to the bone—growing out of his own experiences as a WPA, a faculty member, and a human being.

Acknowledgments

My special thanks to the Tarleton State University Organized Research Committee for funding my research activities in the Hopkins Archives. Very special thanks, too, to University of Kansas archivists Barry Bunch and Ned Kehde for guiding me in profitable directions.

Notes

1. A bit of clarification is needed to establish Hopkins's credentials as a WPA, especially in light of Edward P. J. Corbett's assertion that the first WPAs didn't come along until 1946. Using a model based on Fred Newton Scott's program at Michigan, in 1902 the Kansas Department of English Literature, Language, and *Belles Lettres* was divided into a Department of English Literature and a Department of Rhetoric and English Language. Hopkins, who lobbied aggressively for this configuration (Letter to Frank Strong, 17 July 1909), was named chair of the latter department, which consisted primarily of the first-year rhetoric classes. Thus, in many ways his responsibilities resembled those of a modern WPA.

However, at the end of the 1909 school year, the two departments reunited. Still, without the official title, it appears that Hopkins continued to administer the first-year composition courses, although he also took on a growing number of other administrative responsibilities in graduate studies and in the English education program.

2. According to the *Annual Catalogue of the University of Kansas* for 1890-91, three of the available six degree options at KU for the 1890-91 term required the first-year composition-rhetoric course; from the list of students taking these degree options, it appears that 81 first-year students were enrolled in these three programs and, thus, all would have been in Hopkins's class (204).

3. Of course, as a prominent figure on campus, Hopkins also found himself deep in a number of non-composition related responsibilities. For

instance, he was inundated with committee assignments. During the period of a year and a half from 1913 to 1915, Chancellor Frank Strong appointed Hopkins to the following: Administrative Committee for the College of Liberal Arts (Strong, Letter to Hopkins, 8 Nov. 1913); University Senate (Strong, Letter to Hopkins, 13 Apr. 1914); Special Committee to reply to the Communication from the Asiatic Institute (Strong, Letter to Hopkins, 7 May 1914); Administrative Committee of the School of Education (Strong, Letter to Hopkins, 28 Sept. 1914); and Commencement Committee on Music (Strong, Letter to Hopkins, 7 Apr. 1915). Hopkins was also often called upon to serve his University in other capacities. For instance, he lectured on Emerson and Transcendentalism at the Montgomery County Kansas Teachers Association Meeting on December 12, 1895 (Hopkins Scrapbook 19); he spoke across town at the Haskell Institute on May 3, 1903 (Hopkins, "Purpose of Education"), at the meeting of the Lawrence Ladies Literary League on February 13, 1909 (Hopkins Scrapbook 19), and at the dedication of a new high school in Atchison, Kansas, on May 20, 1910 (Hopkins Scrapbook, 19).

It may well have been that Hopkins had such a sense of commitment to his university that he over-committed himself. For instance, Hopkins also helped to develop the program in intercollegiate athletics at Kansas, serving as the university's first football coach for the 1892 season. He was also a frequent speaker and organist at chapel services held on campus.

4. From time to time Hopkins had taught graduate education courses and helped with certification in English, so the connection was tangible.

Works Cited

Annual Catalogue of the University of Kansas, 1890-91. Lawrence: University of Kansas.
Annual Catalogue of the University of Kansas, 1901-02. Lawrence: University of Kansas.
Annual Catalogue of the University of Kansas, 1906-07. Lawrence: University of Kansas.
Annual Catalogue of the University of Kansas, 1917-18. Lawrence: University of Kansas.
Annual Catalogue of the University of Kansas, 1920-21. Lawrence: University of Kansas.
Annual Catalogue of the University of Kansas, 1925-26. Lawrence: University of Kansas.
Berlin, James. *Rhetoric and Reality*. Carbondale: Southern Illinois UP, 1985.
"Big Colleges Like KU Man's Report." *Daily Kansan*, January 7, 1914. Hopkins Archives, Spencer Research Library, University of Kansas. Hopkins Scrapbook. (32).

Bryant, Frank Egbert. *A History of English Balladry, and Other Studies*. Boston, R. G. Badger, 1913.

—. *On the Limits of Descriptive Writing Apropos of Lessing's Laocoon*. Ann Arbor, Michigan: Ann Arbor P, 1906.

Callahan, Raymond E. *Education and the Cult of Efficiency: A Study of the Social Forces that Have Shaped the Administration of the Public Schools*. Chicago: U of Chicago P, 1962.

Connors, Robert. *Composition-Rhetoric*. Pittsburgh: U of Pittsburgh P, 1997.

—. "Rhetoric in the Modern University: The Creation of an Underclass." *The Politics of Writing Instruction: Postsecondary*. Ed. Richard Bullock and John Trimbur. Portsmouth: Boynton/Cook, 1991. 55-84.

Corbett, Edward P. J. "A History of Writing Program Administration." *Learning from the Histories of Rhetoric: Essays in Honor of Winifred Bryan Horner*. Ed. Theresa Enos. Carbondale: Southern Illinois UP, 1993. 60-71.

"E. M. Hopkins." Hopkins Archives, University of Kansas, 1935. Miscellaneous Folder.

"E. M. Hopkins (Personal Record): September 8, 1919." Hopkins Archives, Spencer Research Library, University of Kansas. Miscellaneous Folder.

[Edwin M. Hopkins] Scrapbook. Hopkins Archives, Spencer Research Library, University of Kansas.

Griffin, Clifford. *The University of Kansas: A History*. Lawrence: U of Kansas P, 1974.

"Hopkins." University of Kansas News Bureau Press Release, June 13, 1946.

Hopkins, Edwin. "Can Good Composition Teaching be Done Under Present Conditions?" *English Journal* 1 (1912): 1-8.

—. "Cost and Labor of English Teaching." *National Education Association* (1915): 114-19.

—. "The Cost and Labor of English Teaching." *Proceedings of the NEA*, 50 (1912): 750.

—. "English in Grammar Schools." Address. NCTE. 15 Dec. 1913. Hopkins Archives, Spencer Research Library, University of Kansas.

—. "The Forthcoming Report of the Committee on English Composition Teaching." *English Journal* 1 (1912): 568.

—. "Forty Years of College English: History and Prophesy." *English Journal* 20 (April 1931): 320-30.

—. *Handbook on the Teaching of English*. Chicago: Scott, Foresman, 1904.

—. *The Labor and Cost of the Teaching of English in Colleges and Secondary Schools with Especial Reference to English Composition*. Chicago: NCTE, 1923.

—. Correspondence with Chancellor Frank Strong. Spencer Research Library, University of Kansas. Series 2/9/5.

—. "The Need of Improvement in the Conditions Surrounding the Teaching of Composition" *College English* 1 (1912): 41-42.

—. "Present Status of the English Teacher." *Journal of Education* (13 Feb. 1913): n. pag.

—. "Purpose of Education." Address at Haskell Institute, 3 May 1903. Hopkins Archives, Spencer Research Library, University of Kansas. Miscellaneous Folder.

—. "Salary List, English Departments; 1908-1909." Correspondence with Chancellor Frank Strong. Spencer Research Library, University of Kansas. Series 2/9/5.

—. "Should English Teachers Teach?" *Education* 42 (1921): 12-18.

—. *Suggestions for the Teaching of English Classics in the High Schools*. Lawrence: U of Kansas P, 1897.

—. "Wanted: A Bureau of Definition." *English Journal* 6 (March 1917): 131-45.

Mason, William. Letter to Edwin Hopkins. 9 Jan. 1920. Correspondence with Frank Strong. Spencer Research Library, University of Kansas. Series 2/9/5.

"A Recognition." *Lawrence Gazette* 13 Nov. 1913. n. pag. Hopkins Archives, Spencer Research Library, University of Kansas. Hopkins Scrapbook.

Rose, Shirley K, and Irwin Weiser. "Introduction: WPA Inquiry in Action and Reflection." *The Writing Program Administrator as Researcher*. Ed. Shirley K Rose and Irwin Weiser. Portsmouth, NH: Boynton/Cook, 1999. v-ix.

Russell, David. *Writing in the Academic Disciplines*. Carbondale: Southern Illinois UP, 1991.

Strong, Frank. Correspondence with Chancellor. Spencer Research Library, University of Kansas. Series 2/9/5.

Taylor, Frederick. *The Principles of Scientific Management*. Norwood, Mass: Plimpton P, 1911.

Taylor, Warner. "A National Survey of Conditions in Freshman English." *The Origins of Composition Studies in the American College, 1875-1925: A Documentary History*. Ed. John C. Brereton. Pittsburgh: U of Pittsburgh P, 1994. 354-62.

Templin, Olin. Letter to Frank Strong. 13 Nov. 1917. Correspondence with Chancellor Frank Strong. Spencer Research Library, University of Kansas. Series 2/9/5.

Whitcomb, Selden Lincoln. *Chronicle Outlines of American Literature*. NY: McMillan, 1894.

—. *Outlines for the Study of English Drama*. Iowa City: Iowa College P, 1901.

—. *Outlines for the Study of Modern Prose Fiction*. Ames: Iowa State UP, 1898.

—. *The Study of a Novel*. New York: D.C. Heath, 1905.

2

"Replacing Nice, Thin Bryn Mawr Miss Crandall with Fat, Harvard Savage": WPAs at Bryn Mawr College, 1902 to 1923

D'Ann George

The first two decades of the twentieth century were pivotal years for Bryn Mawr College's writing program and its WPA. During these years President M. Carey Thomas negotiated with Regina Crandall her role as Director of the Essay Department, in terms of her status, authority, and responsibilities. As Crandall continually lobbied for a seat on the faculty, for more control over the curriculum and for better working conditions for writing faculty, she became a thorn in Thomas's side. In its best moments, her story challenges us to demand equal pay and prestige for work that has historically not received such consideration. At other moments, however, she reminds us how lack of a secure, well-defined professional status can suffocate even the most dedicated writing teachers. As I read records of the often nasty negotiations between Crandall and Thomas, I noted again and again how Crandall linked her lack of autonomy and that of the Essay department to her inability to innovate and introduce change to the writing program.

Thomas's Education Goals

A brief description of M. Carey Thomas's educational philosophy and goals provides an important context for understanding her view of the role of a writing director. When Thomas began the task of creating Bryn Mawr in the early 1880s, she wanted it to be more ambitious than other colleges that admitted women, most of which still claimed to prepare women to be good wives and mothers. Thomas envisioned Bryn Mawr as battling domesticity and gender stereotypes by preparing women to be scholars. This educational philosophy was radical at the turn of the century and threatened many leaders of co-educational and men's institutions, including Charles W. Eliot, President of Harvard. In her opening address to the college in 1899, Thomas summarized Eliot's views on women's education and then defended Bryn Mawr against them:

> President Eliot said that the president and faculty of a women's college have no guide from the past, that the great tradition of learning existing from the time of the Egyptians to the present existed only for men and that this vast body of inherited tradition was of no service to women's education, that women's colleges simply imitated men when they used the same educational methods instead of inventing new ones of their own. Such a statement only shows us that as progressive as one may be in education or other things there may be in our minds some dark spot of medievalism, and clearly in President Eliot's otherwise luminous intelligence women's education is this dark spot. (141-42)

Thomas goes on to claim that classical literature, history, and languages belong as much to women as to men and that women scholars would begin to compete with men very soon. To an admirable extent, Bryn Mawr helped Thomas to realize her dream for women to share equal academic footing with men: between 1889 and 1908, 61 percent of Bryn Mawr graduates pursued some sort of advanced study, and the college produced fifteen times the average number of professional women scholars in proportion to its enrollment figures (Frankford 55). Thomas achieved these impressive numbers by creating graduate fellowships to support women seeking advanced degrees and by recruiting a world-class research faculty. She attracted prestigious faculty by paying them well and relieving them of administrative work.

Thomas and the Writing Faculty

As Sue Ellen Holbrook has shown in "Women's Work: The Feminizing of Composition," the study of modern languages—particularly English—gave women the strongest professional foothold in academic departments in the early twentieth century. However, as academic disciplines continued to professionalize, English studies evolved into a two-tiered system: the more prestigious, better paid work focused on the creation of abstract knowledge through literary study while the lower-tiered work focused on concern for pedagogy, student writing and the administrative tasks associated with running a writing program. Women found it easier to find jobs in the lower tier, demonstrates Holbrook, because of the widespread belief among department heads that women were good at "drudge" work and that teaching composition and WPA work was just that (207).

At Bryn Mawr, Thomas concerned herself with minute details of the writing program and once claimed that the three required semesters of composition were the foundation of undergraduate education at Bryn Mawr. However, she refused to admit that teaching writing or directing a writing program were legitimate academic work, perhaps because treating such work as legitimate would threaten her plan to promote women's intellectual ability. Thomas couldn't legitimize Crandall's position because the male-dominated academic culture branded her work drudge work, unintellectual work, and therefore women's work, and as a turn-of-the-century feminist, Thomas's way of battling gender stereotypes was not to challenge patriarchal value systems but to use Bryn Mawr to find a place for women—though not all women—in those systems. To value Crandall's work and position, in Thomas's eyes, would be to condemn all women to subordinate positions. A letter to Thomas in 1912 from Lucy Donnelly, a member of the literature faculty, reveals a telling assessment of Bryn Mawr's Writing Director, Regina Crandall: she is "clever and painstaking," "responsible," "popular [. . .] with the students" and "content to keep the subordinate position." Compare her character sketch of Crandall to a stereotype of women writing teachers held by many English department heads. As reported by Ella Lonn in a 1924 issue of *The Journal of the American Association of University Women,* English department heads reported that "women do a better job of routine work, such as freshman composition, than men, as they are 'painstaking, conscientious, and enthusiastic'" (Holbrook 207).

Because she did not believe that writing instruction was legitimate academic work, Thomas strongly discouraged both the writing director and instructors from making composition their career. She capped instructor's salaries at $1,000, one-third the pay of literature faculty and a meager living wage. Crandall likewise received only $1,500 for directing the Essay department, $1,500 less than the salary of the literature chair. Though writing teachers were not allowed to teach literature, those who nonetheless managed to show what she called "literary ability" could be promoted to the literature department and receive full pay and faculty-status. In fact, Thomas viewed the Essay department as a vehicle for promoting fledgling faculty who showed a strong interest in literature.

During the early years of the college, Thomas fired or replaced women who wanted to teach writing while promoting those whose real interest was in teaching literature. From 1886 to 1909, four women climbed their way from instructorships in the Essay department to professorships in the English department. Most teachers who were not promoted to teaching literature left the college—some for careers in college preparatory schools where they continued to teach composition. As Director of Composition, Crandall escaped the fate of other composition teachers because while Thomas did not recognize her work as intellectual, she did recognize the importance of her work as an administrator. Crandall presided over placement tests, sought and found qualified teachers, handled cases of plagiarism and academic dishonesty, and assigned teachers to courses and sections of courses. In recognition for this administrative work, her salary was higher and more secure than that of an instructor. However, in a 1913 letter, Thomas issued a stern warning to Crandall in a letter outlining the limitations of her position:

> I think, however, that I ought to state frankly that if at any future time we should succeed in calling a Reader here or if we should succeed in developing among the Readers who are here anyone with a strong literary interest such as was exercised by Miss Donnelly, Miss King and Mrs. Gerould when they were in the [Essay] department and if it should seem best for the good of the department to place the direction

of the second year work in her hands the College is
entirely free to do so.

As an additional reminder of her temporary status, Crandall was denied a seat on the faculty and a salary equal to that of other department heads.

In addition to wanting a cheap writing faculty who would leave after a year or two, Thomas expected writing teachers to handle large workloads that drove more than one instructor to an emotional breakdown. In 1906, for example, Thomas refused to renew the contract of Miss Marsh when she heard that the woman was in a "broken down and overworked condition" and complained of being "very much overworked in the Essay department." Marsh, explained Thomas's letter to the instructor, was "unable to manage large classes" and the department needs "readers on whom we can call in an emergency to do extra work without fear of breaking them down." Likewise, Thomas's own sister, who taught in the Essay department in the early 1890s, complained in tears to Thomas that she was severely overworked. There is evidence that Thomas's lack of sympathy for overworked writing teachers could be linked to her failure to understand the intellectual work of responding to student writing. Her letters often refer to instructors as "correctors," as though the mental processes involved in responding to student writing were limited to a superficial level. The in-depth comments on student writing made by several instructors in the Bryn Mawr department show that they were not.

Crandall Fights Back

While Thomas implemented policies to keep writing faculty temporary, low paid, and subordinate to the literature department, Crandall agitated for salary increases and decreased workloads for her faculty, an autonomous composition program, and an increase in the authority of her position as Director. In a lengthy letter addressed to Thomas in January of 1916, after she had served as Director of the Essay Department for eight years, Crandall detailed her history as a WPA and her many grievances. First, there was the matter of workload and compensation. "Every year I have found occasion to say that the readers are overworked," she noted. As able teacher after teacher quit the job, she had long argued that "it ought to be recognized that the teaching life of the teacher of Composition is shorter than that of the teacher of any other subject and that Composition, like trades accounted 'dangerous,' ought to command a premium." She reminded Thomas that her own contract—an annual rather than long-term arrangement at her insistence—was "in itself a protest, relieving me from further insistence, against a salary that does not accord with the scale of salaries paid at Bryn Mawr."

Crandall also argued that a forced link between composition and literature debilitated the writing program. The defects of a curriculum tied to courses in literature, she wrote Thomas, was that it was "protracted, rigid, and severe": students were forced to read texts that had been deemed important to the history of literature, but which had little value in teaching them writing skills. "Students who are learning to write English," she asserted, "will profit more by parallel reading of modern English than by study of early English masterpieces from Beowulf." Crandall went on to claim that a composition course tied to a course in literary history

> will incur the reproach of monotony [. . .] so long as students, traversing the same course in literature, year after year write papers which constitute about two thirds of the requirement in Composition on works of English literature previous to Shakespeare.

In contrast to the required course in Composition, Crandall's elective course in Daily Themes responded to the immediate rhetorical needs of students and was one of the more popular elective English courses.

Crandall believed that the writing director's lack of authority and status adversely affected the writing program. Before 1908, when Thomas first gave Crandall the title Director of English Essay Work (which eventually became Director of the Essay Department), a different woman held the position almost every year, making it impossible, in Crandall's opinion, to effect any innovative changes to the curriculum. In the 1916 letter, Crandall notes that when she took charge, "the framework of the course was rigidly prescribed, and except for reduction in amount of writing required, was the same as in 1902-03," the year that Crandall began as an instructor at Bryn Mawr. And even in 1908, the new title "represented an effort" only "for the sake of convenience, to give a name to a position in many respects anomalous, in a Department that itself is in an anomalous position," noted Crandall.

Crandall connected this lack of innovation to the fact that the writing director was often helpless to change the curriculum or to present problems directly to the college's board of directors because she lacked the proper status and authority. She repeatedly asked for a position that was more than "merely administrative" only to meet with the response that Thomas and Lucy Donnelly, the department chair, "were active members of the Department and represented it in the Faculty." Her one victory was convincing Thomas to list her name in college catalogues as the Director of the English Essay work. But the title failed to give her any real authority. Her only authorized job was "to systematize and coordinate the work." Because her role was limited to that of an administrator, with no control of the "principle and framework of the course," the composition work deteriorated in to "a kind of established form," she lamented, with few changes made to the curriculum over a fourteen-year period. Crandall concludes her January 1916 letter with a bit of ironic understatement, noting that "an arrangement that gives authority only to persons having no part in the actual work is most disadvantageous."

The Writing Program in Crisis: Harvard's Howard Savage to the Rescue

Because of the continual conflict in the ways the two women viewed the Essay Department and the Writing Director, the writing program was often in turmoil. In 1916, it experienced a defining crisis that triggered not only Crandall's bitter letter but several others from prominent alumnae who came to her defense. Thomas, tired of Crandall's insubordination and the expense of the Essay department, strongly suggested to Crandall that she resign. When she refused, Thomas demoted her from the position anyway and replaced her with Howard Savage, fresh from teaching and training in English A at Harvard. Like Thomas, Savage believed that writing teachers need only possess common sense and be willing to subordinate themselves to literary faculty. In a 1921 *English Journal* article that listed the qualities of the good composition instructor, Savage made it clear that "an interest in things literary is [not] a sure qualification for the teacher of composition" (444). Instead, Savage advocated patience, tolerance, sympathy, physical strength and endurance, and "plain, horse sense." The most essential of these qualities for Savage seems to have been "physical strength":

> The teacher of composition [. . .] must exercise for long hours at a stretch a constant vigilance against errors of detail, even the most minute, and at the same time "hold his standard", take an occasional glance at those eternal values which he must apply and correlate to the case of his individual student. For such constant application he must have a strong body, which from time to time he must refresh by exercise and physical relaxation. (445)

Hiring Savage strengthened Thomas's long-held position that writing teachers should work harder than other faculty and make less. Until Savage's entry into the department, Thomas found it difficult to support this injustice, largely due to Crandall's efforts and to a tight group of teachers who stuck together on important issues such as work loads. By 1916, three teachers in addition to Crandall had reached the maximum salary paid to composition teachers and still appeared determined to remain. Savage promised to cut the department in half simply by instituting a more efficient, standardized grading system. After studying the department for a year, the following was the substance of Savage's report to Thomas in a letter of March 1916:

> The chief crux has come in the correction of papers and the use made of these corrections. In the past I am convinced that readers have spent an inordinate amount of time in writing out corrections which might far better have been made by symbols. In no elementary course is it profitable to attempt to turn out finished writers, because there is not the remotest possibility of teaching more than the "respectabilities," as they should be taught.

Savage's solution to the problem involved a set of symbols teachers could use in correcting student papers, which the college printed in a manual students bought for 25 cents. This new method, Savage appears to have thought, justified increasing the number of students per class to eighty, reducing the number of semesters in which composition was taught from four to two, and reducing the teaching staff from seven teachers to four teachers and one half-time teacher. Savage also chose to retain the least experienced—and therefore cheapest—teachers. He recommended that Thomas retain Miss Hill, who "modestly considers other readers from their experience to have a stronger claim to re-appointment than she; but says that she should enjoy the work as presented to her and that she would heartily co-operate" ("Letter to M. Carey Thomas," Feb. 1916). Savage's own salary as Director of the Essay Work, interestingly, equaled that of literature faculty. In addition, he maintained a seat on the faculty and taught literature courses, which no other writing instructor had been allowed to do since the creation of the Essay Department. Still, the total cost of the Essay Department was less after Savage's changes.

Savage's ideas about quickly and efficiently commenting on student papers might have come from Chester Noyes Greenough, his dissertation director and mentor at Harvard. In a 1913 article titled "Grades that Explain Themselves," for example, Professor Percy Long explained the method he and his colleague, Greenough, devised for commenting, which used an elaborate system of symbols, each of which told a student whether or not he measured up to a set of abstract standards. "If one attempts to explain these things by either written or oral comment," explained Long, the attempt "usually proves both tedious and taxing" (489). Percy proudly quotes a student who remarked that 'B$^{v\ spcoh}$' is "almost equivalent to a conference" (491).

Crandall's Response to Savage

Shortly after Savage began to direct Bryn Mawr's writing program, alumnae, students, and some faculty began to pressure Thomas to restore Crandall to the directorship. Several former students and alumnae went directly to Thomas to complain that the Bryn Mawr tradition of writing was being thrown out and that Savage's approach to teaching writing was "too mechanical," to use the words of one alumna, Elizabeth Sergeant, a leader of the alumnae association in Philadelphia. In a response to Sergeant, Thomas begged her to stop rumors that the college is "replacing nice, thin Bryn Mawr Miss Crandall with Fat, Harvard Savage." "Other letters to Thomas praised both Crandall's teaching and her leadership of the writing program. Margaret Hobart, for example, claimed that Crandall's "illuminating criticism and her patient teaching grounded me in the fundamentals of English composition and of clear, logical argumentation." Those skills, claimed Hobart, laid the foundation for her work as Educational Secretary of the Episcopal Board of Missions, which required her to be "constantly writing short articles, reviews etc. for the Church Weeklies and The Spirit of Missions." In January of 1916, Thomas complained in a letter to Mrs. Fitzgerald that "the agitation among the alumnae has reached Boston" and asked that the former student "help [her] in giving a correct statement of the facts."

Catching wind of the controversy, H. B. Brougham, editor of the Philadelphia *Public Ledger*, solicited faculty and alumnae for complaints against Thomas's administration of the college. The resulting frontpage article, headlined "Bryn Mawr Alumnae Inaugurate Plans for Reform," featured a letter by Evangeline Andrews, a prominent alumna who had vigorously protested Crandall's demotion. Andrews's letter accused Thomas of micro-managing the faculty, who had no way to challenge her since she alone spoke with the board of directors about college affairs. The editorial claimed that Crandall's firing was one more instance of Thomas's despotic rule over departments (Horowitz 417). An editorial the following day reported on a meeting of Bryn Mawr professors who were discussing the need for more faculty autonomy and self-governance. The paper then printed several inflammatory letters from professors who had already left Bryn Mawr (Horowitz 419).

The college's board of directors responded to the crisis by fundamentally reforming the way the college was governed, giving faculty members three permanent seats at board meetings, for example. Meanwhile, after it became clear that Crandall had strong support among influential alumnae, Thomas decided to promote her to associate professor. Until then, her title had been only Senior Reader and Director of the Essay Department. In addition, Thomas allowed her to retain the salary that she had made as Director of the Essay Department, rather than reducing her salary to that of an instructor, as she had previously planned to do.

Though Crandall's position was secure by mid-February, she continued to lobby for lighter workloads for writing teachers and remained critical of Savage's focus on mechanical correctness. In late February of 1916, perhaps emboldened by the strong show of alumnae support, she challenged Thomas and Savage concerning their treatment of composition instructors. "You cannot have realized the number of papers that a reader must correct if the work of the department is to be done by four people," her letter to Thomas began. Crandall reminisced that when she first came to Bryn Mawr in 1902, instructors worked 990 hours a year and that this was "found to be an impossible schedule to carry." She pointed out that readers at present work more than 600 hours, and that Savage's scheme would require 1240 hours. Crandall then warned Thomas about the devastating pedagogical effects of such overwork:

> If they are given twice as many papers to read and correct, the evil result will appear not merely in hasty, unhelpful comment, such as I see constantly in the papers of other colleges, but in the readers' attitude toward their work. One cannot perform drudgery without becoming to some extent a drudge.

Thomas, replying to Crandall's warning of overwork, asked her "not to assume in advance that there will be overwork as it is so easy to produce anything like that by predicting it." She then tried to persuade Crandall that "if Dr. Savage wishes a little different form of correction it is, I think, only in accordance with our understanding that he should be given a free hand in trying this experiment." She did concede, however, that "in thinking over the matter I believe that we shall get the best results from a forty-hour week which is at the present time, I believe, exceeded."

Crandall also argued that Savage's plan threatened to discard valuable traditions of teaching and writing at Bryn Mawr. The courses were unique at Bryn Mawr, she believed, because while professors in other departments lectured to undergraduates about topics in a specialized academic discipline, writing teachers centered their courses around student observations and interests. They also listened as students read their own work aloud, gave frequent oral and written response, asked students to comment on each other's writing, and encouraged them to publish their writing. Scores of themes from required composition that were published in *The Lantern* and the handful of surviving freshman essays and daily themes support Crandall's claim for the ability of writing teachers to connect course work to students' interests and to engage them intellectually. Topics included sports games, settlement work, social and religious concerns, college friendships, college slang, as well as more academic subjects such as literary criticism.

Crandall's administrative and teaching ability was appreciated by her former students, many of whom wrote to protest her demotion. One student in particular, Margaret Haskell, felt that Crandall's teaching fostered "intellectual alertness" and "the ability to get at the meat" through her "daily contacts" with students. This student was so impressed with the incongruity between Crandall's teaching and her status at Bryn Mawr that she and her father stepped forward during the summer of 1917 to establish the *Margaret Kingsland Haskell Professor of English Composition* for Crandall. In a formal letter to Crandall that same month, Thomas notified her of the gift and made an unqualified offer of a full professorship, "at a salary of $3,000 or whatever may then be the salary of a full professor." She closed the letter with an offer for Crandall to teach "elective, advanced, and graduate courses [. . .] on the same basis as the elective and graduate courses given by other members of the department of English." Though Thomas did not note the historical significance of the appointment in her letter or in the minutes of the Board of Directors meeting, the Haskell Chair is very likely the first chaired professorship of rhetoric and composition held by a woman.

Letters between Thomas and Regina Crandall after 1917 are scarce, as are other college records concerning Crandall. Course catalogs indicate that she continued to teach courses in argument, daily themes, and expository writing. Furthermore, personal interaction with students continued to be important to her. In the 1919 *Bryn Mawr College Calendar*, her course in intermediate composition's description stated that "the work is carried on through class meetings and personal interviews." A seminar class that year emphasized "discussion and criticism of the students' own writing" and specified that "the subject of study in each year is adapted to the purpose and interests of the students." When Savage joined the United States Army in 1918, Crandall again briefly directed the Essay department but turned the reins back over to Savage when he returned in 1919. In 1930, she became Professor Emeritus of English Composition.

Howard Savage did not fare so well at Bryn Mawr. While Thomas claimed to be thrilled with his reorganization of the required coursework in composition, and welcomed him back to his job after World War I ended, he was not promoted to full professor in 1922, as he had been promised in his initial appointment letter. Instead, after numerous petitions to the board of directors in which he reminded them of their unfulfilled promise, he was granted a salary increase and the promise of a future promotion when a full professor in English left or retired. The board felt that there were too many full professors in English, Thomas explained. Another instance may indicate Savage's loss of status within the department and college. In 1922, when Crandall and Savage both applied for sabbaticals for the 1923-24 year, Savage's request was deferred by the board since, according to Thomas, "it would not be for the best interests of the college for two professors of English Composition to be away in the same year." In 1923, Savage resigned from the college to take a position at the Carnegie Foundation for the Advancement of Teaching.

Works Cited

The Bryn Mawr College Calendar. 1918-1919. Bryn Mawr College Archives, Bryn Mawr College.
Crandall, Regina. Letters to M. Carey Thomas. Microfilm reel 161. The Papers of M. Carey Thomas. Bryn Mawr College Archives, Bryn Mawr College.
Donnelly, Lucy. Letter to M. Carey Thomas. 14 July 1912. Microfilm reel 160. The Papers of M. Carey Thomas. Bryn Mawr College Archives, Bryn Mawr College.
Frankford, Roberta. *Collegiate Women: Domesticity and Career in Turn-of-the-Century America.* New York: New York UP, 1977.
Haskell, Margaret. Letter to M. Carey Thomas. 10 July 1916. Microfilm reel 161. The Papers of M. Carey Thomas. Bryn Mawr College Archives, Bryn Mawr College.
Hobart, Margaret. Letter to M. Carey Thomas. 18 Dec. 1915. Microfilm reel 161. The Papers of M. Carey Thomas. Bryn Mawr College Archives, Bryn Mawr College.
Holbrook, Sue Ellen. "Women's Work: The Feminizing of Composition." *Rhetoric Review* 9 (1991): 201-29.
Horowitz, Helen Lefkowitz. *The Power and Passion of M. Carey Thomas.* New York: Alfred A. Knopf, 1994.
Long, Percy W. "Grades that Explain Themselves." *English Journal* 2 (1913): 488-93.
Savage, Howard. "Personnel for College Composition." *English Journal* 10 (1921): 439-49.
—. Letters to M. Carey Thomas. Microfilm reel 161. The Papers of M. Carey Thomas. Bryn Mawr College Archives, Bryn Mawr College.
Sergeant, Elizabeth Shepley. Letter to M. Carey Thomas. 5 Mar. 1916. Microfilm reel 161. Bryn Mawr College Archives, Bryn Mawr College.

Thomas, M. Carey. The Papers of M. Carey Thomas. Bryn Mawr College Archives, Bryn Mawr College.

—. "Notes for the Opening Address at Bryn Mawr College, 1899." *The Educated Woman in America: Selected Writings of Catherine Beecher, Margaret Fuller, and M. Carey Thomas*. Ed. Barbara M. Cross. New York: Teachers College P, 1965. 141-42.

3

Cooperative Writing "Program" Administration at Illinois State Normal University: The Committee on English of 1904-05 and the Influence of Professor J. Rose Colby

Kenneth Lindblom and Patricia A. Dunn

Though much work has been done on the teaching of writing at prestigious northeastern universities, particularly Harvard, not enough has been done in the way of exploring writing instruction outside of the Northeast. David Russell surveys courses of study at several colleges from the late 1800s to the present in his well-regarded *Writing in the Academic Disciplines*, but even his work centers mainly on the so-called Harvard narrative.

One reason for the dominance of the Harvard narrative is the emphasis on research, which American universities and professors have adopted as a result of the influence of the German model of graduate education. The focus on research has, for decades, enabled a disrespect for composition practice that is by now well rehearsed in our field. Less explored is how that research-focus has enabled a disrespect for administrative work, particularly writing program administration, and we applaud this volume's move to address that lack in our field's history. At the same time, we have also become intensely aware of the ways in which the myopic focus on research at American universities has allowed an even more widespread lack of attention to scholarship on pedagogy and, in particular, institutions that have taken as their priority the production of teachers: namely, normal schools.

It is to composition's disadvantage that we have for so long ignored our historical connections to normal schools. In her recent Braddock Award-winning article, "A Rediscovered Tradition: European Pedagogy and Composition in Nineteenth-Century Midwestern Normal Schools," Kathryn Fitzgerald suggests that contemporary composition's democratic impulses may "have precedent in the normal schools" and that "normal schools were established in a completely different social and educational environment from the elite schools on which historians have primarily focused so far" (225-26). For example, she says, "normal schools were intended to be inclusive, democratic institutions" that operated according to "a unique normal school *ethos*" (244). Normal school *ethos* holds much promise for contemporary composition-rhetoric scholars and practitioners, and we intend our archival study to contribute to that promise.

Drawing from the rich yet little studied history of normal schools and intending to address this volume's interest in writing program administration before 1976, we present relevant findings from the Illinois State Normal University (ISNU) archives. Primarily, we present the history of a short-lived committee at ISNU, the Committee on English. This Committee explored and implemented a program for teaching language in 1905 that has much to teach WPAs today.

What we present is a community of teacher-scholars working together to provide an effective education in writing and English for students who would go on to become teachers themselves. As our research will show, this cooperation is not without some disharmony—if one looks closely. But it remains a cooperative effort. As we will describe, these efforts have similarities with the Cooperation Movement in Education in the early twentieth century taken up by Russell, but there are two distinct differences: 1) the professors at ISNU were teacher educators in the normal school tradition whose aims were similar to the contemporary aims of compositionists such as ourselves, who work in graduate composition programs and undergraduate English education programs producing teachers; and 2) the influence of one especially prescient teacher, June Rose Colby. Due to these differences, the model of cooperation developed at ISNU exceeds the examples Russell examines. We believe this and other case histories from normal schools provide an important resource for the contemporary aims of writing program administrators.

The Cooperation Movement in Writing Instruction and Administration

Much of the work completed by the Committee on English can be viewed consistently with the Cooperation Movement in education described by David Russell (140-55). Though cooperation had been suggested as early as 1892, by the national Committee of Ten, Russell dates the first "coherent formation" of cooperative language instruction in 1901 with the publication of a leaflet by the New England Association of Teachers of English. For the next twenty years, Russell says, "dozens of articles appeared on the subject [. . .] [h]undreds of programs began [. . .and i]n 1924, teachers at the NCTE convention ranked cooperation as the highest priority for improving instruction" (144).

The Cooperation Movement aligned with the notion that "every teacher should in some sense be an English teacher" (144), and pedagogical and programmatic experiments abounded. In some programs, teachers of subjects other than English would teach writing in their courses while in others, the faculty as a whole would create standards for writing while English teachers retained responsibility for teaching writing. In still other programs, the entire faculty would be involved in a language instruction program devised by the administration. Classroom experiments had English teachers "correct" papers written for other courses and use texts from content areas in their English class (144-45). In some schools, social studies and English teachers used the same books and co-planned, co-graded, and sometimes team-taught courses (154).

While much of the work in the Cooperation Movement sounds very promising for contemporary mores, Russell claims there were many problems with the movement and that ultimately it was not positive for writing instruction. Primarily, the problem was that cooperation was created by "administrative progressives" as a way of making language instruction more efficient and easier to cost-justify. The separation of disciplines that accompanied the research orientation carried to American universities from Germany was actually a "boon to cooperation in language instruction," says Russell, "if only a rational means could be invented to organize efficiently cooperative efforts across disciplines, to take advantage of economies of scale and efficiency of specialized organization" (146).

Thus the Cooperation Movement in language instruction amounted to an administrative rationalization for a differentiated curriculum, and,

> never confronted the issue of language and discipline because most administrative progressives [. . .] saw writing as a generalizable skill, independent of disciplinary content and context: thus, the mandated page requirements, the error counting, the papers graded for 'content' in one class and 'form' in English class. By viewing writing as a discrete skill, administrative progressives were able to quantify and rationalize its instruction, while ignoring its complex relation to disciplinary learning. (146)

A second major problem for the Cooperation Movement was its foundational link to remediation. In most schools, cooperation amounted to an organized method within which teachers across disciplines could refer students deficient in language to a remedial English course (149). Russell describes Harvard's commission of a Committee on Use of English by Students in 1914 as a typical and influential model of remediation. In this case, a standing committee was created to serve as "the writing police," who were supposed to be sent any student work that "has demonstrated the writer's inability to express his thoughts" (150). Students whose skills in writing could be shown to have declined in the years after taking Harvard's English A would be required to take a remedial course trenchantly called "English F" (150-51). Russell is understandably negative about the possibilities of progressive writing instruction given the models of "cooperation" he studies. Had he examined a normal school, he might have concluded on a more optimistic note.

We believe that the Committee on English at Illinois State Normal University illustrates a far more productive version of the Cooperation Movement in language instruction. Russell says that "cooperative language instruction often made more headway [in vocational schools] than it did in comprehensive schools," and he credits this advance to vocational schools' "clear goals and relatively homogeneous student bodies" (154).[1] We believe the more sincere and productive cooperation that occurs under the auspices of the Committee on English occurs not because of the reasons to which Russell points, but rather because of ISNU's thoroughness and responsibility to a coherent and consistent respect for pedagogy. Far from being a problem for composition, we believe the connection to pedagogy was a boon for language instruction.

To complete this history, we drew on the materials of the Illinois State Normal University archives.[2] In particular, we quote from several logs of faculty meeting minutes, most of which are handwritten but some of which are typed-up sheets that have been pasted in. We also cite ISNU catalogues, yearbooks, and histories.

Before we discuss the specifics of the Committee on English, we must introduce the role of probably its most influential figure at ISNU, Professor June Rose Colby. Our understanding of Professor Colby's work and ideas comes from her published and unpublished manuscripts, which are kept at the ISNU archives.

A Central Figure: June Rose Colby

A central figure in the making of policy, curricular design, and major goals of the English department was June Rose Colby. The first person to receive a PhD in English from the University of Michigan in 1886, Colby came to ISNU in 1892. She was Preceptress and Professor of Literature, holding those positions until she became Emerita Professor of Literature in 1931 and continuing to teach until she was seventy-six years old. In many of the documents and policies regarding language use in English and across the university, we can see Colby's influence. She believed schooling, especially the study of language, had social and ethical purposes, among them "making language tell the truth" ("What Does the Department of Literature and Rhetoric Contribute?" 26). She greatly admired intellectual curiosity and courage, and she believed language study could promote self-respect in learners, the full living of life, and the joy that comes from doing so. Most importantly, she believed language study was needed not only in literature classes but in classes across the curriculum. Her views on language, literature, and learning helped shape ISNU's writing program administration (though it wasn't called that, obviously) at the turn of the twentieth century.

It is intriguing to think about what English PhD students at the University of Michigan were discussing together in the mid- to late 1880s. Fred Newton Scott, whom Robert Connors calls a "truly great figure" in the teaching of rhetoric, was himself a graduate student there (182-83). Rose Colby was also there and received her PhD in 1886, three years before Scott did. Is it possible that Fred Newton Scott, whose "genius lay in pedagogy and language issues rather than in rhetorical theory" (Connors 339, fn #5) was influenced by June Rose Colby? She was an advanced doctoral student in the same department, already an experienced teacher and deeply, passionately interested in issues of pedagogy and language. Space does not allow further speculation in this essay, but it is certainly an important question for future research.

Colby's vast influence can be seen in the testaments to her when she retired in 1932; in the many, many references to her in the *Indexes* (yearbooks) from the time she arrived in 1892 until she retired forty years later; in her textbooks and other publications; and in her unpublished works. Colby viewed children as thinking, feeling beings as worthy of respect as adults. She had both an Arnoldian humanistic view of the role literature could play in broadening students' lives—in fact, her masters' thesis was on Matthew Arnold—and a fierce belief that language study was necessary for maintaining democracy and preventing warfare.

Though she taught Shakespeare and other courses in literature, much of the responsibility for assessing themes and other papers fell to her Department of Literature and Rhetoric. She spoke and wrote much about the need for teachers of other subjects to concentrate also on students' writing. Her motivation for this view may have been influenced partly by her belief in the importance of language in all learning and partly by frustration and exhaustion at the extra paper load carried by English faculty.

As the next section describes, Colby is of immediate concern to this project as she was one of five members of the Committee on English at Illinois State Normal University.

Summary of the Work of the Committee on English 1904-05

At the September 13, 1904, meeting of the Illinois State Normal University faculty, it was voted that "a committee consisting of five members of the Faculty be appointed by the President to make investigation and, if necessary and advisable, make recommendations for the promotion of more effective education in the use of the English language" (*Faculty Meeting Minutes*).

It was unusual for five faculty members to be appointed to such a committee; more commonly it was three. The numbers, and the extent of the committee's work, as will be shown, indicates that the Committee on English's work was of primary importance to the faculty. The five members of the Committee were Manfred. J. Holmes (teacher of general method and psychology),[3] J. Rose Colby (professor of literature), Elizabeth Mavity (head of the practice school and teacher of elementary pedagogy), Orson L. Manchester (professor of foreign language and economics), and Frederick. D. Barber (teacher of physical science) (Manchester et al. 354-55). The Committee apparently met often until it was dissolved—upon the completion of its work—on May 16, 1905. During its eight month lifetime, the Committee on English completed the following tasks:

1. Established the specifics of its charge.

2. Issued a university-wide call for data regarding student use of English language.

3. Established detailed recommendations to improve instruction in English language use.

4. Charged the Committee on Course of Study with implementing a remedial program for students not meeting the standards for language use.

The initial report of the Committee on English (see Appendix A) recommended a university-wide examination focusing on two questions: "What is the present status of English in our school?" and "Can the standard be improved? If so, how?" (*Faculty Meeting Minutes*).

The report suggests that the input of the entire faculty was necessary to answer the questions. Thus, the Committee suggested that to answer the first question, each faculty member should hand in "a list of common defects in the language of his pupils in oral expression and written expression" (*Faculty Meeting Minutes*). A long list of defects was attached and included enunciation, correct grammatical usage, force, delivery, penmanship, and "extent of acquaintance with good literature." Significantly, faculty members were not expected to categorize the defects: "But the faculty are not asked to classify under these headings. The committee will do this, if it seems necessary, after the lists are in." Each faculty member was also asked to submit "a statement showing what he does to improve his pupils' English in oral work and in written work." Specifically, teachers were asked to report the "Amount and frequency of written work," "Extent and character of corrections made," and "Extent to which these corrections lead to improvement" (*Faculty Meeting Minutes*).

The faculty members were given about six weeks to turn in their reports, and they appear to have taken the requests quite seriously. The October 11th meeting of the faculty reportedly included much "time spent discussing the nature of the work to be done by the faculty in furnishing data for the committee on English." And, an item at the January 1905 faculty meeting suggests that either faculty members were not turning in statements to the Committee on English or, perhaps, that the faculty members wanted more input on the Committee's work: "Motion carried that the members of the Faculty be requested to hand to the Committee on English a statement of what in their judgement [sic] can yet be done to improve the standard of English in our school" (*Faculty Meeting Minutes*).

The Committee on English issued its relatively detailed final report at the April 4, 1905 meeting (See Appendix B). The Committee claimed to have taken up the "problem of English in our school" in a "four-fold division":

1. The present status of English in our school.

2. Causes and conditions that prevent the most desirable results.

3. What is now being done to secure and maintain best results in English?

4. What can yet be done to improve the standard of oral and written language in our school? (*Faculty Meeting Minutes*)

Next in the report, and in surprisingly passive and elusive language, the Committee announced that it decided not to report anything at all on the first three divisions, those very divisions which might have sparked interesting and controversial debate (and perhaps did). In making this announcement, the report states:

> It has not been thought necessary to report on divisions "1," "2," and "3"; but to carry the study forward

> to the most helpful and permanent results in the life of the school the following recommendations arising from the study of division "4" are submitted for adoption or rejection by the Faculty. (*Faculty Meeting Minutes*)

Having moved immediately to the question of what could be done to improve the standard of language in the school, the report includes three sets of recommendations: 1) "Recommendations That Concern General Means and Conditions" (philosophical and practical suggestions for the teaching of writing and speaking across the curriculum); 2) "Recommendations That Bear Upon Classroom Work" (recommendations that seem somewhat more directly related to individual classroom teaching practices); and 3) "Recommendations That Concern The Course of Study" (recommendations that sought to impact the university-wide culture regarding interest in language study).

The final note of the report reads, "Recommendations relating directly and especially to the work of our special English courses, and all initiative toward change or improvement in these courses have been left to the teachers of the special English branches and the Committee on Course of Study" (*Faculty Meeting Minutes*).

At the close of the delivery of the report, one member of the faculty moved that the report be voted upon item by item, which suggests to us that there was at least some controversy over one or more of the items in the report. The motion to vote item by item was seconded, but then failed to carry. The report was approved as a whole, though the tally was not recorded. It was also voted that each faculty member be given a copy of the report.

The Committee on English was officially dissolved at the next meeting, May 16, 1905.

On May 30, 1905, the Committee on Course of Study issued a report that followed up on the Committee on English's recommendation regarding "special English courses." They reported no need for a change in the special English courses. Rather what was needed was "a plan to make effective" the policy as it was already published in the University Catalogue:

> Inasmuch as the teacher's own example is likely to be the most potent influence in determining the quality of the pupil's reading, penmanship, and English

style, all students notably deficient in clear and accurate expression, spelling, punctuation, idiom or division into paragraphs, will be required to take additional work in spelling or English composition until such deficiency is removed. Similarly students may be required to take additional courses in reading or penmanship. Correction of such deficiencies must receive early attention in the course. (qtd. in *Faculty Meeting Minutes*)

As a normal school producing teachers, it was in the interest of the entire Faculty to be sure that their students—who would go on to be teachers themselves—were responsible role models in their use of English language. Thus, the Committee on Course of Study recommended the following procedure for deciding who would be assigned to Special English:

1. That the teachers of any student at any time previous to the student's senior year, constitute a committee, which may be called together by any of its members, and which shall have power to warn the student, for the Faculty, that his English is in certain specified particulars so poor that marked improvement in it must be made; that he must expect to be assigned early in his senior year to extra work in case his deficiencies have not (been) remedied before that time. Whenever a student has been so warned, the fact shall be reported at the next faculty meeting.

2. It shall be the duty of the Secretary of the Faculty to keep a record of such reports and to read at the first faculty meeting of the fall term the names of any students reported as warned or who have only one year's work or approximately that to complete before graduation.

3. The teachers of each student whose name is read shall constitute a committee that shall report at the faculty meeting in the sixth or the seventh week of the same term what extra courses, if any, should be required of the student.

The minutes indicate that this policy was adopted at that very meeting.

Productive and Cooperative Language Instruction at Illinois State Normal University

Faculty Cooperation and Early Writing Across the Curriculum.

Russell's major critique of the Cooperation Movement is that it was instituted for administrative efficiency. The Committee on English at Illinois State University was founded upon a request from the faculty as a whole who directed President Felmley to appoint a committee. As already described, Felmley appointed an interdisciplinary committee of five, rather than three, indicating the Committee's work was of substantial importance to the university as a whole.

Fortuitously for us, the Committee on English's final report suggests much in the way of cross-disciplinary cooperative efforts for language instruction. In fact, one suggestion recommends directly that "there be more general and continuous concerted cooperative action on the part of the Faculty" in language instruction. There is, however, some division of labor between English teachers and teachers of other subjects.

According to the report, the English department should prepare "a style sheet to serve as a standard in all essentials of composition form;"[4] "a list of simple rational (self explanatory) abbreviations to be used in correcting student work;"[5] and "directions for theme writing, use of examination paper;"[6] and "comments and suggestions with regard to common errors." These resources would then be useful to all faculty members as they participated as language teachers in their content courses in the following ways:

1. That the adopted "form and style of paper for written work" be "used for all written work";

2. "That all members of the Faculty place an appropriate and adequate value upon the general execution of all expression work"; and,

3. "That written work below the standard be more frequently returned for revision before being accepted."

Such recommendations imply a philosophy of cooperation and describe precise classroom practices recommended for carrying out productively cooperative language instruction. In particular, we believe the recommendation that content area teachers have their students "revise" their work more often places firmly in the hands of each teacher the responsibility for teaching writing. (We acknowledge that "revision" was probably defined then closer to what we would think of as "correction.")

Russell also faults the Cooperation Movement for resulting in a view of writing "as a generalizable skill, independent of disciplinary content and context" (146). Although ISNU obviously employed its English professors in the work of generating university-wide standardized forms, they did not create naive standards that ignored disciplinary difference. In fact, the report includes a caveat to recommendation #1 above. While the standardized forms for writing should be used for all written work, an exception is made "when special requirements make its use impossible" (*Faculty Meeting Minutes*). This exception makes clear that the Committee theorized that a standard form might unproductively constrain writing in the disciplines. If our interpretation seems too generous, consider the following data we've also collected from the ISNU archives.

Incidental Composition

At a May 12, 1903, meeting of the ISNU faculty, the Committee on Course of Study in the Practice School proposed a new description for a course in grammar and composition. The descriptions for seventh and eighth grade, presented by Instructor of Grammar, Chestine Gowdy, seem especially important for demonstrating the school-wide philosophy that all teachers are responsible for helping students learn to write well. In particular, the concept of "incidental composition" is important: "Incidental composition work, both oral and written, is still done in all classes, and each teacher is held as definitely responsible for the language of his pupils as for their mastery of the subject matter of his course" (*Faculty Meeting Minutes*). In fact, Gowdy's report contains specific details for how subjects other than English may be useful for the student of writing.

> The science note book work gives opportunity for practice in clear and simple description; the explanation of problems in arithmetic, and the analysis of sentences in grammar for exposition. The geography work involves both description and explanation; and history recitation makes necessary narration, expla-

nation and occasional argument. All styles of discourse enter in the work of the literature classes (oral and written) and this study offers, perhaps, the best opportunity for original thought. (*Faculty Meeting Minutes*)

The inclusion of these details suggests that perhaps some of the faculty needed convincing as to why they should see their work in science or geography, for example, as attending simultaneously to composition. Or, it is possible that as a normal school, the faculty attended regularly to the specifics of their pedagogical decisions. Such thoroughness may be seen throughout the archived ISNU faculty meeting minutes.

Of course, the composition courses described in Gowdy's report were for the practice school, not the university students who were being taught to teach at the practice school. But we find that this is one of the very promising and unique strengths of the normal school tradition: they articulated their pedagogical theories from the youngest students to the most advanced. The same faculty members who worked out the philosophies for teaching composition in grades three through eight also worked those out at the university levels, as evidenced by work of the Committee on English. We believe it was this careful attention to the depth and breadth of language instruction that allowed ISNU to invent a cooperative method that excelled beyond those described by Russell.

Colby's Influence on Cooperative Language Instruction

Also lending evidence to our positive interpretation of cooperative writing instruction at ISNU is the work of Professor Rose Colby. In "English in the School," Colby writes what might be seen as an early call for writing across the curriculum. She sees accuracy of expression in other courses as inextricably connected to mastery of a particular subject. She calls for conferences between faculty in different disciplines, contending that the subject for compositions should arise out of the course of study. Colby emphasizes the complexity of writing, always calling on her colleagues across the curriculum to step up, not to view English as a service department any more than any other department: "The end to be attained, the honest mind thinking intelligently and expressing itself in words adequate to its thought, is a thing too great, too many-sided, too difficult to be attained without the service and cooperation of every subject in the course [of study]" (6).

She also demonstrates her awareness of the dangers of separating form from context, which Russell claims was endemic to the Cooperation Movement (146). With admirable directness, Colby writes, "As soon as [language] becomes a distinct subject, inanity in teaching it usually begins" ("English" 2).

Colby's is not a philosophy that jettisons intellectual rigor to buoy administrative efficiency. Rather, she expresses succinctly and passionately a view of language that is both empowered and informed by a rhetorical understanding of disciplinarity: "My plea, then, is that we shall not lift language to be an end in itself, but use it always in intelligent *ministry to the special ends which each subject serves* in securing the great general purpose of education" (6, emphasis added).

Colby values the "special technical vocabulary" of each subject and claims that a "really sympathetic understanding of the modern world and its problems is perhaps impossible without a fairly comprehensive grasp of the most important technical terms in many fields" (6). To demonstrate her point, Colby explains in a paragraph each why the specialized terms of math, science, history, economics, political and social science, the fine and domestic manual arts, and literature are essential to education.

Russell considers David Sneeden's advocacy of teaching writing "in specific genres for specific activities" (140) as the one positive exception in the Cooperation Movement. We would point to Colby's work—published nineteen years earlier—as another example.

A Complicated Definition of Language and Language Use and Student Error

The "Recommendations That Bear Upon Classroom Work" from the Committee on English's report in some ways reflect a complicated view of language. The recommendations also suggest the faculty had a relatively complicated sense of student error. Faculty members are asked to be attentive to "both the formative and the corrective aspects of language training," suggesting that the faculty members perhaps understood error as a necessary part of the learning process. Different kinds of errors are identified and are recognized as requiring different reactions from effective teachers: some errors "arise from a lack of clear understanding," while others "prevent sufficiently effective communication of thought." Harvard professors come to the same conclusion about their own students' errors nine years later (Russell 150).

Yet we should be careful not to view ISNU as somehow free from the influence of less complicated views of language and from its own tradition of rigid philosophy of language and error. ISNU was infamously tough and unforgiving of error. Faculty members in the earliest days of the University shared respect for military precision—discipline for discipline's sake—and a belief that misspellings and mispronunciations were manifestations of moral corruption. (For examples, see Harper. For a more detailed analysis, see Lindblom et al.) We see vestiges of these old attitudes in at least two of the Committee on English's latest recommendations.

In one recommendation, the committee states "that the most important thing in language training is fidelity to the truth" and in another, "that in all ways possible our students be brought to a sense of the true relation of thought and language" (*Faculty Meeting Minutes*). In the second recommendation, there is room for a more rhetorically complicated sense of that relationship, including attention to audience, purpose and forum, but most of the other recommendations and traditions of ISNU instruction make it doubtful that such a degree of complication operated. And although we claim that the Committee on English's mention of "formative aspects" of error might indicate a progressive instructional philosophy, it is also possible that the "formative" referred to is the soul or good taste of the student, which, again, has a long history at ISNU. It's impossible from this context to tell exactly how they intended the word "formative."

Perhaps an examination of committee-member Colby's views on language can help illuminate some of the recommendations in that report. Colby had complex opinions on language. To us, they might seem at times contradictory.

In some of Colby's writings, her view of writing seems to be premised on the view that all speech and writing simply presents what is already in the mind:

> the first, most fundamental principle of composition—[is] that thought must precede speech, that the sole business of composition, the most elaborate or the most simple, is to present thought, to convey to others the thought of the speaker or writer exactly as it exists in his mind [. . .] ("What?" 14)

She also says, "[. . .] when the writer really knows what he thinks and what he feels the problems of composition are reduced to the one problem of making language tell the truth" ("What?" 26). The phrase "fidelity to the truth" in the Committee on English's report may have come directly from Colby.

Ironically, however, the more she insists on the necessity of "making language tell the truth," the more interesting Colby's view of writing becomes. That is, if truth or beauty or *pathos* is so important for the writer to convey accurately to the reader, Colby seems to imply that work will be needed (revision?) to sculpt the writing so that it does its job of "truth telling." In a speech to the Faculty Club in 1899, Colby says:

> I believe that if a man's thought be clear and well-defined in his own mind his utterance of it will be clear; that if he sets himself always the task of presenting to his reader just his thought, that and nothing else, and his thought is beautiful or pathetic or sublime, he will be dissatisfied with any utterance of it that does not present it with beauty or *pathos* or sublimity. I believe that the man who understands the organic laws of composition, and has really grasped the truth that language is nothing but the symbol by which thought is conveyed, and is worse than nothing if it does not present thought truly, *will not rest until he compels language to present his thought truly*. ("What?" 31, emphasis added)

That a writer "will be dissatisfied" or "will not rest" until his thoughts are rendered satisfactorily opens the door to a concept of revision intended to make a text more effective for a particular audience.

In another passage from "Significance of the Study of Language," her view of thought preceding language again seems complicated by her view that language use promotes thought. These passages may intersect with the Committee on English's use of the word "discovery" [of truth] or with the phrase "the true relation of thought and language." Note how Colby here discusses the need for learners across the curriculum to study the language practices of a particular field: "If there is time, it certainly follows that no student of education, of art, literature, science, pure or applied, of history, economics, politics, philosophy, ethics, manual training or agriculture, or mathematics can afford to ignore the study of language" (22). Later in the same passage, she mentions reading, language as discovery, and language study as a stimulant to thinking:

> It is equally true that it is through the language constructions thus shaped in the speech and writings of others that we must detect and follow the logical structure of their thoughts, discover the truth of things *as it appears to them*, build again the universe of fact and truth, of thought and emotion in which they live. To study language therefore in any serious sense is to follow the thought process in all its subtlest windings. It is to get a severe and rigid training in thinking. (28-29, emphasis added)

Despite the Committee's emphasis on correction and error, Colby critiques the focus on fault:

> And in the language class even the primary teacher grows critical of speech forms—critical possibly in the narrow and popular sense of merely fault-finding. It is commoner certainly to meet here with corrections of faulty forms than with incitements to adequate and vigorous expression. In some cases 'written language' becomes mainly a drill in spelling, capitalization, and punctuation. ("English" 3)

Note the distinction she is making here (in 1908) between language as mere expression and language as a means of learning—a distinction usually credited to the language across the curriculum movement in 1960s Britain and one that would seem to contradict her oft-stated views on language as simply an accurate representation of thought. She calls for teachers to help students "make language and composition not merely a means of expressing what they know but a real instrument in the acquiring of further knowledge in the same or related fields" (3).

A Student-Centered Pedagogy and Respect for Students

Larry Cuban describes student-centered instruction as occurring when "students exercise a substantial degree of responsibility for what is taught, how it is learned, and for movement within the classroom." He also lists a number of "observable measures" that need to be present, such as much student talk, student-determined curriculum, furniture arrangement conducive to group work, etc. (7). By these standards, ISNU was probably a long way from student-centered instruction. However, clues from the Committee on English's report, and, more especially, Colby's views on children and teaching, suggest that elements of student-centeredness may have existed on the ISNU campus at this time.

In "English in the School," Colby calls for teachers to focus on "the real language of children" and that

> children should gradually be made conscious of their needs and put in possession of means to meet them. Then, if the time in these classes is too short, the work may be carried over into a special hour, but in such wise [ways] *as always to keep in mind the occasion out of which the need rose.* (3, emphasis added)

Colby's view that language skills should be taught in conjunction with what students were learning in all their courses is partly reflected in the 1901 ISNU Catalog description of how "Language-Spelling-Writing" were taught in the practice school:

> Language, spelling, and writing are taught in connection with the other studies, especially geography, literature, and science. These furnish abundant, familiar, and interesting subject matter, and the motive for either oral or written expression. The aim is fluency, freedom, variety. Corrections spring wholly from the child's needs. (59)

One of the Committee on English's recommendations regarding language training is "to its expression; whether this be in spoken or written words, in graphic representation, embodiment in material forms, or other modes of the expressive art" (*Faculty Meeting Minutes*). Another passage from Colby's "English in the School" essay also connects student language learning to activities other than the written word. Children's need for expression can come from "their games, their nature classes, their handwork of all kinds, even in their 'number work'" (3). This centering of learning on a wide variety of children's activities perhaps reflects Colby's interest in, and adoption of, the philosophies and practices of her contemporaries: Francis Parker, John Dewey, and especially Ella Flagg Young.[7] At the turn of the century, Young was a supervisor of instruction at Dewey's Laboratory School, which emphasized "reading and writing learned through activities rather than through isolated tasks [. . .]" (Cuban 41-42). According to a tribute Colby wrote after Young died, Young was also a twenty-five year member of ISNU's Board of Education. It's clear that Colby knew and admired Young's work. In the preface to her book, *Literature and Life in School*, Colby thanks Young "for help of many kinds freely given." Colby also thanks Dewey "who has read much of the manuscript" (iv).

In another manuscript "Training Teachers of Appreciation," Colby touches on what entering school children already possess. The following passage seems very student-centered. It seems, in fact, to anticipate Paulo Freire's critique of "banking model" education:

> And now for boys and girls. I believe in them. They are not receptacles to be filled. They are not embryos waiting to be born into life, 'to enter upon life,' as at graduation from high school they are often told. They are already living, have been living for some years when they come to us, even if we are primary or kindergarten teachers. (14-15)

The spirit of this passage can be seen in a description of fourth-year work in reading and literature, from the 1901 ISNU Catalogue (*ISNU Catalogues 1897-1904*). Though there is some reference to word drills and correctness, there are also references to enjoyment of life, student empowerment and free expression of thought, choice, and individual needs:

> Thru the substance and form alike [of literature] he [the pupil] gains increase of life and an increased capacity to enjoy good literature. On the other hand he gains in power to give to others what he himself gets from the book. The teacher seeks to remove whatever obstacles physical or mental stand in the way of the pupil's free expression of his thought. By constant attention in connection with the reading and by special word drills he works for correct pronunciation and articulation, fluency of speech, clear, sweet, and nat-

> ural tones, and a good position of the body in reading. The material provided for the grade is meant to be ample and varied enough to permit choice with reference to the special needs of classes and individuals. (59-60)

The last sentence of this passage reads like a version of what Lev Vygotsky later refers to as a "zone of proximal development": "Part of it [the reading] is easy enough to be well within the pupil's already acquired power of getting at the thought and rendering it; and part of it is as [sic] once hard enough and interesting enough to stimulate effort and growth" (59-60).

We see, then, that "language training" at ISNU under the influence of J. Rose Colby and others has elements of humane, progressive pedagogy.

Attempts to Impact the University-Wide Culture of Interest in Language, Social/Cultural Change, and Public Policy

Some of the most interesting recommendations of the Committee on English are the ones that attempt to effect university-wide cultural changes. Besides fostering cooperation among the entire faculty, the committee recommends that all faculty work to interest more of "the best" students in oratory and debate, that "general exercises be given on some aspect of language to help keep alive a school interest in language," and that they bring outside speakers who are "stimulating and suggestive." A new sensitivity to the pressures of workload on the ISNU students also existed. The university was traditionally very rigorous, requiring so much work that students often fell ill (Lindblom, Banks, and Quay), so this attention to the students' workload was probably quite necessary and also unusual. Teachers were cautioned to require extra work "only when [they] know that the student's program will enable him to meet the requirement well without undue pressure and distracting haste" (*Faculty Meeting Minutes*).

Onerous "extra work" must have been an ongoing problem. Five years before these recommendations were recorded, a piece called "Retrospect and Prospect," from the 1900 *Index* points out changes in the university culture regarding writing:

> There has come, too, more freedom in the school life,—less pressure, more spontaneity. [. . .] Spelling

> has ceased to vex the soul of the student whose sense of uniformity and whose abiding faith in the reign of law are constantly violated by the absurdities of the English tongue. The course [of study] has been made flexible to suit the varying needs of all grades of students that seek the Normal School. (7-9)

The outbreak of World War I gives us further clues to at least one faculty member's view on the role education could play—beyond the classroom or even the campus—in achieving world peace. In a Founder's Day speech by Colby, she writes:

> It falls to me to-night to ask you to consider what the public school can do through its curriculum to further the world peace we are all seeking. To further this possible influence of the public schools is the obligation and the opportunity of the normal school. [. . .]
> If through knowledge [the public school attempts] to replace the sense of strangeness and unlikeness to ourselves, which we now feel in contact with men and things foreign, with a sense of familiarity and even of likeness to ourselves underlying the strangeness, it will have gone far toward uprooting dislike and hostility and planting in their place sympathy and friendliness. As I see it, this is exactly the task of the school. This is its proper contribution toward world peace. ("The Public" 3, 6-8)

While we do not know, finally, how relevant students' language training seemed to them in their lives outside of school, these snippets indicate some attempt to make it so.

The Limitations of Cooperative Language Instruction at Illinois State Normal University

In no way do we wish to imply that ISNU's was a utopic writing program without tension or controversy. In fact, much evidence implies that ISNU created a forward-looking program for language instruction in spite of heavy controversy, and that it was subject to the same professional problems that writing programs suffered nationally.

Close readers will note that the first report of the Committee on English requests a list of student language "defects," but that the committee decided not to ask the faculty to classify them in any way. We are given no indication why the committee decided not to ask the faculty to classify the students' errors. Are the faculty members nervous about their ability to classify? Are they worried about using up too much of the their time? Does the committee think such categorization is unnecessary but isn't going to fight about it? Any of these answers imply controversy and make clear that the committee decided it was better to sidestep the issue. Similar issues of grammar and style affecting the work of contemporary WPAs are—to put it mildly—legion.

In the final report, the Committee on English completely ignored three-quarters of the charge they assigned themselves by deciding not to make any claims at all about what the present status of English use was at ISNU, what the major impediments to better usage were, or what faculty were currently doing to improve students' language use. There was some discussion of errors, if we can trust the parenthetical note in the report—"(Some suggestions made by members of the faculty have been deferred by the committee for future consideration)"—but we find no follow-up at all in the faculty meeting minutes to support that any such future consideration took place. We lament the committee's decision to deem these charges "unnecessary." Had the committee followed through, they might have produced the very first university-wide systematic study of error. But we also acknowledge how ambitious the committee was to suggest them in the first place, and we can imagine that asking faculty to report on the successes and failures of their own teaching practices would have been especially foreboding at a normal school. Thus we understand the committee's administrative savvy in side-stepping what might well have been unproductively tense issues and instead deciding to move immediately to changes that could be made in the future to improve the teaching of writing and speaking.

It is also worthwhile to note that the language instruction program at ISNU did follow along with the context of remediation that Russell points out most Cooperative models of writing instruction did at the time. While the call for cooperation in the instruction of writing aligns with Colby's published work and with other curricular efforts at

ISNU (such as Gowdy's report on composition in the practice school), the Committee on English was generated as a way to address student deficiencies in writing and speaking, just as Harvard's Committee on the Use of English by Students was nine years later. And while the ISNU Committee on English brought a complicated understanding of language and error to bear on their recommendations, they also left all matters of the remedial "Special English" course to the Committee on Course of Study. The Committee on the Course of Study's recommendation that students who are deficient in language use be reported to the whole faculty and be assigned to "Special English" follows very closely the typical model of faculty as "writing police" rightly criticized by Russell.

Despite the policing aspect, that teachers from all disciplines would be willing to serve together as arbiters of each individual student's language use indicates a continuing desire to have the faculty cooperate as writing and speaking instructors. This would have require a great deal of work for ISNU teachers. Perhaps the ambition proved too much. The only mention we find of any follow up on this recommendation occurs in the November 20, 1906, meeting minutes: "Informal discussion of the English of certain students." Never again in the faculty meeting minutes is any mention made of student use of English.

Another limitation in the cooperation at ISNU concerns a recommendation that is completely struck out in the Committee on English's final report: "That in every way possible we do what we can to raise the standard of instruction in English in the schools from which our students come." It is important that the committee had initially recommended meaningful communication with local schools concerning language instruction, something that remains to this day too rare. We wonder why the recommendation was struck out and if this recommendation was the reason for the request to vote item by item on the report. What were the concerns? Did the faculty believe it was not their place to tell local schools their business? Were the faculty not interested in working directly with local schools? Was the recommendation simply too radical or ambitious? One hundred years later, some college writing program administrators continue to wrestle with how to effectively communicate with K-12 schools, while others would never think of doing so.

Colby also had a complicated relationship with the idea of "cooperative" language instruction herself. We know that she was sensitive about the undue workload given to English teachers. In one speech, Colby talks about the heavy paper load of English faculty, pointing to "the critical reading of an average of almost fourteen thousand words of MS, five nights in the week for twelve weeks" ("What?" 39). Through most of it, Colby makes the argument that there is not enough time to focus on students' present needs.

We must also acknowledge that part of Colby's motivation toward a version of writing across the curriculum was to free literature from the demands of language instruction. She claimed students were denied the "joy" of literature "because the teacher of literature is made to be first of all a teacher of English, and is therefore forced to treat literature merely as a means to serve the ends of training in composition, rhetoric and maybe grammar" ("English" 4). Colby sounds a great deal like the literature professors Russell describes who asserted that the primarily role of an English Department is to teach literature and who lamented, resented, and resisted administratively imposed "cooperative" efforts in the teaching of writing and speaking (147). Still, Colby is more complicated. In "English in the School," she acknowledges both sides of the problem:

> [N]othing is commoner than to find all training in English relegated to the department that is responsible likewise for all development through literature. This often results in a double misfortune. The essential function of literature is ignored [. . .] . The loss to the student of literature is immense. But so also is the loss to the student of English. He gets the notion that English is a thing of value in one classroom only. (4-5)

Near the end of her article, Colby complains about teachers of English being given the responsibility of marking papers from other courses—a practice not uncommon to early WAC programs almost eighty years later.

> Sometimes teachers of English are called upon to read a certain proportion of the papers prepared in other classes and mark them as exercises in English, the other teachers being thus largely freed from responsibility for English. Now while this new vigilance is greatly to be desired, and the end sought a

> most necessary end, yet certain things in the means are unfortunate in themselves and seem to spring from a lingering misapprehension of the function of English throughout the curriculum. Organization of thought and form of expression in a geography paper are evidences of a pupil's really practical master of geography and its language; and should be credited, not to English, but to geography itself. (10)

Colby goes on to call for practices that sound very much like twenty-first century WAC/WID programs:

> Not a mere teacher of English but the special teacher of the subject is the person pre-eminently fitted to perceive both the adequacy and the inadequacy of his pupil's English in talking and writing about the special subject. If any teacher is not so fitted to recognize the strength and the weakness of his pupil's expression and the source of each, he is so far ill fitted to teach his subject. And very much of our loose and unsatisfactory teaching in all subjects springs from this very lack on the part of special department teachers. (10)

Colby also presents the need for much communication between and among all teachers regarding students' individual language needs:

> Nevertheless, while the English teacher should not be held primarily responsible for the English employed and the skill in composition manifested in various classrooms, the connection and interchange between the English room and all other rooms should be close and constant. Peculiar language needs and weaknesses that come to light in case of individuals or whole classes in other subjects should be reported to the teacher of English that in his special classes he may keep them in mind and direct a part of his work to meeting the needs and overcoming the weaknesses. Conferences between English teachers and other departments will be mutually helpful. The English teacher may sometimes help a colleague to discover

an ill and its remedy. He will certainly himself be helped thereby to remember that language is only a means of expression, and that all training in language and composition is necessarily a training in thinking in some definite field and expressing a body of related thought belonging to that field. And this is the only solid ground for the teacher of English. (10-11)

Our research demonstrates that there were indeed turf-battles and unproductive tensions in the cooperative language instruction developed by the Committee on English at Illinois State Normal University and that these tensions result in many ways from the same larger problems well examined by David Russell. But the research also demonstrates that the cooperative spirit was sincere and intellectually rigorous. There is much for us to learn from the ideas and debates of the ISNU faculty as they struggled with many issues of writing instruction that we continue to wrestle with today.

Conclusion: Embracing Composition-Rhetoric's Historical Connections with Pedagogy

In *The Origins of Composition Studies*, John Brereton posits rhetoric's historical connection with pedagogy as the root of its problems.

> [. . .] I would argue that the real damage [to composition] occurred in the relegation of composition to pedagogy. [. . .] Once it was determined that composition work was to be considered pedagogical, not the product of research or a province of the aesthetic imagination, writing instruction's place at the bottom was sealed. (22)

In the early twentieth century at Harvard, for example, Brereton says that rhetoric suffered from the "art/science divide," and that "[t]o argue rhetoric was not a science, not a way of knowing, was to consign it to training, to an introductory level of college, to pedagogy" (10).

Of course Brereton is right. In a university system that privileged research, taking pedagogy on as a serious consideration had severe consequences for rhetoric (24). But that is true only in the context of an exclusively research-driven university, such as Harvard. Research universities were not the only types of university contexts that existed. Since the early nineteenth century, normal schools have proudly engaged in the training of pedagogues; there, we find faculty members who began with the assumption that pedagogy was a legitimate scholarly practice. In such a context, composition-rhetoric's pedagogical connections would not be treated with contempt but celebrated as central to the intellectual mission of the university. Rather than lament composition-rhetoric's historical connections with pedagogy, we should *embrace* them. We have far better models for our contemporary WPA practices in normal schools than the Harvard narrative provides. As a field, we should begin to take this rich history more seriously ourselves.

Students at Illinois State Normal University provide us a model of this intellectual attitude as well. In 1903, a group of them took a trip to their University's younger sister, the University of Illinois at Urbana-Champaign, which had become the flagship institution in the state by then, having been established as a research university and taken the lion's share of funds in higher education. About their trip, the students write:

> Although we acknowledged that the University of Illinois has splendid equipments, buildings and grounds, we think that our institution, with its difference of purpose, does not suffer in comparison with it. We stand by you, You bet we do, Old I.S.N.U. ("The Champaign Trip" 88-89)

While our research at Illinois State Normal University shows that composition did not thrive unfettered in normal schools, we believe we have made the case that further study of the history of composition and writing program administration at normal schools may well pay dividends for our field, for enriching our own historical narratives and informing our contemporary scholarly, pedagogical, and administrative efforts, many of which are remarkably similar to the efforts of normal school professors over one hundred years ago.

Notes

1. Russell discusses schools of commerce, technology and industrial arts, but makes no mention of normal schools.

2. We are grateful to Illinois State University Archivist, Dr. Jo Rayfield, for her consistent help with our projects. We also acknowledge the assistance of Rise Quay, whose archival research assistance in the summer of 1999 continues to be useful to us. Quay's assistance was paid for with funds from an Illinois State University College of Arts & Sciences Small Grant for Research.

3. Holmes had also been a teacher of rhetoric and composition at the Minnesota State Normal School in Winona, Minnesota, from 1891 to 1897 ("Faculty Register" 355).

4. At the February 10, 1902, meeting, the faculty had adopted the NEA Style Sheet, but there is no mention of this style sheet ever again in the minutes, including in all of the work of the Committee on English.

5. The only mentions of symbols for correcting student work in the minutes occurs in two meetings in 1917. At the January 16 meeting, a text entitled "Symbols for Correcting Written Work" from an unidentified text is pasted into the minutes and adopted. At the November 22 meeting, a committee of three (including Colby) is charged with creating new symbols, though no further discussion is mentioned.

6. Directions for theme writing are included in the faculty meeting minutes of May 30, 1905. The directions, about one-page in length, cover only such concerns as measurement of margins, paragraphing, heading, and other surface standards.

7. It is possible that this pedagogy, in its fledgling student-centeredness, was influenced indirectly by John Dewey's work regarding education and the social. Cuban points out that Dewey himself was greatly influenced by Francis Parker (Dewey's son and daughter attended Parker's "Practice School" in the 1890s), who promoted child-centered education as well as the connections between courses across the curriculum, and employing in pedagogy such things as art, gardening, and music (Cuban 40). Colby begins her "English in the School" article with this quote from Ella Flagg Young, given in an address at Oberlin College. Young's words here are Colby's "English in the School" argument in a nutshell:

> English must come to stand not for chill exercises exemplifying principles of rhetoric, grammar, and logic, but for the application of the mother-tongue in all its accuracy, vigor, and beauty to other fields of study, in order that we may speak with persuasion and effectiveness. [. . .] I concede that the work should be specialized in academic as in vocational courses, but on the contrary, I insist that the specialization is in large measure unprofitable if its work originates and terminates in isolation from problems in related subject matters.

When Young died in 1918, Colby wrote "Ella Flagg Young: Teacher, Soldier, Patriot," apparently a speech or other tribute. What Colby says about Young in this tribute gives us a glimpse of Colby's own beliefs about and values regarding education and society. In turn, Colby's beliefs and values are woven into the curricula and practices of ISNU, which she helped shape at that time.

Works Cited

Brereton, John. C., Ed. *The Origins of Composition Studies in the American College, 1875-1925: A Documentary History*. Pittsburgh: U of Pittsburgh P, 1995.
Colby, J. Rose. "Ella Flagg Young: Teacher, Soldier, Patriot." Ms. June Rose Colby Papers. Box 1. Illinois State University Archives. Normal, IL.
—. "Ella Flagg Young." Ms. June Rose Colby papers. Box 1. Illinois State University Archives. Normal, IL.
—. "English in the School." *The Educational Bi-Monthly* (October, 1908): 1-11. June Rose Colby papers. Box 1. Illinois State University Archives. Normal, IL.
—. *Literature and Life in School*. Boston and New York: Houghton, Mifflin and Company, 1906.
—. "Significance of the Study of Language." Ms. June Rose Colby papers, Box 1, Illinois State University Archives. Normal, IL.
—. "The Public School Curriculum and Peace." Ms. June Rose Colby papers. Box 3. Illinois State University Archives. Normal, IL.
—. "Training Teachers of Appreciation." June Rose Colby papers. Box 4. "Misc. Manuscripts." Illinois State University Archives. Normal, IL.
—. "What Does the Department of Literature and Rhetoric Contribute?" Ms. June Rose Colby papers. Box 1. "Faculty Club 1899." Illinois State University Archives. Normal, IL.
Connors, Robert J. *Composition-Rhetoric: Backgrounds, Theory, and Pedagogy*. Pittsburgh: U of Pittsburgh P, 1997.
Cuban, Larry. *How Teachers Taught: Constancy and Change in American Classrooms 1880-1990*. 2nd ed. New York: Teachers College P, 1993.
Faculty Meeting Minutes, Illinois State Normal University. (Four Volumes) Illinois State University Archives. Normal, IL.
Fitzgerald. Kathryn. "A Rediscovered Tradition: European Pedagogy and Composition in Nineteenth-Century Midwestern Normal Schools." *College Composition and Communication* 53.2 (December 2001): 224-50.
Harper, Charles A. *Development of the Teachers College in the United States, With Special Reference to the Illinois State Normal University*. Bloomington, IL: McKnight & McKnight, 1935.
ISNU Catalogues 1897-1904. Illinois State University Archives. Normal, IL.

Lindblom, Kenneth, William Banks, and Rise Quay. "Mid-Nineteenth-Century Writing Instruction at Illinois State Normal University: Credentials, Correctness and the Rise of a Teaching Class." *Alternative Histories of Composition*. Ed. Patricia Donahue and Gretchen Flesher Moon. Unpublished manuscript.

Manchester, O. L., David Felmley, J. Rose Colby, Manfred J. Holmes, John A. H. Keith, and William T. Bawden, eds. "Faculty Register." *Semi-Centennial History of the Illinois State Normal University 1857-1907*. Normal, IL: Illinois State Normal University, 1907. 349-57.

"Retrospect and Prospect." ISNU Index. 1900. 7-12. Illinois State University Library, Normal, IL.

Russell, David R. *Writing in the Academic Disciplines: A Curricular History*. 2nd Edition. Carbondale: Southern Illinois UP, 2002.

"The Champaign Trip." *ISNU Index*. 1903. 88-89. Illinois State University Library, Normal, IL.

Vygotsky, Lev. *Thought and Language*. Ed. A. Kozulen. Cambridge: MIT UP, 1987.

Young, Ella Flag. "Address at Oberlin College." Oberlin College. n.d.

Appendix A

From the Illinois State Normal University Faculty Meeting Minutes: September 27, 1904
[Report One of] The Committee on English

The work of this committee falls under two questions:

1. What is the present status of English in our school?

2. Can the standard be improved? If so, how?

To answer the first question the committee recommended the following action which was approved and adopted by the faculty Sept 27.

1. That each member of the faculty hand to the committee a list of common defects in the language of his pupils.

   a. in oral expression,

   b. in written expression

Note. These language defects may cover the whole field of language expression including limitations in—

   enunciation, quality of voice,

pronunciation,
correct grammatical usage (oral and written)
accurate and discriminating use of words. Provincialisms? Slang?
good sentence structure (oral and written)
clearness
force
fluency
delivery
ability to read intelligently and intelligibly
punctuation
capitalization
general execution, proper composition forms, penmanship, neatness, etc.
extent of acquaintance with good literature

But the faculty are not asked to classify under these headings. The committee will do this, if it seems necessary, after the lists are in.

2. That each member of the faculty furnish the committee a statement showing what he does to improve his pupils' English.

   a. in oral work

   b. in written work—Amount and frequency of written work (about how many times a term)? Extent and character of corrections made? Extent to which these corrections lead to improvement?

3. That common errors in language be made the basis of a general exercise now and then before the whole school. (This is to be arranged for by the President.)

The data under the first and second items of the committee's report should be handed in any time before October 31.

Appendix B

From the Illinois State Normal University Faculty Meeting Minutes:
Regular Meeting April 4, 1905
Report [Two] of the Committee on English

To the President and Faculty: Your committee appointed to conduct a study of the problem of English in our school submits the following report.

The study has been conducted under a four-fold division:

1. The present status of English in our school.

2. Causes and conditions that prevent the most desirable results.

3. What is now being done to secure and maintain best results in English?

4. What can yet be done to improve the standard of oral and written language in our school?

It has not been thought necessary to report on divisions "1," "2," and "3," but to carry the study forward to the most helpful and permanent results in the life of the school the following recommendations arising from the study of division "4" are submitted for adoption or rejection by the Faculty. (Some suggestions made by members of the faculty have been deferred by the committee for future consideration.)

I. RECOMMENDATIONS THAT CONCERN GENERAL MEANS AND CONDITIONS.

[The following is struck out:] 1. That the Committee on Course of Study devise a plan by which students who have passed English courses but whose English becomes unsatisfactory shall be reassigned to such course or courses as they may need.

4. That written work be given only under conditions favorable to satisfactory (i.e., wholesome) results. This chiefly means (1) adaptation of work to classroom conveniences, and (2) the giving of no more work than can be done well within the time allowed. (The assembly room might be used more generally for the longer written exercises.)

5. That collateral reading and written work in addition to the regular class work be required only when the teacher knows that the student's program will enable him to meet the requirement well without undue pressure and distracting haste.

6. That a form and style of paper for written work be adopted by the school, and used for all written work excepting when special requirement makes its use impossible. (This is already referred to committee.)

7. That the Department of English prepare a leaflet, or brief handbook for use of students, which shall contain (1) a style sheet to serve as a standard in all essentials of composition form; (2) a list of simple rational (self-explanatory) abbreviations to be used in correcting written work; (3) directions for theme writing, use of examination paper, etc.; (4) comments and suggestions with regard to common errors, mooted suggestion, etc., that might be appropriately included in such a student's handbook.

II. RECOMMENDATIONS THAT BEAR UPON CLASSROOM WORK

1. That we give due weight and emphasis in thought and practice to the fact that the most important thing in language training is fidelity to the truth; (1) to its discovery or discernment; (2) to its expression; whether this be in spoken or written words, in graphic representation, embodiment in material forms, or other modes of the expressive art.

2. That in all ways possible our students be brought to a sense of the true relation of thought and language.

3. That all members of the Faculty place an appropriate and adequate value upon general execution of all expression work.

4. That, if possible, there be more general and continuous concerted cooperative action on the part of the Faculty in both the formative and the corrective aspects of language training; that in no case and in no subject a student be allowed to fall back to lower ideals and standards.

5. That as early as possible the student's personal interest and rational self-discipline be enlisted in freeing himself from bad language habits, and on substituting new correct ones.

6. That all fundamental errors in language should as a rule be corrected promptly; this refers (1) to those errors that arise from a lack of clear understanding, and (2) those that prevent sufficiently effective communication of thought.

7. That as students advance in their course they be given fair opportunity and be made responsible for the organization and

presentation of larger and larger units of thought in their integrity independent of the teacher's constant help.

8. That written work below standard be more frequently returned for revision before being accepted.

III. RECOMMENDATION THAT CONCERNS THE COURSE OF STUDY

1. That more concerted action of the part of the Faculty be enlisted in getting more of the best students into the work of oratory and debate.

2. That occasional general exercises be given on some aspect of language to help keep alive a school interest in language.

3. That we bring before the school more frequently the most stimulating and suggestive readers and speakers.

4. That in every way possible we do what we can to raise the standard of instruction in English in the schools from which our students come. [Recommendation #4 is completely struck out.]

Recommendations relating directly and especially to the work of our special English courses, and all initiative toward change or improvement in these courses have been left to the teachers of the special English branches and the Committee on Course of Study.

Respectfully submitted, by the Committee [on English]: M. J. Holmes, J. R. Colby, Elizabeth Mavity, O. L. Manchester. F. D. Barber [all original signatures]

4

Building a Career by Directing Composition: Harvard, Professionalism, and Stith Thompson at Indiana University

Jill Terry Rudy

For many decades, composition directors have held an often-conflicted professional status in modern universities. Research in the last decade has helped illuminate and contextualize the professional conflicts faced by composition directors. Evan Watkins in *Work Time*, for example, discusses the social organization that affects the people, and the cultural values, circulating in and out of composition classrooms and English departments (258-60). In contrast, Susan Miller in *Textual Carnivals* examines composition administration as a conflicted position embedded in the emerging ideologies, disciplinary status systems, and institutional structures of English departments and universities (159-73). Focusing on pedagogical theory and classroom practices, Robin Varnum in *Fencing with Words* gives insights into the work of Theodore Baird and his associates, who devoted much of their careers to writing instruction at Amherst College beginning in 1938. Varnum describes English 1–2, the course directed by Baird, in terms of how instructors built relationships in the classroom and enhanced students' abilities to discover and convey meaning through language and reflection (247). Collectively, Varnum, Miller, and Watkins suggest that issues connected with professionalism have affected composition directors for much of the twentieth century.

Because professional careers and disciplinary status systems were still emerging in the early twentieth century and doctoral degrees in composition were rare, it is difficult to identify one professional track leading to the position of composition director. It becomes important, then, to know more specific information about the training and working conditions of composition directors during this time frame. Stith Thompson (1885-1976) had a career path that illustrates some of the particular benefits and limitations of directing composition in the early twentieth century. After Thompson became an English instructor in 1914, his work in composition helped him ascend the professional career ladder. After seven years of teaching freshman composition and literature courses at three universities, Thompson moved to Indiana University where he directed and taught composition from 1921 until 1937; during these years, he also taught graduate seminars in folklore and published his most renowned folklore research. From 1938 until his retirement in 1955, Thompson received international accolades for his folktale scholarship while he also taught graduate students and built an interdepartmental folklore doctoral program at Indiana. Although his career culminated with institutionalizing folklore, both composition administration and literary history scholarship affected Thompson's career trajectory.

Thompson's active pursuit of career opportunities in both composition and folklore provides a telling commentary on internal disciplinary status systems and external affiliations with professional organizations, universities, and the general public. I do not intend merely to push back the timing of the professionalization of the field from the 1960s or 1970s to earlier in the twentieth century. I also prefer not to critique attitudes from the past in order to posit some new, positive alternatives to a beleaguered history or the status quo (see Watkins *Work Time*, 274-75). Rather, I want to study the details of Stith Thompson's career to examine how representations of professionalism, in part, constituted his experiences teaching and directing freshman composition. A memoir written at his retirement in 1955 and an oral history interview provide the filter for Thompson's experiences. Although these details will not be replicated exactly in other locations and times, they can be instructive about how professionalism affects occupational choices and about why composition still experiences status conflicts. As agents of professionalism, it seems imperative that composition administrators and instructors better understand the ideals and effects of a culture of professionalism.

Career Aspirations, Thompson's Harvard Training, and Composition as Apprenticeship

Burton Bledstein in *The Culture of Professionalism* gives a thorough discussion of the assumptions and actions that played into emerging ideas of a career in the mid-nineteenth century. Bledstein explains, "Career meant scheduled mobility, from the distinct and ascending levels of schooling, to the distinct and ascending levels of occupational responsibility and prestige" (111). Thompson's decisions and behavior in the early twentieth century appear to enact these emerging ideas. Thompson combined the memoir genre and the emergent culture of professionalism to narrate his life in terms of his career advancement. As documented in the memoir, his progress from bachelor's degree to doctorate and from English instructor to Distinguished Service Professor neatly matches middle-class career aspirations that appeared decades earlier. In chapter four of the memoir, Thompson establishes his father's lack of career opportunities as an impetus for his own decisions to obtain security through schooling and career advancement. He mentions that his father traded cattle in the Midwestern markets and experienced financial highs and lows in this precarious enterprise. In a stark one-sentence paragraph, Thompson writes, "The lean years were the years of my teens and they affected me profoundly" (25). Thus, the notion of "scheduled mobility" upward through a career appealed particularly to Thompson by seeming to assure him that the extended time spent obtaining credentials would be rewarded with meaningful and secure work. As such, Thompson attended Butler College, University of Wisconsin, Berkeley, and Harvard. He also taught high school English, first in Kentucky between years at Butler and Wisconsin and then in Oregon before his MA work at Berkeley.

As an aspiring professional in the early twentieth century, Thompson gravitated toward Harvard University as a pinnacle of advanced training and doctoral credentials. It is significant that Harvard doctoral training prepared new English faculty for literary research with an option to take a course in composition teaching. The atmosphere at Harvard impressed on these apprentice professors a hierarchal relationship between the fields. Most of Thompson's course work followed the Harvard commitment to philological research with classes in early languages, oral genres, and the medieval period; however, Thompson also took the graduate course on teaching composition. Thompson's doctoral training suggests that he picked up on the early distinctions between literary research and composition teaching evident in the career of Harvard English professor, Francis James Child (1825-1896), the mentor of Thompson's dissertation director, George Lyman Kittredge (1860-1941). Child is currently remembered for giving up the Boylston Chair of Rhetoric to become Harvard's first professor of English (Graff, Miller). This change in position removed Child from teaching composition courses and allowed him more time to teach upper-level literature courses and research the English and Scottish ballad.

Several institutional histories have posited explanations about why rhetoric lost status as literary history ascended and why composition emerged as a distinct, but lower status academic enterprise (Kitzhaber, Graff, Miller, Winterowd, Scholes). Miller gives evidence that "points toward how a cooperative brotherhood within English studies first *necessarily* separated and subordinated the teacher of composition in those departments that were well enough supported to establish a division of necessary labor" (126). To explain the necessary separation between the fields, Miller compares the heights of canonized literary expression with the struggling efforts of freshman writers to conclude that literature held more cultural value than freshman writing. However, Miller ignores the fact that the study of vernacular literature and language conducted by Child and Kittredge brought folk literary genres into the mix of cultural values claimed by English departments (Rudy). Because of scholarly interest in literary history and folklore as the presumed foundation of literature, Harvard was the leading institution in the United States for the study of literary folklore (Zumwalt). Thompson's career confirms that Child's example helped establish a pattern of professional status that rewarded research over undergraduate teaching, with composition teaching in particular becoming the apprentice work of English professors.

While underappreciated in English, composition at the turn of the twentieth century had public value outside of the university. The constructed literacy crisis of the 1892 Report on the Committee of Composition and Rhetoric submitted to the Harvard Board of Overseers and the interest in writing as the display of merit influenced the creation of freshman composition programs across the nation (Douglas). However, the assumption that freshman composition was remedial work for secondary school failures made teaching the subject a tenuous activity within emerging disciplinary hierarchies of the English department and the university. Because of this tenuous status, Brereton concludes that "English departments would gain their renown from scholarly work in literature, not work in composition" (132). But, as William Riley Parker and others acknowledge, university officials and the general public also came to assume that writing instruction would be a significant activity in university English departments.

Thompson structured his memoir in a way that reflects his disciplined assumptions about the hierarchal relationship between composition teaching and literary research. In the memoir he did not list a course on teaching composition with most of his doctoral courses; rather, he mentions the course when he discussed his first teaching position after his doctoral degree. The memoir chapter titled "Harvard: 1912-1914" describes the training in literary history that Thompson experienced and details his dissertation research and final examination. In the "Apprenticeship: Texas, 1914-1918" chapter, Thompson discusses his first full-time teaching position as instructor at the University of Texas at Austin. He describes a course load weighted toward writing instruction, "The young instructors all had three sections of beginning composition and one section of sophomore English literature" (64). In this "apprenticeship" chapter, Thompson finally mentions that he prepared for this aspect of his career by taking a course in teaching composition. He explains, "I had just come from Harvard where I had taken the course in the teaching of elementary composition under Chester N. Greenough and I was still enthusiastic about trying out new methods" (64). This organization of the memoir suggests that Thompson considered composition as part of an apprenticeship in an early phase of a professorial career, distinct from research training but worthy of a graduate course on teaching techniques.

Although Thompson moved on to teach upper-level and graduate courses in his literary specialties, composition became part of his professional identity. He taught freshman composition courses for much of his career. As an instructor of freshman composition with a new Harvard PhD, Thompson had certified academic training and an affiliation with a reputable university. Teaching composition at Texas was a more professional occupation than teaching high school and a step up the career ladder. The field also had some training methods and organizational structure by 1910. Although the graduate program in rhetoric established by Fred Newton Scott at Michigan was probably the most effective and best theorized approach to scholarly study at the turn of the twentieth century (Berlin 55), the Harvard approach of an atomized rhetoric with a focus on correctness and the modes of discourse influenced more attitudes toward rhetoric and composition in general (Stewart). Berlin asserts that "Chester Noyes Greenough's course at Harvard" was the "most conspicuous" graduate course to prepare students to teach composition (55). Thompson also did not give many details about taking the course; however, he was prepared to enjoy teaching composition. He explains in his memoir, "I felt from the very beginning [at Texas] that my work with these classes was successful; the rapport with the students was always excellent" (64). His Harvard training also introduced Thompson to professional expectations about publishing.

Thompson's Composition Textbook and Name Recognition in English

Although a conflicted genre in English disciplinary status systems, the composition textbook has served as a means of professional advancement for the field and for professors. Composition textbook publication suggests the connection and conflict of internal and external affiliations for English professors. Connors explains: "Modern composition-rhetoric was firmly in place, carried forward almost exclusively in textbooks, which represented the only organ of tradition in the field of composition teaching" (14). The general public would assume publishing a composition textbook to be a valuable contribution of a new English faculty member, while to Thompson, as the Harvard-trained English professional, the textbook was only an initial foray into academic publishing before getting his dissertation research into print. Connors describes the status of composition textbooks and the field of composition-rhetoric as a "scholarly backwater and a professional avocation, a drudgery, and a painful initiation ritual" (14-15). However, both Thompson's graduate training and apprentice work as an English instructor encouraged his textbook aspirations. He explained his ideas about publishing a composition notebook in the memoir:

> I began to think about a method of correcting themes discussed in Greenough's class at Harvard. The idea was to make a list of mistakes in any particular theme, to classify them into various categories, and then in a space opposite the error to make the correction. (65)

Greenough's composition course at Harvard and the teaching load of three freshman composition classes at Texas led directly to Thompson's *Manual and Notebook for English Composition.*

Greenough's manual for English A suggests that the Harvard freshman English course went beyond the more dire elements of mechanical correctness eventually identified with the Harvard program by Berlin (7-9). Students in English A wrote on diverse topics, conferenced with instructors, read in a variety of literary and nonfiction genres, and revised themes for meaning and form—not only to correct mechanical errors. However, the focus on errors was part of the required student notebook. Giving the detection and correction of errors more prominence, Thompson's notebook provided a format for listing errors in a left-hand column and corrections in the right-hand column. By emphasizing correctness in his composition notebook, Thompson probably selected an issue of general public value over and against his literary history training that valued vernacular expression for itself.

The attempt to publish a textbook indicated more than Thompson's Harvard training and methodological tendencies; the effort illustrated his professional aspirations and lack of status in the field. Thompson was an unknown English instructor at the University of Texas, and he approached more than one publisher before getting a positive response from Scott, Foresman and Company. To get published and used in classrooms, the manual needed name recognition, a sign of professional reputation that Thompson had not yet established in his career. To solve this problem, Thompson needed to collaborate with a more well-known professor to get the project in print. He explained in the memoir: "They liked the manuscript but suggested that since I was only a beginner and had no reputation, I invite Professor James F. Royster to be joint author. Royster consented and gave the manuscript a good reading and also helped with the proofs" (65). The project was published as *Manual and Notebook for English Composition* in 1916. The publishers soon let Thompson know that "many teachers did not like the notebook idea but did like the manual part of the book" (65). Not overly attached to his unique contribution of a notebook for corrections, Thompson, along with Royster, prepared a *Guide to Composition* in 1919. Evaluating the monetary and academic value of these publishing efforts, Thompson concluded that the textbooks "were not making me much money but even two or three hundred dollars a year was worth while, and I felt that I had at least broken the ice in the publishing of books" (65). Although his notebook idea did not catch on and he was listed as second author, Thompson considered producing the textbook as a useful entry into academic publishing and reputation building.

Thompson's composition textbook demonstrated some expertise in the field and invited more opportunities to establish name recognition and career advances. Although the composition manual did not link Thompson's name with key new ideas in the field, as in Kaufer and Carley's discussion of authorial handles (376), the textbook associated Thompson's name with composition. This association, along with collegial contacts, brought him the job offer to direct freshman composition at Indiana University. Unable to make salary or other advances at Texas, Thompson left the university in 1918 for a position at Colorado College, but bad faculty and administration relations had him looking for other opportunities when he attended the 1920 MLA meeting (76). At MLA, Thompson presented a paper related to his dissertation work, and he visited with John Rea, the English department head at Indiana University, whom Thompson had met "years before at a Radcliffe function" (77). Thompson noted the significance of the conversation: "Rea discussed with me something of my work at Texas and he already knew my textbooks. This was to be important later" (77). Tapping into connections with another former colleague, Thompson took a one-year job at the University of Maine, where he "was put in charge of the organization of the freshman composition course" (79). This position helped Thompson the next spring when Rea contacted him about a job directing composition at Indiana University (81-83). Publishing textbooks, attending a scholarly conference, and networking with colleagues all combined to help Thompson achieve the position at Indiana. Given public interest in writing instruction and Indiana University's interest in growth and improvement, it is not surprising that Thompson drew on all of his Harvard training to build his career as an English professor.

Composition, Literary Folklore, and the Professionalization of English

Not only did the emerging culture of professionalism associate career success with ascending responsibility, rewards, and security, but professionalism linked an individual's life with increasing engagement with the subject matter of the profession. Bledstein's career model posits an almost one-to-one correspondence between one's specialty and one's professional success. However, the demands of instruction and administration in most English departments required general acquaintance with various fields of language, composition, and literature. By the late nineteenth century, the need for skilled writers and willing employees helped entrench freshman composition in English departments and universities (Parker, Douglas, Miller). Composition offered some graduate training, publication venues for textbooks, and a potential supervisory role over instructors; thus, the field afforded some English faculty limited opportunities to claim a measure of professional status and career advancement.

For example, Thompson stepped up the career ladder when he began directing freshman composition at Indiana. Because most of the faculty taught two or three sections of freshman composition each semester, he held a leadership position over much of the department (Gray 122). In an oral history interview in 1968, Thompson described his position as composition director as being the "number two man in the English department," second in influence to the department head (Clark and Winther 26). Work in composition during the first half of the twentieth century, however, did not offer English professors acceptable ways to develop a scholarly reputation. Thompson attained the highest career advancement available to a professor, the rank of Distinguished Professor of English and Folklore, by pursuing international scholarship on the folktale and founding a new doctoral program; he could not achieve this career status for directing composition.

Professionals work to obtain credentials and status in order to achieve autonomy and to receive the benefits granted to doctors, lawyers, educators, and other occupations that meet the public need for expertise. Sociologists Kevin Leicht and Mary Fennell discuss professionalism in terms of "the status of the expert" that stems from "the professional's control over formal knowledge systems" (25). These knowledge systems are time-consuming, costly, and often difficult to enter, yet they provide useful, even necessary, services to an untrained public and allow perquisites and privileges for successful professionals. Professional careers, therefore, have a built-in tension between internal and external interests and affiliations—between self-promotion and public service. The internal interests of professionals encourage efforts to recruit and credential peers and to maintain the status, privileges, and specialized knowledge of the profession itself. These internal interests may or may not correspond with the outside interests of clients or other non-professionals who receive and pay for professional services.

Professional careers began to flourish under assumptions that professionals would subordinate the potential to monopolize necessary knowledge and services by accepting certain privileges and by sublimating internal interests to the external interests of society. Some social commentators in the early twentieth century, such as R. H. Tawney, Emile Durkheim, and Charles Peirce, promoted professional disinterestedness as an antidote to excessive self-interest encouraged by business and the marketplace. However, Thomas Haskell finds that businessmen competed for pecuniary rewards of capital and profit, while professionals accepted lesser financial remuneration by competing for non-pecuniary rewards of status and reputation (184, 216-17).[1] Professionalism did not inherently displace self-interest. For example, receiving the reward of academic status and reputation usually requires faculty to publish and promote work that is accepted by knowledgeable peers. Professors interested in professional advancement, therefore, might focus excessively on research and on developing an "authorial handle" (Kaufer and Carley 376, 380). Although peers in the scholarly discipline evaluate and award reputation, the ranking process is not solely internal; outsiders often grant financial and other benefits, such as tenure, based on the status a member holds within the profession and on the status of the disciplinary field itself.

As an eager and savvy new English professor, Thompson recognized the public and institutional value of composition and worked across disciplinary fields in English to establish professional status as a composition director and as a folklore scholar. He explains in the oral history interview, "I was very happy in managing the freshman composition. [. . .] I was definitely interested in folklore, but I realized that coming here I would have to work hard on that job [directing composition]" (Clark 4). While valuable to university administrators and the public, however, composition administration in Thompson's situation did not conform to internal standards in English to publish scholarship and establish a reputation in a specialized field. Directing composition brought Thompson a certain visibility at Indiana University that allowed him to maintain and extend his literary folklore research. When affiliations with professional societies, such as the American Folklore Society and the Congress for the Study of the Folktale, brought Thompson international acclaim, he achieved status as a renowned scholar in the eyes of university administrators. Given his reputation for research and his ability to administer programs, he was appointed dean of graduate studies in 1947, and university officials offered him more resources to institutionalize folklore at Indiana University (Thompson 243-58). Thompson's ultimate career success as a folklorist, therefore, shows the force of discipline building in mid-twentieth century universities.

Directing Composition and the Limits and Benefits of Professional Status

Thompson's career moves may look like a bait and switch, portraying himself as a composition director to get in the English department when he really viewed himself as a folktale scholar. While Thompson's memoir, his publishing record, and university documents indicate his preference for the folklore research, these sources also show how the daily and seasonal rounds of his work linked the two fields. According to accounts of how Thompson divided his work time in the memoir, he focused on the freshman composition course during the fall and spring, while he also continued his folktale research in the summers or during a sabbatical (83-86). A view of the bait-and-switch, then, holds only so far as a logic of disciplinary purity can be maintained. The assumption of disciplinary purity and professional disinterest also tends to obscure the social relations that embed professorial work in contexts of labor issues, institutions, and the distribution of resources.[2] While Thompson could attain status as a folktale scholar from peers within the discipline of literary scholarship, he obtained library resources, travel funds, and graduate courses in his specialty from contacts with his department head and the university president. Because of Thompson's supervisory role over an important area of public and institutional value, at least at the department level, he came in close contact with university leaders as he administered the freshman composition course, and this contact directly supported his career achievements.

As director of freshman composition at Indiana University in 1921, Thompson immediately drew the support and attention of university leaders because he accepted the charge to standardize the composition courses. Over the next sixteen years as director, Thompson continued to make career advances by supervising the composition program, conducting and publishing folk literary research, and maintaining supportive relationships with university administrators. For example, the charge to standardize the freshman composition program came directly from the university president. Thompson described the way President William Lowe Bryan supported more organization and rigor:

> Up to that time the teaching of freshman composition had never been really organized and I found that it was being badly handled. [...] When I called upon President Bryan he told me that he hoped I would take hold of the reorganization with vigor. He anticipated that I might find opposition among the faculty of the department, and he was right . [...] He came to my first meeting with the staff and gave a talk about what he hoped would happen and asked for the hearty cooperation of the staff in the reorganization. I had to improvise quickly the whole plan for sectionalizing the incoming freshman class so that the easy teachers would not get all the students. I found that the standards of marking papers were, on the whole, very low, and set about to try to raise them. (83)

Thompson's work as director carried more status than stigma, as indicated by the fact that the university president appeared at the initial staff meeting to support the reorganization of the Indiana writing program.

The more professional status of composition at Indiana is reinforced by the fact that Thompson was intentionally hired in 1921 to direct composition. Although Indiana was still a small school, with only three thousand students when he arrived, Thompson linked his charge to organize the freshman composition course with the university president's desire to enhance the university. Twice during the oral history interview, Thompson mentions his hiring interview with President Bryan. He reiterates each time the charge he received from the president to organize, even professionalize, the composition course. First he explains

> Dr. Bryan told me what he had in mind. They wanted to reorganize freshman composition on a basis of a large university. Up to that time, freshman composition was taught in a very informal way. All the lazy students went into certain soft spots, and often a man would have only six or seven students because he was a hard marker. (2)

After discussing several other issues including his marriage and attitudes toward several faculty members prominent in the university at his hiring, Thompson was asked to restate his opinion about Bryan as a person and university president. He replied, noting that Bryan told Thompson in his hiring interview, "One of the reasons that we're asking you to come is because you have worked in a large system at the University of Texas. You have written text books [sic] in the field. We want this [composition] organized on the basis of a big university" (15-16). Clearly the university president was aware of freshman composition as a site that needed to be standardized and needed a faculty member with experience and publishing credentials to administer the course.

By assuring that "the easy teachers would not get all the students," Thompson helped the Indiana composition program fulfill an important aim of professionalism: to train, sort, and credential future professionals—essentially, to circulate and assess human capital. He did this by instigating placement tests and monitoring grades, but professionalism in English also had a claim on contributing to cultural knowledge. The acquisitiveness of early English departments in claiming literature and composition allowed both cultural and human capital to circulate through courses and other work-related activities. English departments organized faculty labor around the evaluation of diverse discursive forms and literate practices, such as oral ballads, Shakespearean plays, and freshman compositions. As Watkins asserts in *Work Time*, there is a certain uniformity of labor in English that levels the playing field between these discursive forms: what circulates in English that matters most to outsiders is students and grades (6). Miller explains, "Outsiders to English did not recognize composition as separate, as they still do not" (127). The idea that social relations in English center around the distribution and evaluation of cultural and human capital helps explain why composition was both constitutive of and resistant to professionalism as Thompson pursued it in his career.

Briefly remembering the career of Francis James Child may be a helpful corollary to Thompson's career trajectory as it relates to cultural and human capital, social relations in English, and the limits of professionalism in regards to composition. Although there are many interpretations of the event, it is generally agreed that Child declined an offer from Johns Hopkins and stayed at Harvard when university president Charles Eliot Norton agreed to shift Child's title and work from evaluating student themes to literary teaching and research. As composition developed at Harvard shortly after this event, freshman composition became associated with an assessment of what would currently be called human capital. In turning from these evaluative duties to teach literature and compile *The English and Scottish Popular Ballads*, Child indicated a personal, and soon to be professional, preference for the cultural aspects of work in English. At least in terms of the internal rationale of the discipline, composition became a "deniable subtext" distanced from the circulation of cultural values as literary study promised to become "the guardian of national 'ideals'" with valid claims on resources and "time for academic research" (Miller 127). Composition administration was constitutive of professionalism to the degree that administrators like Thompson standardized syllabi and grading criteria so the course provided a valid way to sort and evaluate student potential. Composition administration was resistant to professionalism to the extent that instrumental assumptions about the field restricted opportunities to establish a scholarly reputation.

The details of Thompson's career considered here show that, for him, the culture of professionalism served to bring the meaningful and secure work that he learned to desire as an adolescent. Composition provided several important rungs on his career ladder, but internal and external forces at work in English departments limited the possibility of attaining the highest professional status without a literary research project that could be expanded into a new specialty. Professionalism still affects individual careers and composition administration in universities, but composition, universities, and professionalism have changed significantly since Thompson's day. Discipline-building the way Thompson pursued it for folklore may still be a viable professional attainment and career move; but the expansion of new specialties and the maintenance of old disciplines face severe constraints, given current economic trends. Thompson's career considerations were not hampered by issues of gender, race, and class. At the same time that increasing awareness of diversity opens professional opportunities to more groups of people, it is obvious that professionalism no longer offers the certainty and rewards that it seemed to proffer even a few decades ago. It also is clear professionalism never was the equitable meritocracy many hoped it to be. But the desire for secure, substantive work represented by an academic career like Thompson's deserves serious consideration, some critique, and perhaps, generous lines of defense.

What will be new in the early twenty-first century, as Watkins suggests in *Everyday Exchanges,* is the trend that some professionals in composition may have better career opportunities and more status as universities streamline departmental structures to provide human resource services to potential employees and their employers (161-64). The organized teaching of writing and critical thinking skills will remain an important service in our society both as a way to sort for merit and to update skills for specific work tasks and projects. Composition can perhaps more persuasively be connected with the development of human capital than literary study can be connected with a need to develop cultural capital. However, numerous people may be affected negatively because of prevailing employment practices that challenge work autonomy by encouraging temporary hiring and the constant assessment of productivity, trends that definitely affect composition. These trends may dismantle the benefits of a sustainable career for many professionals who might hope to achieve successes similar to those of Stith Thompson. Even under critique and attack, the loftiest goals of professionalism for secure, meaningful work that ethically provides needed services need not be abandoned. Composition administration remains a place to promote and protect classrooms and work environments that encourage opportunities to learn to use language to reach potential through meaningful work and other forms of service.

Notes

1. Evan Watkins in *Everyday Exchanges* offers a more recent discussion of connections between professions and the marketplace. He notes the proliferation of professions during the twentieth century, moving beyond university credentials in medicine, law, and other fields to leverage many kinds of economic practices into "a claim for publicly recognized authority" (185). Thus, a professional carpet cleaner or other professional listed in the yellow pages can claim authority both to provide a particular service and to give that service a certain "general public value" because it is called a professional service. The general public has come to rely on the symbolic assurances that "professional" certifies a desired level of service, as well as to value being able to become professionals at some type of work (184-85).

2. Here again, Watkins offers a useful discussion of how the distribution of economic resources connects with more than financial concerns. Watkins argues that people facing economic constraints have "been busy constructing economic alternatives that work [. . .] despite how capitalist common sense has made their economic resources seem invisible" (63). Many disciplinary and institutional histories also keep the acquisition and distribution of resources rather invisible; however, it seems important to a discussion of professionalism and composition administration to identify how a composition director combined professional behaviors with occupational networks to obtain resources.

Works Cited

Berlin, James A. *Rhetoric and Reality: Writing Instruction in American Colleges, 1900-1985*. Carbondale: Southern Illinois UP, 1987.

Bledstein, Burton J. *The Culture of Professionalism: The Middle Class and the Development of Higher Education in America*. New York: Norton, 1978.

Brereton, John C., ed. *The Origins of Composition Studies in the American College, 1875-1925: A Documentary History*. Pittsburgh: U of Pittsburgh P, 1995.

Child, Francis J. *The English and Scottish Popular Ballads*. Five vols. Boston: Houghton Mifflin, 1882-1898.

Clark, Thomas D, and Oscar O. Winther. *Oral History Interview with Stith Thompson*. Papers of Thomas D. Clark. University Archives. Indiana U, Bloomington, 1968.

Connors, Robert J. *Composition-Rhetoric: Backgrounds, Theory, and Pedagogy*. Pittsburgh: U of Pittsburgh P, 1997.

Douglas, Wallace. "Rhetoric for the Meritocracy: The Creation of Composition at Harvard." *English in America: A Radical View of the Profession*. Ed. Richard Ohmann. Hanover, NH: Wesleyan UP, 1996: 97-132.

Durkheim, Emile. *Professional Ethics and Civic Morals.* Trans. Cornelia Brookfield. London: Routledge, 1957.
Haskell, Thomas L. "Professionalism versus Capitalism: R. H. Tawney, Emile Durkheim, and C. S. Peirce on the Disinterestedness of Professional Communities." Ed. Thomas L. Haskell. *The Authority of Experts.* Bloomington, IN: Indiana UP, 1984. 180-225.
Graff, Gerald. *Professing Literature: An Institutional History.* Chicago: U of Chicago P, 1987.
Gray, Donald J., ed. *The Department of English at Indiana University Bloomington, 1868-1970.* Bloomington: Indiana University Publications, n.d.
Kaufer, David S., and Kathleen M. Carley. *Communication at a Distance: The Influence of Print on Sociocultural Organization and Change.* Hillsdale, NJ: Lawrence Erlbaum, 1993.
Kitzhaber, Albert R. *Rhetoric in American Colleges, 1850-1900.* Dallas: Southern Methodist UP, 1990.
Leicht, Kevin T., and Mary L. Fennell. *Professional Work: A Sociological Approach.* Malden, MA: Blackwell, 2001.
Miller, Susan. *Textual Carnivals: The Politics of Composition.* Carbondale, IL: Southern Illinois UP, 1991.
Parker, William Riley. "Where Do English Departments Come From?" *College English* 28 (1967): 339-51.
Peirce, Charles Sanders. *Collected Papers.* Ed. Charles Hartshorne and Paul Weiss. Volume VI-290. Cambridge: Harvard UP, 1931-60.
Royster, James Finch, and Stith Thompson. *Guide to Composition.* Chicago: Scott, Foresman, 1919.
Royster, James Finch, and Stith Thompson. *Manual and Notebook for English Composition.* Chicago: Scott, Foresman, 1916.
Rudy, Jill Terry. "Considering Rhetoric's Wayward Child: Ballad Scholarship and Intradisciplinary Conflict." *Journal of Folklore Research* 35.2 (May-August 1998): 85-98.
Scholes, Robert. *The Rise and Fall of English: Reconstructing English as a Discipline.* New Haven: Yale UP, 1998.
Stewart, Donald C. "Harvard's Influence on English Studies: Perceptions from Three Universities in the Early Twentieth Century." *CCC* 43 (December 1992): 455-71.
Tawney, R. H. *The Acquisitive Society.* New York: Harcourt, 1921.
Thompson, Stith. *A Folklorist's Progress: Reflections of a Scholar's Life.* Ed. John H. McDowell, et al. Bloomington, IN: Special Publications of the Folklore Institute No. 5, 1996.
Varnum, Robin. *Fencing with Words: A History of Writing Instruction at Amherst College during the Era of Theodore Baird, 1938-1966.* Urbana: NCTE, 1996.

Watkins, Evan. *Everyday Exchanges: Marketwork and Capitalist Common Sense*. Stanford: Stanford UP, 1998.
—. *Work Time: English Departments and the Circulation of Cultural Value*. Stanford: Stanford UP, 1989.
Winterowd, W. Ross. *The English Department: A Personal and Institutional History*. Carbondale: Southern Illinois UP, 1998.
Zumwalt, Rosemary Lévy. *American Folklore Scholarship: A Dialogue of Dissent*. Bloomington: Indiana UP, 1988.

Part II: Communities

5

The "Advance" Toward Democratic Administration: Laura Johnson Wylie and Gertrude Buck of Vassar College

Suzanne Bordelon

> Here were two women [Wylie and Buck] of the highest distinction, either one of whom, alone, would have made an English department, in the same sense that Mark Hopkins alone, as it was said, would have made a university. Together, they achieved something which I believe was quite without parallel, then or perhaps since, in the field of American college English teaching; something, moreover, which has lived on as a sound creative influence, through the students who have gone out to become leaders in many corners of the country.
>
> —*Elisabeth Woodbridge Morris*[1]

In the past few decades, feminist historians of rhetoric and composition have transformed the traditional canon by rewriting it to include women.[2] As Cheryl Glenn explains, this regendering of history "entails our rethinking texts, approaches, narrative—and history itself" (3). One area that has experienced burgeoning growth is research on nineteenth-century women's rhetorics. Recent works have explored the significance of dress and appearance for women speakers, the gendered nature of "parlor traditions," and the role of women and African-Americans in the abolitionist movement.[3] These texts show the diversity and richness of research on nineteenth-century women's rhetorics. However, one site that has been overlooked by this rewriting/regendering effort has been women's administrative efforts in the nineteenth and early twentieth centuries. Writing program administration scholarship has tended to focus on its recent history. In so doing, such scholarship has virtually ignored earlier examples of writing program administration, including histories that focus on women administrators (L'Eplattenier 2).

This analysis expands the revisioning efforts by exploring the administrative efforts of Laura Johnson Wylie and Gertrude Buck, English professors at Vassar College during the Progressive Era (1890-1920). For twenty-four years, both women worked together and crafted a collaborative model of administration that encouraged members of the English department to take an active role in running the department. As chair of the English department, Wylie oversaw literature while Buck coordinated rhetoric and writing. (The department also included the study of language and eventually grew to include Spoken English and drama.) Wylie and Buck viewed the teaching of literature and rhetoric/writing as equally important and organically connected, which typically was not the case within other English Departments across the nation (Connors, "Overwork/Underpay").

This chapter explores how Wylie and Buck developed a democratic model of administration that was inextricably connected to its Progressive Era context.[4] More specifically, it examines how Wylie and Buck enacted their ideas in the administration of the English department and how they responded to clashes with the administration during tight budgetary times. This analysis demonstrates that although the administration of a writing program and a college may seem to share similar goals, they often are in direct conflict with each other. At the same time, this study shows how Wylie and Buck's model anticipates current approaches, such as those advocated by Jeanne Gunner.[5] One difference, though, is that Gunner's model advocates a decentered writing program, whereas Wylie and Buck's approach demonstrates a collaboratively administered English Department, with equal literature and writing components.

Wylie and Buck: An Overview

To better understand Wylie and Buck's administrative efforts at Vassar, it is necessary to know something about their lives and social philosophy. Both Wylie and Buck were among the early generations of women to graduate from college, women who "felt they had to prove their rights to a higher education by doing something important" (Davis 37). This led many, like Wylie and Buck, to have a strong sense of social responsibility. Both women were involved in social justice movements, particularly women's suffrage, and both believed in advancing democratic relationships, both at the college and within society. Although Wylie and Buck's vision of democracy viewed everyone as equal, it tended to privilege those with their class, status, education, and race.

Wylie (1855-1932) began her career at Vassar as an English instructor in 1895; two years later, she became the chair of the English department and remained chair from 1897 to 1922. Valedictorian of Vassar's class of 1877, Wylie was among the first women to receive a PhD from Yale, and Yale published her dissertation, *Studies in the Evolution of English Criticism*, in 1894 (Wylie File). Most of her energy focused on administrative and teaching duties, rather than publishing. Thus, she was not as prolific a scholar as Gertrude Buck. According to Elisabeth Woodbridge Morris, Wylie was "a talker rather than a writer, because she was never wholly willing to let her ideas stiffen into the printed phrase" ("Pioneer and Humanist" 68). Personal communications and teaching were Wylie's preferred mediums.[6]

Wylie also "combined teaching with community involvement work and a commitment to suffrage and social reform" (Gordon 130). She was the president of the Poughkeepsie Suffrage Party, and she founded and served as president of the Women's City and County Club, a reorganized version of the suffrage party after New York women won the vote in 1917 ("Women's City and County Club" 2). She also served as a faculty vice-elector and an honorary member of the Vassar College Chapter of the College Settlement Association (*Vassarion*, 1889 94). After her retirement, Wylie continued to be involved in women's issues, teaching at the Bryn Mawr Summer School for Women Workers in Industry,[7] which began the American workers's education movement and "drew its primary inspiration from the thriving women's social justice movement of the progressive era" (Heller 4).[8]

Similar to Wylie, Buck (1871-1922) was active in suffrage and social reform. Buck's involvement in women's issues was supported through her relationship with Wylie, her longtime professional associate, friend, and housemate.[9] The devotion of the two women to each other is evident in many ways, particularly in Wylie's establishment of a Gertrude Buck fund after Wylie's death in 1932.[10] Wylie also directed that "her body be cremated and the ashes buried in the grave of her friend, Gertrude Buck, in Woodlands Cemetery, Philadelphia" ("Miss Wylie's Will Probated"). As colleague Elisabeth Woodbridge Morris points out, "The cooperation of these two was unique, and it is impossible to separate their fields of achievement" ("Laura Johnson Wylie" 13).

A member of the Poughkeepsie Suffrage League and later the Board of Directors of the Women's City and County Club, Buck published two limericks, "Anti-Suffrage Sentiments," in *The Masses*, and she and Wylie participated in suffrage parades and activities. According to Vassar President Henry Noble MacCracken, Wylie and Buck's home "in the center of old Poughkeepsie became a rallying place for suffrage and for many other movements" (150).[11]

Buck, like Wylie, was distinguished in her field. Buck was the first person in the United States to receive a PhD in composition-rhetoric, the first PhD student in rhetoric to graduate from Fred Newton Scott's program at the University of Michigan, among the first teachers to pioneer the "Dewey school of thought," among the first women to attend George Pierce Baker's playwriting and stage production course, and among the first teachers to implement the new playwriting curriculum in women's colleges (Connors, "Teaching and Learning" 137; J. Campbell, "Gertrude Buck" 1; Snyder 118; Flanagan 16).

However, Buck was also very much a product of the progressive society of the time, benefiting from her background and education. She received her bachelor's (1894), master's (1895), and doctorate (1898), all at the University of Michigan, where she came under the influence of two powerful intellectual figures—John Dewey and Fred Newton Scott.[12] In her dissertation, Buck acknowledges her debt to Dewey, "for the fundamental philosophic conception embodied in it" and to Scott, "for much stimulus and criticism" in preparing her thesis (iii). As Joan Shelley Rubin points out, Buck's acknowledgment of Dewey "was no frivolous compliment, but rather the key to her [. . .] political perspective" (12). Quoting Lawrence A. Cremin, Rubin adds that for

Dewey and progressive educators like Buck, the goal of education in a democracy is "'to make human beings who will live life to the fullest' by continuously enlarging their participation in society" (12).[13] Education is not a neutral activity but serves the political function of creating a democratic society.

While completing her doctorate, Buck was hired as an English instructor in 1897 at Vassar College. She taught at Vassar until her death at age fifty. She suffered a stroke in August 1921 and died after a second stroke on January 8, 1922 (Reed, "In Memoriam" 128-29).

Both women viewed education as a way of bringing about their organic theory of society, which emphasized a reciprocal relationship between the social and the individual. Wylie and Buck revised the traditional power of the chair by developing a collaborative model that emphasized the role of department faculty in the administrative process. In this way, the department became more inclusive and democratic.

Wylie: "Experiments in Democracy"

In a June 1921 presentation at the fiftieth anniversary of the Vassar Alumnae Association, Wylie discusses "the advance toward Democratic Government at Vassar" (12).[14] Wylie traces this advance from the late 1870s, when she was a student at Vassar, to her return to the college in 1895, to the present in 1921. If asked to summarize the changes at Vassar, Wylie explains that she "should call them experiments in democracy, experiments in democratic government" (12). In her presentation, Wylie constructs Vassar's identity as a college that has a long history of developing a democratic consciousness. More specifically, she discusses different stages in this movement, emphasizing that it is a positive and continuing development at Vassar. In addition, she suggests that this advance toward democratic government did not just involve Vassar but was the ultimate question for Progressive Era society. She concludes with a strong argument for the importance of this movement: "Educationally, it means free power [. . .] . It means that better people are going to come to teach, if they have a chance to shape a larger teaching policy themselves" (23). For Wylie, the development of a democratic consciousness in administration is much more important than "even the most essential question of bread and butter" (23). Wylie's presentation is significant because it gives us insight into her own "democratic consciousness" and her belief in cooperative forms of administration.

Wylie's introduction, similar to her conclusion, echoes the significance of this advance, which she describes as "perhaps the most important line of educational development" (12):

> When I say that I am going to speak about the advance toward Democratic Government in Vassar, it seems at first as though it might seem as though I were stepping out of my proper educational field into an administrative, purely governmental position. That is very far, to my mind, from being true, because, as in the world around us, the achievement of some sort of real Democratic administration of life, in whatever form we take it, is the supreme question, so I believe in college to-day [sic] the establishing of a truly democratic sentiment, of a truly democratic administration is the crucial point. (12)

Wylie establishes her credibility to speak on the topic by linking the issue of forming a more democratic administration at Vassar to the broader question of creating democratic relationships within society. Wylie sees this as "the supreme question" facing Progressive Era society, affecting everyone.

In this movement toward democratic administration, Wylie argues that the major challenge is no longer simply having a voice:

> It wasn't so very many generations ago when we thought that a voice was enough, if we could say what we wanted, and if enough of us said it, we were fairly sure to get it. We don't feel that way now. We know that besides the voice, we have to have the technique, the method. (13)

Wylie recognizes that a voice without power is as meaningless as no voice at all. The problem, then, was gaining the power and influence to create organizational structures that foster democratic relationships. This is still a challenge that administrators face.

In the early years at Vassar, Wylie notes the college was "isolated" and, as a consequence, "[w]e were not very conscious of ourselves" (14). Assessing the early days, Wylie says, "the thing that I can see that we got toward that democratic consciousness which has underlain our later progress was that tremendous sense of solidarity" (15). During this early period, the college was "a solid family." The president lived on campus, "and we all lived around him, and almost all the members of the faculty, and almost all of their children lived in Main Building" (Wylie 14). In many ways, Wylie says the isolation "was exceedingly bad," but, on the other hand, "it tremendously concentrated our group feeling toward the college. And I think one reason was that we didn't have any sense of class or sub-groups within it, we were a single unit" (16). One result of this isolation was a lack of self-awareness of how radical the college was:

> We didn't feel our radicalism very much because we didn't know that we were radical. It is really amazing, when I look back on it, to think that we were not very far from reaching, when I was in college, what I suppose ought to be the most radical venture, the thing that was going to do much, to do more than any other thing to change the position of women in the economic world. We didn't think about that. We thought the world was all right, and we would live just the same and the world would be just the same when we were educated. If anybody had told us what was going to happen, we would simply have scouted the idea. (16)

This isolation allowed the college to carry out "the most radical venture" of educating women without much outside interference. Wylie emphasizes how radical educating women truly was in the 1870s and how this education could, in turn, dramatically alter society.

Wylie then discusses changes she noticed at Vassar when she came back as a teacher in 1895: "it was a new world that I came into, absolutely different from the one that I had left" (17). In this advance toward democratic government, Wylie singles out two developments as significant. First, "the group consciousness" remained strong, "but it developed into a perfect class consciousness" (18). Second, the faculty had became more aware of the students' needs (18).

During this period, Wylie points out that "[t]he administrative machinery of education" became more sophisticated, and it had developed "in the one necessary way strictly parallel to the way that any business up to that time had been developing" (18-19). So, when Wylie first became the chair of the English department in 1897, she and other chairs "were all given free hands" (19):

> We were to be managers and we were told explicitly that we were to be managers. It was our business to manage our departments. It was our business to know the advanced thought in our departments, it was our business to organize and be responsible for the work. (19)

Chairs "managed" their departments using a top-down approach similar to the ways businesses were managed during this period.

The formation of distinct departments at Vassar is significant because it meant the development of a new administrative layer in the educational process. In her description of Vassar from 1870 to 1880, Mary Augusta Jordan (Vassar, Class of 1876) emphasizes that during this period

> there was a marked absence of rigidity in administrative order. Vassar illustrated easily the best aspects of what may be called academic quantivalence. Teaching Greek did not unfit an officer for usefulness in the library, and the instructor in gymnastics might teach German. The watertight compartment treatment of learning, or even scholarship, would not have seemed dignified to the aspirant for culture in those days. (57)

Ada F. Snell, a Mount Holyoke English professor who completed an unpublished history of the college's English department in 1942, notes similar changes brought about by departmentalization in the late nineteenth century (Mastrangelo 94): "Previous to this period, as for all colleges, each subject had been a single course; now each subject unfolded into many courses clustered in departments administered by highly specialized instructors" (qtd. in Mastrangelo 111). Departmentalization resulted in dramatic changes in how learning and the curriculum were conceived and administered and in the level of specialization required of its instructors.

Wylie's report notes that during the 1890s, the different classes within the university also became more distinct: "There was the faculty feeling among the groups at the top. There was the faculty group of workers who were under the group at the top" (19). Wylie says she is discussing the class distinctions that developed only to emphasize

> that this group consciousness into which the college was at that time largely divided was an inevitable thing in the course of progress. It was on a parallel with the outside world. It was the thing that, for efficiency, had to be. And I think it led us farther and better than could possibly have been done by any other method at that time. And when you talk of the democratic consciousness, it was not excessively democratic, it was the strengthening of feeling, it was a heightening of responsibility at different points; it was not inclined to draw the community very much closer together. (19-20)

Wylie views the managerial stage in department administration as a necessary step in the seemingly inevitable "advance" toward a more democratic administration. This phase allowed for certain efficiency in moving departments forward in the early years. However, with the development of separate classes within the college came "a very keen sense of the need of a closer co-operation" (20). According to Wylie, a recent change was the belief that

> the whole college should be represented and people who live here should appear in the political life. That went through a few weeks ago, and there wasn't [a] ripple, nobody minded that employees of the college had a chance to be members of the political life. Yet, when I came to the college it was only spoken of with bated breath, behind closed doors. (21)

She suggests that this change is significant in terms of the movement toward democratic administration.

A second major change occurred at the department level:

> Quite a number of us found that, if our positions allowed us to be bosses, we rather were guilty of benevolent despotism and we found that that didn't go far in getting departmental teachings done. We found, if we were going to have good departments, if we were

going to have good teachers, we simply had to have democratic organizations. And so gradually the departments in many cases made their own experiment toward a real and genuine democratic government. (21-22)

Here, we get a sense of Wylie's own philosophy in terms of chairing the English department and how she viewed the department administration as an "experiment" in democracy.

According to Wylie, the

> third very hopeful sign outstanding was the first joint-committee, when Dr. Taylor [then President of Vassar] [. . .] asked some of the students, two or three members of the faculty, and a few student representatives to meet to talk over that burning question how we could simplify social life at Vassar. [. . .] I didn't realize at all at the time that that was really the beginning of the solution that is going on so well to-day [sic]. (22)

In each administrative level of the college, Wylie emphasizes this movement toward more cooperative and inclusive organizations. This movement, though, was not as seamless as Wylie depicts it. Wylie and Buck were among twelve faculty members who signed a statement or petition in March 1913 calling for a more democratic college administration ("Statement to President"). The petition was in response to a December 1912 Board of Trustees resolution that some faculty members thought denied them any participation in the college's administration and educational policies (Vassar College Faculty Meeting Minutes, 9 Dec. 1912). Although it seems that the petition was not circulated or forwarded to the board, it did disturb and offend President James Monroe Taylor. In February 1913, Taylor notified the college trustees that he planned to resign within the year, claiming he was "tired of administration" (Daniels, *Bridges* 68). He left Vassar shortly after.

Many of those who signed the petition also were active in the suffrage movement, and there had been a major clash with President Taylor in June, 1908, when he prohibited a number of Vassar suffragists from organizing and meeting on the college campus during commencement activities. The following year, Taylor explained his stance toward "the progressive movements of the day" in a speech entitled "The 'Conservatism' of Vassar," presented before an annual meeting of the alumnae, later published as a pamphlet and distributed nationally. In the speech, Taylor emphasized that he did not specifically oppose any one cause, but that he was concerned that such movements were potentially exploitative of students. Reiterating what first Vassar President John Howard Raymond said in 1875, Taylor asserted that "the mission of Vassar College was not to reform society but to educate women." Thus, Taylor contended that "plain old-fashioned preparatory education, opening up all of these questions but under the influence of the spirit of teaching and investigation, and not of agitation, has some claim upon the undergraduate mind." In her presentation, Wylie fails to mention these earlier conflicts; however, they were integral to the faculty's effort to gain political power.[15]

Wylie concludes her presentation by discussing what Vassar had become in 1921. Wylie suggests that the ideas that were developed in the 1890s and early twentieth century are continuing. For the past two years, Wylie says that all sectors of the university

> have been working at the very center to try to get at that question of how we can get together. Educationally, it means free power [. . .] . It means that better people are going to come to teach, if they have a chance to shape a larger teaching policy themselves. It isn't only lack of money, it isn't only poverty that has made teaching for the last ten years in a great majority of cases rather a lean profession. It is because people have been placed in positions where they don't control their lives, their own activities, and this working out of a democratic government and democratic consciousness seems to me far and away more important than even the most important and most essential question of bread and butter. (23)

The leanness Wylie describes was felt at Vassar. The 1921 Report of the Department of English states that the tight budget at Vassar meant "the failure of five members of our department to get the promotion, with corresponding increase in salary and intercollegiate dignity, to which long and recognized service should have entitled them" (1). The current budget constraints hindered this advance toward democratic government and subsequently made the need for it all the more apparent.

Democratic Organization: The English Department at Vassar

The records of the English department indicate Wylie enacted many of the ideas she discussed in her 1921 presentation. Although Wylie was nominally the chair of the department, it is evident from department reports that in the first twelve years, Wylie and Buck collaboratively administered it. In Wylie's last twelve or so years as chair, the faculty took an even more active role in the department's administration. In the 1911-12 Report of the Department of English, for instance, Wylie writes that "the general administrative work of department has been more effectively done than ever before <I think>[16] because the members of the department have done more of it and taken more responsibility in it" (3). Wylie details the different duties of faculty members: scheduling department lectures; overseeing the commencement essays; supervising tutors; attending meetings with the Poughkeepsie teachers of English; re-examining students needing "special attention;" running a "special spelling class weekly;" managing the English Book Club; and arranging department and journal club meetings (4). In addition, faculty members presented and discussed their research during regular department meetings and during journal club meetings (2). Although Wylie's aim was a democratically run department, her actual practices may have emphasized responsibility and "efficiency" over personal freedom as is evident in the following quotation from Vassar President Henry Noble MacCracken:

> She [Wylie] was not a radical as the term is generally understood. She liked organization. A born commander, this advocate of personal freedom expected and obtained a willing obedience and service from all her associates. The members of the Department of English were her loving aids long after her resignation from active work, yet her training was really a training in freedom and in administrative efficiency, and every teacher in the Department of English was given some executive responsibility. (149)

Despite this apparent contradiction, a key aspect of the department was an interconnected view of literature and writing. In "Retrospect, 1924," written upon Wylie's retirement, Katherine Warren describes the organic philosophy that was central to the department's organization:

> The ideas upon which this [the development of the department] rested were definite, and original both in themselves and in their application. Chief among them was her conception of the field of English as a single territory of art and scholarship, the "branches" of which were not separate, but were merely different aspects or approaches, emphasizing one or another element without detaching it from the rest. From this it inevitably followed that the department itself should be an organic whole in the main trend and character of its teaching [. . .] . (83-84)

This organic view of the department was particularly evident in the collaboration between Wylie and Buck. For instance, in the 1905-06 Report of the Department of English, Wylie emphasizes Buck's significant value to the department in asking that she be appointed to a full professor: "Miss Buck's arduous service for the college both as a teacher and as an administrator imperatively demand this recognition, while her standing outside the college and her influence with the students add possibly less weighty reasons for it" (4). Wylie reiterated her request in a 1906-07 report, and Buck was appointed a full professor in 1907, according to the student yearbook, the 1921 *Vassarion* (15).

The joint significance of their equal efforts within the department also became evident in their salaries. In the 1908-09 Report, Wylie asks that Buck's "salary be made equal to that of the head of the department" (2). Here again, Wylie underscores Buck's important role as a teacher and administrator in the English Department, emphasizing the benefits this collaboration has for the college:

> This [the salary increase] has for some time seemed just to me, because of the size, and consequent administrative work of the department of English. Of this administrative work, Miss Buck does her full share, relieving me entirely of a great deal of it. Indeed, if we did not work to-gether [*sic*] in entire har-

> mony, it would be necessary either for me to do considerably less teaching, or to divide the department, as has been unfortunately done in many places, into the departments of English or Rhetoric, and Literature. The present union of the two subjects in a single department has many advantages of economy and efficiency, and it seems unfortunate that in order to preserve these, one of the people concerned should suffer serious and permanent financial loss. (2)

Wylie emphasizes the inherent unfairness of the current salary scale, given Buck's department responsibilities. She also highlights how this collaboration benefits the college because it would be much more costly to have two separate departments. This issue has not gone away; today, we still struggle over potential rhetoric/English departmental splits.

In addition, as Barbara L'Eplattenier points out, the collaboration of the women is visually evident in several of the department reports and draft reports. Wylie and Buck were often both involved in drafting them, even though they are signed, "Respectfully submitted" by Wylie. For example, the 31 January 1908 Report of the Department of English is typed, and both Buck's and Wylie's corrections are evident throughout the report. As L'Eplattenier explains, "[o]pen, sweeping, rounded and bold, Buck's handwriting is easily recognizable and clearly different from Wylie's tight, scrawling, chicken scratch" (83). Wylie and Buck also probably discussed the reports and their contents since they lived together for many years. Another indicator of their close working relationship is the fact that Buck served as the chair during the 1913-14 academic year when Wylie was on leave. The department documents demonstrate the close collaboration between Wylie and Buck.

The collaborative nature of the department is particularly evident in the 1920-21 Report of the Department of English, submitted by Wylie (2 May 1921). A committee consisting of Wylie, Alice Snyder, and Amy Reed wrote the report, and then a draft was read to the entire department and "had the benefit of much suggestion and criticism" (13). Wylie's emphasis on democratic organization and budgetary constraints, evident in her earlier presentation, is echoed in this document. This report is important because it was Wylie's last before stepping down as chair, a position she had held for the past twenty-four years; she resigned as chair, shortly after Buck's death in January 1922. In the 1921-22 report, Amy Reed, who became the department chair, explains the significance of the document, noting the report is "in some sense a summary of accomplishment during her [Wylie's] administration, and an analysis of needs for the future" (1). Reed notes that Buck's death "meant a revolution for the Department" (2). JoAnn Campbell points out that Wylie's 1921 report "differs in tone considerably, for she [Wylie] holds nothing back in giving [President] MacCracken her opinion of the way finances have been handled by the college" (*Toward a Feminist Rhetoric* 253).

The report was written in response to President MacCracken's request that the English department "consider plans and methods in relation to the budget, with a special view to retrenchment wherever such retrenchment was possible" ("1920-21 Report" 13). However, according to Wylie and the members of the department, the "financial pressure" had increased over the past five years to the point "where there must be not merely amelioration of a bad situation, but a radical change in policy towards the department, involving a considerable enlargement of our resources" (1). They explain, though, that it is "in no spirit of rebellion" that they present their findings, but instead so that the President and Trustees "should have a chance to know what seem to us the educational issues involved in [the] present retrenchment" (1). The first part of the reports details how the department is "suffering from a long-continued pressure of overwork, with little prospect of relief" (7). The remaining pages "prove the fallacy of the current impression that the department of English is among the most expensive in the college" (8). The department demonstrates this fallacy through a statistical analysis of the "student-hours per teacher" (8-9), which shows that the department "not only rank[s] fourth from the lowest in money spent, but that only five departments carry a larger number of students, or of student-hours, per teacher" (9).

The report also includes a table showing the number of students per teacher within the English department from 1898 to 1921. During the 1920-21 year, teachers taught an average of 150.1 students per year and 75 students per semester. Based on the number of students taught, Wylie and the other department members contend that they are being asked "to work a fifth harder than we did six years ago, when we, for the first time in our history, even approached our early estimates as to numbers—an estimate which, as we were even then convinced, was too high for truly efficient teaching" (10). The situation at Vassar was not unusual. For instance, according to Wellesley's 1895 President's Report, Sophie Chantal Hart (who became chair of the English department) and a "Miss Weaver" "were responsible for the theme writing of 200 students apiece. Weaver, in addition, taught another twenty-six students in a course in Theme Writing" (Mastrangelo 145). Hart's heavy workload apparently continued and was the primary reason she resigned her chair position in 1935. In her resignation letter, she writes that her drama course has more than one hundred students, her history of criticism has seventy, and her advanced composition course is "'full to the limit'" (qtd. in Mastrangelo 157). This course load was in addition to her duties as the chair. Similarly, at Harvard, the average freshman class size had increased to more than two hundred students by 1870; the class size jumped to more than six hundred students by 1903. In many colleges, the average freshman class was two hundred plus students, and similar to Vassar, many teachers were required to meet individually with students to discuss their work (Connors, "Overwork/Underpay" 112). At Vassar, teachers devoted an average of three or more "interviews" to each student each semester, and the interviews typically lasted twenty-five minutes ("1911 Report of the Department of English" 2).

Calling the budget situation "the present regime of drastic retrenchment," the report emphasizes some of the major consequences: the failure of five department members to gain promotions and salary increases (1). The budget crisis was made worse by World War I and the fact that members of the department and faculty "have been giving liberally of our time and strength to help the college bear the financial burdens inevitable in time of war" (2). Instead of relief, though, the workload had become even heavier than it was during the war:

> We are also keenly aware that the budget for labor and for material equipment has been exceeded again and again. In other words, the administration will face a deficit to meet material, but not spiritual or intellectual, necessities; and it would seem that a cooperative spirit on the part of teachers makes them inevitable victims of retrenchment when coal dealers or hand workers get their price. (2)

Wylie and other members of the English department felt that the administration had taken advantage of their cooperative nature for its own cost-cutting benefits. Because of "a situation educationally precarious we have felt it necessary to review, with especial reference to the budget, the principles on which, so far as money and personnel allow, we have as a department hitherto tried to work" (2). Thus, the report outlines the key principles of the department.

The first department principle was that "English is primarily an art, and that, whether considered from the point of view of literature or of writing, it should be so studied and taught" (2). One "practical consequence" of viewing English as an art is that "it must be taught as individually as possible and must concern itself with the imaginative and perceptive hardly less than with the intellectual training of the student" (3). The department had "made every effort to have small classes, and to allow opportunity for individual teaching" (3). Thus, class teaching and individual conferences were emphasized. As President MacCracken notes, "[t]his basic and simple face-to-face relationship [. . .] formed the basis of training for generations of Vassar writers such as Margaret Culkin Banning, Constance Rourke, Edna St. Vincent Millay, Mary McCarthy, Elizabeth Bishop, Eleanor Clark, and others" (qtd. in Daniels, *Bridges to the World* 58). According to the report, "[t]he striking difference," though, between Vassar and Princeton, which had used a preceptorial system since 1905, and Harvard, which adopted a tutorial plan for its class of 1917, was that the same teacher did the classroom teaching and conferences (4). This difference was because the department held the "conviction that all our teaching must be done by the best people" (5).

Wylie then emphasizes why the department needs "the best" teachers:

> The need of an experienced staff is the more important because the second article of our educational creed is the co-operative or democratic organization of the department.
>
> From 1896 at least, we have worked co-operatively whenever co-operation was possible. Matters affecting the interests of the whole group have in every case been made subjects for joint discussion, and whenever it was practicable have been jointly determined. (5)

In other words, because the department is democratically organized, the department needs experienced faculty. In practice, "the best" often meant upper-class white women like themselves, with several being former Vassar graduates.

Later in the report, Wylie contends that the "co-operative management of the department, though at first sight remote from questions of budget, is in fact intimately bound up with it" (7). She then clarifies the direct connection between democratic management and budgetary issues. In the early years, Wylie says "the English staff co-operated rather in carrying out policies outlined by Professor Buck or me than in initiating activities or modifying those suggested" (7). However, in the past twelve or more years, department faculty members

> have increasingly taken a vital share in the management of the department, with the natural result that, while I carry less personal responsibility than formerly, the other members carry considerably more. Such departmental organization as ours seems to me to be just now especially necessary if Vassar is to advance towards the democratic government rapidly developing in most of our colleges and universities. Democratic government—i.e. general departmental and faculty control of educational policies—is possible only when the members of the faculty share in ultimate educational responsibility. Such responsibility requires time and energy as well as interest; and if the college is to benefit by the best services of its faculty, the work involved in joint management of common business must be recognized as an integral part of the teacher's task. Such work can assuredly not be done by people exhausted by excessive demands whether of the classroom, of the additional conference-hours made necessary by sections that are too large, or of an over-burden of administrative detail. It is true, too, that these more general activities, essential as they are both to the well-being of the college and to the teacher's grasp of large educational polities, ordinarily meet with scanty recognition either administrative or scholarly. (7)

We get a sense of Wylie's anger and frustration at the administration's lack of understanding of the "time and energy" required to create more democratic organizations. She sees the current budget crisis as severely hindering this movement because the faculty is "exhausted by excessive demands." Here, similar to her presentation, Wylie emphasizes this democratic movement is happening beyond Vassar and that the college needs to keep up with this "advance."

Conclusion

I have contextualized Wylie and Buck's democratic approach to administration within the Progressive Era, showing how both women were influenced by a strong sense of social responsibility felt by many upper-class white women during this period. In their administrative practices, Wylie and Buck emphasized the importance of social responsibility and democratic government. Although the contexts are markedly different, we can see how the situations that Wylie and Buck faced anticipate current administrative circumstances. Issues such as teaching load, pay, and promotion remain central to English departments and writing programs. Questions about whether rhetoric and composition programs should be in English departments or separate and how to gain recognition for the kinds of service so often involved in writing programs also are relevant. Wylie and Buck's administrative efforts remain vital to us because their work can be illuminating to today's administrators grappling with similar concerns.

As Cheryl Glenn reminds us, inherent in revisionary history

> is the necessary historical inquiry that empowers political action [. . .], for historical inquiry helps people situate problems in a broader context and discover the available means of persuading their communities to act from their shared historical experiences and needs. (17)

How might Wylie and Buck's story serve to "empower political action" today? We can see that the lean budget times they faced severely hindered their efforts to foster democratic organizations. As Wylie emphasizes in her 1921 report, such efforts take time and money and they "ordinarily meet with scanty recognition either administrative or scholarly" (7). Wylie's words seem prophetic, given today's tight economic situation. Efforts toward more democratic administration will, no doubt, be difficult. This situation makes the need to gain recognition for such efforts that much more necessary and the analysis of prior models and alternate means of persuasion all the more significant. Although many priorities vie for importance during tight times, as Laura Johnson Wylie reminds us, the development of more democratic administration is more important than "even the most essential question of bread and butter" (23).

Notes

1. A friend and colleague, Woodbridge edited a tribute to Wylie and co-authored *A Course in Expository Writing* (1899) and *A Course in Narrative Writing* (1906) with Gertrude Buck.

2. The feminist project of writing women into the history of rhetoric is quite extensive, and this list is not meant to be a complete record of all contributions: K. Campbell 1989; Biesecker 1992; Lunsford 1995; Wertheimer 1997; Glenn 1997; Logan 1999; Sutherland and Sutcliffe 1999; Royster 2000; Mattingly 1998, 2001 and 2002; Ritchie and Ronald 2001; Donawerth 2002.

3. See Mattingly 2002, Johnson 2002, and Bacon 2002.

4. In so doing, this study extends the work of Barbara E. L'Eplattenier, who in her 1999 dissertation, examines how Wylie and Buck "negotiated and garnered fiscal and political power within their university and for their department" (x).

5. See Gunner's "Decentering the WPA." *WPA: Writing Program Administration* 18.1/2 (Fall/Winter 1994): 8-15.

6. Despite her heavy teaching and administrative load, Wylie was a scholar. In addition to her dissertation, Wylie published *Social Studies in English Literature* (1916) and "What Can Be Done About It?" (1918). She also edited *Poems and Plays* by Buck (1922), and she edited school editions of the following texts: *The Winter's Tale, Adam Bede,* and *The Sir Roger de Coverly Papers from* The Spectator (*Miss Wylie*, Woodbridge n.p.).

7. Information on the Bryn Mawr Summer School for 1921-27 indicates that Wylie served as an instructor during the years 1924, 1925, and 1926. See Hilda Worthington Smith's *Women Workers at the Bryn Mawr Summer School*, 295.

8. For further information on the Bryn Mawr Summer School for Women Workers, see Rita Rubinstein Heller's "The Women of Summer: The Bryn Mawr Summer School for Women Workers: 1921-1938" (1986). See also Smith (1929) and Hollis (1994) and (2001).

9. Buck and Laura Johnson Wylie had a very close personal and professional relationship. In her dissertation, Barbara L'Eplattenier discusses how

President Henry Noble MacCracken "specially refers to Miss Wylie and 'her great friend, Miss Buck'" (Daniels, *Bridges to the World* 182). After carefully reviewing various archival material, L'Eplattenier says that she "is compelled to argue that 'her great friend' was the code word for what we today would call a domestic partner—that is, recognition of the lesbian relationship, sexual or not, that existed between Wylie and Buck" (86). As Lillian Faderman points out, during this time female relationships were not "yet widely stigmatized as 'lesbian,'" and the "female twosome was an accepted institution on the faculties of women's colleges in the late nineteenth and early twentieth century" (xiii). See Anne MacKay, ed., *Wolf Girls at Vassar; Lesbian and Gay Experiences 1930-1990* (1992), foreword. See also Carroll Smith-Rosenberg's article, "The Female World of Love and Ritual: Relationships Between Women in Nineteenth-Century America," *Signs* 1 (1975): 1-29. In addition, see her book *Disorderly Conduct: Visions of Gender in Victorian America* (1980).

10. In her will, Laura Johnson Wylie, who shared Buck's love for community theater, created a $10,000 fund to "perpetuate friendly relations between the college and city," achieved by Buck through her work with the Poughkeepsie Community Theatre ("Laura J. Wylie Dies").

11. After Wylie's death, the house that Wylie and Buck shared for so many years was purchased and dedicated as the headquarters for the Women's City and County Club. Buck and Laura Johnson Wylie's former home is now occupied by Hudson River Sloop Clearwater, Inc., a non-profit environmental organization founded by folk singer Pete Seeger.

12. For a detailed discussion of Fred Newton Scott's achievements, see Donald C. Stewart and Patricia L. Stewart, *The Life and Legacy of Fred Newton Scott* (1997).

13. Rubin is quoting from Lawrence A. Cremin's *The Transformation of the School: Progressivism in American Education, 1876-1957* (1961), 118, 121, 123.

14. The presentation was given during the fiftieth Anniversary of the Alumnae Association at the "Conference on Education" (16 June 1921). Speakers at the conference discussed issues related to the following topic: "Education at Vassar, its Ideals and its Methods. Does the Present undergraduate training at Vassar give the student sufficient broad preparation?"

15. For an interesting discussion of suffrage issues and their impact on Vassar, see Elizabeth A. Daniels, "Suffrage as a Lever for Change at Vassar College" (1983).

16. Angle brackets are used to indicate handwritten words inserted by Wylie in the typed report.

Works Cited

Bacon, Jacqueline. *The Humblest May Stand Forth: Rhetoric Empowerment, and Abolition*. Columbia: U of South Carolina P, 2002.

Biesecker, Barbara. "Coming to Terms with Recent Attempts to Write Women into the History of Rhetoric." *Philosophy and Rhetoric* 25 (1992): 140-61.

Buck, Gertrude. *The Metaphor: A Study in the Psychology of Rhetoric*. Diss. U of Michigan. 1898. Fred Newton Scott. Contributions to Rhetorical Theory 5. Ann Arbor: Inland Press, 1899.

Buck, Gertrude, and Elisabeth Woodbridge Morris. *A Course in Expository Writing*. New York: Henry Holt, 1899.

—. *A Course in Narrative Writing*. New York: Henry Holt, 1906.

Campbell, JoAnn. "Gertrude Buck and the Celebration of Community: A History of Writing Instruction at Vassar College, 1897-1922." Diss. U of Texas at Austin, 1989.

—, ed. *Toward a Feminist Rhetoric: The Writing of Gertrude Buck*. U of Pittsburgh P, 1996.

Campbell, Karyln Kohrs. *Man Cannot Speak for Her: A Critical Study of Early Feminist Rhetoric*. 2 vols. New York: Greenwood, 1989.

Connors, Robert J. "Overwork/Underpay: Labor and Status of Composition Teachers since 1880." *Rhetoric Review* 9.1 (1990): 108-26.

—. "Teaching and Learning as a Man." *College English* 58 (1996): 137-57.

Cremin, Lawrence A. *The Transformation of the School: Progressivism in American Education, 1876-1957*. New York: Knopf, 1961.

Daniels, Elizabeth A. *Bridges to the World: Henry Noble MacCracken and Vassar College*. Clinton Corners, NY: College Avenue Press, 1994.

—. "Suffrage as a Lever for Change at Vassar College." *Vassar Quarterly* (Summer 1983): 32-36.

Davis, Allen F. *Spearheads for Reform: The Social Settlements and the Progressive Movement 1890-1914*. 1967. New Brunswick, NJ: Rutgers UP, 1991.

Donawerth, Jane, ed. *Rhetorical Theory by Women Before 1900: An Anthology*. Lanham, MD: Rowman and Littlefield, 2002.

Faderman, Lillian. Foreword. *Wolf Girls of Vassar: Lesbian and Gay Experiences 1930-1990*. Ed. Anne MacKay. New York: St. Martin's, 1992. xi-xv.

Flanagan, Hallie. *Dynamo*. New York: Duell, Sloan, and Pearce, 1943.

Glenn, Cheryl. *Rhetoric Retold: Regendering the Tradition from Antiquity Through the Renaissance*. Carbondale: Southern Illinois UP, 1997.

Gordon, Lynn D. *Gender and Higher Education in the Progressive Era*. New Haven: Yale UP, 1990.

Gunner, Jeanne. "Decentering the WPA." *WPA: Writing Program Administration* 18.1/2 (Fall/Winter 1994): 8-15.

Hart, Sophie Chantal. Private Papers. Wellesley College Archives and Special Collections. Wellesley, MA.

Heller, Rita Rubinstein. "The Women of Summer: The Bryn Mawr Summer School for Women Workers: 1921-1938." Diss. Rutgers U, The State U of New Jersey, 1986.

Hollis, Karyn. "Liberating Voices: Autobiographical Writing at the Bryn Mawr Summer School for Women Workers, 1921-1938." *College Composition and Communication* 45 (1994): 31-60.

—. "Plays of Heteroglossia: Labor Drama at the Bryn Mawr Summer School for Women Workers." Ed. John Trimbur. *Popular Literacy: Studies in Cultural Practices and Poetics*. Pittsburgh: U of Pittsburgh P, 2001. 151-74.

Johnson, Nan. *Gender and Rhetorical Space in American Life, 1866-1910*. Carbondale: Southern Illinois UP, 2002.

Jordan, Mary Augusta. "Spacious Days at Vassar." *The Fiftieth Anniversary of the Opening of Vassar College: October 10 to 13, 1915: A Record*. Chronicler, Constance Rourke. Poughkeepsie, NY: Vassar College, 1916. 47-69.

"Laura J. Wylie Dies Here at 76: Vassar Emeritus Professor had been on the Faculty from 1897 to 1924." *Poughkeepsie Eagle News*. 14 April 1932. n. pag. Special Collections, Vassar College Libraries, Poughkeepsie, NY.

L'Eplattenier, Barbara E. "Investigating Institutional Power: Women Administrators During the Progressive Era, 1890-1920." Diss. Purdue U, 1999.

Logan, Shirley Wilson. *"We Are Coming": The Persuasive Discourse of Nineteenth-Century Black Women*. Carbondale: Southern Illinois UP, 1999.

Lunsford, Andrea A., ed. *Reclaiming Rhetorica: Women in the Rhetorical Tradition*. Pittsburgh: Pittsburgh UP, 1995.

MacCracken, Henry Noble. "Appreciations I." Woodbridge 149-51.

MacKay, Anne, ed. *Wolf Girls at Vassar: Lesbian and Gay Experiences 1930-1990*. New York: St. Martin's, 1992.

Mastrangelo, Lisa. "Stories of a Progressive Past: Early Feminist and Progressive Approaches to Writing Instruction." Diss. U of Albany, State U of New York, 2000.

Mattingly, Carol. *Appropriate[ing] Dress: Women's Rhetorical Style in Nineteenth-Century America*. Carbondale: Southern Illinois UP, 2002.

—, ed. *Water Drops from Women Writers: A Temperance Reader*. Carbondale: Southern Illinois UP, 2001.

—. *Well-Tempered Women: Nineteenth-Century Temperance Rhetoric*. Carbondale: Southern Illinois UP, 1998.

"Miss Wylie's Will Probated: Most of Estate Goes to Gertrude Buck Fund." *Sunday Courier* [Poughkeepsie] 17 April 1932. n. pag. Special Collections, Vassar College Libraries, Poughkeepsie, NY.

Reed, Amy. "In Memoriam: Gertrude Buck." *Vassar Miscellany News* 11 Jan. 1922: n. pag. Rpt. in *Vassar Quarterly* Feb. 1922: 128-29. Special Collections, Vassar College Library, Poughkeepsie, NY.

—. "Report of the Department of English." 1921-22. Special Collections, Vassar College Library, Poughkeepsie, NY.

Ritchie, Joy, and Kate Ronald, eds. *Available Means: An Anthology of Women's Rhetoric(s)*. Pittsburgh: U of Pittsburgh P, 2001.

Royster, Jacqueline Jones. *Traces of a Stream: Literacy and Social Change among African American Women*. Pittsburgh: U of Pittsburgh P, 2000.

Rubin, Joan Shelley. *Constance Rourke and American Culture*. Chapel Hill, N.C.: U of North Carolina P, 1980.

Smith, Hilda Worthington. *Women Workers at the Bryn Mawr Summer School*. New York: Affiliated Summer Schools for Women Workers in Industry and American Association for Adult Education, 1929.

Smith-Rosenberg, Carroll. *Disorderly Conduct: Visions of Gender in Victorian America*. New York: Oxford UP, 1985.

—."The Female Word of Love and Ritual: Relationships Between Women in Nineteenth-Century America." *Signs: Journal of Women in Culture and Society* 1 (1975): 1-29.

Snell, Ada F. "History of English Studies in Mount Holyoke Seminary and College." Unpublished typescript, 1942. English Department Records. Mount Holyoke College Archives and Special Collections, South Hadley, Massachusetts.

Snyder, Alice D. "The Philosophy of an English Teacher." Woodbridge 115-30.

"Statement to President Taylor and the Board of Trustees." 15 March 1913. Special Collections, Vassar College Library, Poughkeepsie, NY.

Stewart, Donald C., and Patricia L. Stewart. *The Life and Legacy of Fred Newton Scott*. Pittsburgh: U of Pittsburgh P, 1997.

Sutherland, Christine Mason, and Rebecca Sutcliffe, eds. *The Changing Tradition: Women in the History of Rhetoric*. Calgary: U of Calgary P, 1999.

Taylor, James Monroe. "The 'Conservatism' of Vassar." N.p.: 1909. N. pag. Special Collections, Vassar College Libraries, Poughkeepsie, NY.

Vassar College Faculty Meeting Minutes, 9 Dec. 1912. Special Collections, Vassar College Libraries, Poughkeepsie, NY.

Vassarion. Poughkeepsie, NY: Vassar College, 1889.

Vassarion. Poughkeepsie, NY: Vassar College, 1921.

Warren, Katherine. "Retrospect, 1924." Woodbridge 81-93. Rpt. of "The Retirement of Miss Wylie." *Vassar Quarterly* Nov. 1924: 1-6.

Werthheimer, Molly Meijer. *Listening to Their Voices: The Rhetorical Activities of Historical Women*. Columbia: U of South Carolina P, 1997.

Woodbridge Elisabeth Morris. "Laura Johnson Wylie 1855-1932." Woodbridge 1-17.

—. "Pioneer and Humanist." Woodbridge 65-71.

—, ed. *Miss Wylie of Vassar*. New Haven: Yale UP, 1934.

"Women's City and County Club Soon to Close a Busy Season." *Poughkeepsie Star* 14 April 1925: 2.

"Wylie File." Special Collections, Vassar College Library, Poughkeepsie, NY.

Wylie, Laura Johnson. "Education at Vassar, its Ideals and its Methods. Does the present undergraduate training at Vassar give the student sufficient broad participation for her future activities?" (16 June 1921.) Quoted in "Stenographic Report," Fiftieth Anniversary, Associate Alumnae, Vassar College. 11-23.

—. "Report of the Department of English." 1905-1921. Special Collections, Vassar College Library, Poughkeepsie, NY.

—. *Social Studies in English Literature*. Boston: Houghton, 1916.

—. "What Can Be Done About It?" *Vassar Quarterly* July 1918: n. pag. Rpt in Woodbridge, 131-42.

6

"Is It the Pleasure of This Conference to Have Another?": Women's Colleges Meeting and Talking about Writing in the Progressive Era

Lisa Mastrangelo and Barbara L'Eplattenier

> Without intellectual curiosity, without the wish to discover and explain something about life, history *is* a dustbin.
>
> —*Robert Connors*

> I do not think of these women as exemplary heroines. Instead, I think of them as sites—historical locations or markers—where crucial political and cultural contests are enacted and can be examined in some detail. To figure a person—in this case, a woman—as a place or location is not to deny her humanity; it is rather to recognize the many factors that constitute her agency, the complex and multiple ways in which she is constructed as a historical actor.
>
> —*Joan Wallach Scott*

In 1919, writing faculty from Mount Holyoke College, Wellesley College, Vassar College, and Smith College came together for the first Intercollege Conference on English Composition to discuss issues of writing program administration.[1] To see them as administrators and as part of a network refutes the notion that these women, like so many other participants in rhetoric and composition's history, were individual actors, toiling in isolation, with little or no support from those around them. Archival documents reveal that these women created social and institutional networks. They collaborated with one another about programmatic issues, pedagogy, work loads and labor issues, and issues particular to women's colleges at the time. They recognized the importance and primacy of writing instruction and expended time and energy on ways of administering and teaching writing well; they reflected on their successes and failures. In short, they were functioning as writing program administrators.

Working with Archival Evidence

The primary pieces of archival evidence that we are relying on in this chapter are the conference programs from 1919, 1920, 1922, and 1924 and a transcript of the 1919 conference proceedings; other archival documents include memorandums and faculty meeting minutes. These documents allow us to include these women in the fabric of women's history, perhaps for the first time. In seeing them as connected to one another, we are able to avoid labeling them as lone mavericks, which Gail Griffin notes "is one means by which women's history is kept in the dark" (31). These documents, instead, shed light on a community of extraordinary women whose history is mostly unknown. When we first discovered the 1919 transcript, we were puzzled, thrilled, and amazed. Unlike other events or incidents, we found little reference to this gathering in the various official minutia that accompanies the administration of a department. The 1919 transcript led us to the documents referring to the conferences of 1920, 1922, and 1924; departmental annual reports also offered occasional references. These archival documents, however, are the only representation we have found thus far of these conferences. The transcript is a record of the discussion of the conference, while the conference programs have topics that were "submitted, not as a formal program to be discussed in detail, but as suggestions indicating the general lines on which exchange of opinions is desirable" (Mount Holyoke College, "English Conference" 1922). As documents within a historical context, the transcript and the conference programs seem to stand alone and, in some ways it is difficult to discuss them without recounting entire histories of the writing programs at the four sisters. Fortunately, work on the writing programs at Vassar, Wellesley, and Mount Holyoke has already been done (see Wagner, Campbell, L'Eplattenier, and Mastrangelo).

The largest piece of archival evidence, the 1919 transcript, remains somewhat of a puzzle to us. The transcript is approximately forty-seven pages long, with an inconsistent typeset, two pages numbered eighteen and an inconsistent format. Equally puzzling—and unfortunate—is that the transcript ends on page forty-six—right in the middle of a discussion on the types of debating questions used in English classrooms. Thankfully, the conference program indicates that this subject was the eleventh out of twelve discussed at the conference. While frustrating, it is heartening to know that we have a record of the majority of the discussions which occurred.

Other aspects of the document also remain a mystery to us. The initial conference took place at Mount Holyoke, which has a copy of the conference program. It is Wellesley's archives, however, that possessed the actual transcript. This transcript is annotated by "C.F.S."—Mount Holyoke's Clara Frances Stevens, who often changed a word or two throughout the manuscript and initialed the entries. How the transcript made its way into the Wellesley archives, and why it is still held there, remains unknown.

Despite its idiosyncrasies, we feel that the transcript's value as a document overrides its difficulties as a historical text. We recognize the validity of Robert Connors's statement when he notes that, regardless of what archival documents may look like, "all of historical work, then, is provisional, partial—fragments we shore against our ruin. We are trying to make sense of things. It is always a construction. It is always tottering" ("Dreams and Play" 21). More important than its oddities, the contents of this document, in conjunction with the later conference programs, help us make sense of an overlooked aspect of our discipline's history. To put it bluntly, these documents reveal that people anticipated our profession—or saw a need for the type of work that writing program administrators do—and worked to establish professional gatherings to establish the intellectual importance of and raise questions about administering writing programs.

Motivation for the 1919 Conference: Admissions Decisions

Although the participants of the conference came together to "find out the policy of each college in regard to the entrance examination; the freshman (required) course in English composition, and the work in Debating" (Wellesley College 1), we believe that the admissions process of women's colleges was a primary source in the formation of the conference. Women's colleges had long had difficulty with how they admitted students. Vassar, for example, accepted students based on a certificate system, where the student's teacher—who might have been a tutor, clergyman, or public school teacher—wrote her a letter of academic accomplishment. Certified students were then admitted on a first-come, first-serve basis, with pre-registration possible. Some parents (and even grandparents) pre-registered their daughters shortly after they were born, so as to ensure a space. Once the class was filled, all other applicants—who were often better qualified—were placed on a waiting list and told to wait for a space. This was a significant problem: C. Mildred Thompson noted that "For entrance in September 1916, the number of applicants reached the six hundred mark on February 1, 1915. [. . .] for 1920, the same number was registered three years before entrance." (Daniels, *Bridges* 101). Henry Noble MacCracken, President of Vassar, recognized the difficulties with such a system. He also knew that the other women's colleges faced the same dilemma; he had seen similar problems in the admissions process during his tenure as an English professor at Smith. On his first official day as the new Vassar President, he began to make changes:

> On the day after the Fiftieth Anniversary [1915], President Burton of Smith, President Pendleton of Wellesley, and President Woolley of Mt. Holyoke [sic] met at my invitation in my office and organized the Association of Four Colleges. We did not dare ask Miss Thomas of Bryn Mawr. She would have haughtily refused. After Miss Thomas retired, however, Bryn Mawr joined, and so later did Barnard and Radcliffe. [. . .]
>
> With these colleges, Vassar would drop the old certificate system, and join men's colleges in trying to raise standards of admission by using examinations

like those used in England.² (*The Hickory Limb* 43-44)

In September 1919, the four colleges, writes Elizabeth Daniels, implemented a "new plan of admissions [. . .] with competitive examinations superseding admissions by certificate" ("Vassar History, 1915-1922").³ While this background information is never specifically mentioned during the 1919 conference, the date of the conference coincides with the new plan of admissions and helps explain the lengthy discussion regarding entrance examination which occurred at the conference. However, it is also clear from the transcript that the participants came together not only to solve the admissions problem but also to discuss the status of writing and debate within their schools. Indeed, they used this meeting as an opportunity for professional development and to discuss the administrative issues surrounding writing at women's colleges.

Conference Participants

Because the only extant transcript is from the 1919 conference, this is the only conference for which we can compile a partial list of the names of the attendees. Although we know that seventeen delegates, and all but one of the Vassar English department faculty attended the 1922 conference, we do not know the names of the participants. In any case, at least twenty-two people—nineteen of them women—participated in the 1919 conference; among these were the three heads of rhetoric departments and one writing program administrator of the four colleges. Clara Frances Stevens of Mount Holyoke spent thirty-seven years as the chair of the department of rhetoric (Mastrangelo 47). Sophie Chantal Hart taught forty-five years at Wellesley, many of them as the chair of the department of English language and rhetoric.⁴ Gertrude Buck administered the writing program at Vassar for almost twenty years—and was recognized for it, both in terms of rank and financial compensation. Mary Augusta Jordan chaired the English department at Smith for a majority of her career (Horowitz 194). The other participants appear to have been the writing teachers at their representative colleges; some, such as Mary Yost, focused their research on writing throughout their career.⁵ The investment of the time and energy needed to travel, present, and participate in such a conference indicates the importance with which these women, departments, and colleges viewed rhetoric and writing.

Table 1. List of 1919 Conference Participants

Mount Holyoke	*Wellesley*
Clara Stevens (Chair, Department of Rhetoric) Ada Snell Helen Griffith Margaret Ball	Sophie Chantal Hart (Chair, Department of English Language and Literature) Elizabeth Manwaring Frances Warner Agnes Frances Perkins Alfred Sheffield Amy Kelly
Smith College	*Vassar College*
Mary Augusta Jordan (Chair, English Department) Elizabeth Hanscom Ada Comstock (acting Smith President) Rose Egan Howard Patch Katherine Woodward Samuel Eliot Margaret Bradshaw	Gertrude Buck (directed Rhetoric side of the department; salary and rank equal to chair) Mary Yost Sarah Hincks Leonora Branch

Additionally, these women had more in common than just meeting and talking about writing at conferences; they also had similar educational backgrounds. During this era, only a small percentage of women went to college at all; approximately a quarter of the doctorates and 40 percent of master's degrees granted at this time were granted to women (Woody 338). Not surprisingly, the majority of the participants—especially those in supervisory positions—were alumnae of the few undergraduate programs that would admit women at the end of the nineteenth century; these schools were often the Seven Sisters colleges. Additionally, an astonishing sixteen of the nineteen female participants had graduate degrees at the time of the conference. Most had MAs at the very least: Mary Augusta Jordan received her MA from Vassar, Ada Comstock received her MA (1899) from Columbia. Some would continue on for additional graduate degrees after the conference.

Their graduate education also created significant connections between the participants. At least six of the participants received their graduate degrees from the University of Michigan. Gertrude Buck (PhD 1898), Clara Stevens (MA 1894), and Sophie Hart (MA 1898) were all at Michigan when Fred Newton Scott was there; the time frame of their degrees suggests that they may have known of each other, if they didn't actually socialize or take classes together. A later group also received their graduate degrees from Michigan within the same time frame: Ada Snell (PhD 1916), Mary Yost (Fellow in rhetoric 1913-14; PhD in Sociology 1917), and Sarah Hincks (MA 1914; PhD 1922). Additionally, the early alumnae of Michigan, like Buck, recognizing the dearth of advanced graduate training available in rhetoric and women's overall difficulty in obtaining admissions to graduate school, sent a small but steady stream of their students to Michigan and other progressive programs for training.

Connected by their education and belief in the importance of rhetoric and writing, these women engaged in a progressive crusade involving the teaching of composition and rhetoric. While rhetoric was quickly coming to be known as the rules of proper grammar and punctuation, the women at these colleges fought against this. In part because of their educational backgrounds, and in part because those with progressive backgrounds trained and conversed with others, the instructors and administrators at these colleges sought a broader picture of the teaching of composition. They did not meet Connors's general description of teachers during this time: "the act of a teacher reading and commenting on the general communicative success of a piece of student writing—form and content—was succeeded by a simplified concept: the teacher as spotter and corrector of formal errors" (142). Instead, faculty in composition at all four colleges created and maintained more complex visions of writing instruction, including attention to small group work, individual conferences, and continued practice with writing itself, rather than its dissected components. Vicki Ricks provides support for this when she notes that

> the [Vassar] department regularly argued for reduced teaching loads so that faculty could teach English as expression controlled by individual experiences and in relation to an audience. In arguing for both these aspects of English composition, the faculty sought student involvement, not merely dictating mechanical 'skills' for future clerks and managers. (74)

It seems in keeping with this model, then, that the women met with other pedagogues and administrators in order to discuss how best to continue their progressive teaching, as well as to maintain standards. Amy Reed of Vassar noted that "the general inference from the meetings seems to be that a general community of ideas exists among these four eastern colleges for women, as to the nature and function of the teaching of English composition" ("1922 Annual Report"). As the 1919 transcript demonstrates, these conferences were *working* conferences—opportunities for teachers and administrators to discover what their colleagues were doing at comparable schools in the area, compare their programs to others, and address the practical aspects of teaching in and administrating fairly large writing programs. These women formed a community on the East Coast that valued writing as a form of self-expression, a method for political advancement, and a component in their students' education. Additionally, they supported and assisted each other in the development and administration of the programs, often serving as judges for various writing contests or the like. Because of this, they had an excellent sense of what other similar schools were doing regarding writing and could, in turn, evaluate their own programs effectively.

The 1919 Conference

The most revealing conference is the first one, held at Mount Holyoke in October of 1919. The existence of both the conference program and transcript offers an unprecedented glimpse into writing program administrative work during the turn of the century. The program reveals that conversations were scheduled over the course of two days and included discussions regarding entrance examinations, the role and place of debate at the colleges, the "real purpose or function of a required course in freshman composition," and trials and tribulations in attempting to work with other departments, as well as suggestions for standardizing criteria for writing courses at all four of the colleges (Mount Holyoke College "The Intercollege Conference"). The transcript's contents reveal writing instructors working on programmatic issues, struggling with pedagogical applications, attempting standardization across the four colleges, and considering the educational implications of their work as teachers and college administrators. As stated earlier, a key reason for the conference was the change in entrance requirements at the colleges; the very first discussions at the 1919 conference are reflective of this.

The Entrance Examinations

The sharing of information regarding the entrance exams at the four institutions was the first item on the 1919 program. Such exams had been required at colleges such as Harvard as early as 1865, and by 1872, included "correct spelling, punctuation, and expression, as well as legible handwriting [. . .] and failure in any of these particulars [could] be taken into account at the examination" (Kitzhaber 34). Harvard's use of the entrance exam quickly spread to other schools and became a standard gatekeeping feature of college life, used to classify students and maintain standards. In addition to addressing the admissions problem, developing and maintaining standards was more than just an institutional activity for women's colleges, it was also an *ethos* issue. As late as 1899, Harvard President Charles Eliot—and other critics—still disparaged women's education and women's abilities to learn; the role and purpose of women's education were still being debated at the time of the conference. Many of the participants were first generation college graduates and were well aware of the controversy that had surrounded, and continued to surround, women's colleges. Competitive admissions through standardized entrance exams would have solved two problems at once; the best applicants would have been admitted while at the same time continuing to increase the reputation of women's colleges.

As a result of the need to improve the admissions process, the four colleges had that year adopted a new standard and method of reading the exams. The Readers of the College Board, a group comprised of school readers and college readers from the various departments of composition, evaluated the essays. According to Mary Yost, who reported on the reading, the two groups' opinions on what was being tested differed radically. The school readers felt "we were going to test for specific information" while the group of examiners at Vassar were interested in whether or not the student seemed able to do college work overall (Wellesley College 2). Grading was also an issue; some felt the numerical method should be used, while other argued for grading holistically, using a rubric, which would "help a great many of the secondary school teachers [. . .] get away from a rigid mathematical basis in marking, and help them to consider the examination in terms of the qualities it shows" (5). These qualities included the "power and ability" of the student (5). Although errors were a component of the evaluation—the quality rather than the quantity was noted—they were not the primary focus of the evaluation, as was the situation at Harvard (Berlin 61). Grading standards were quite strict; anyone who scored less than 60 percent was considered a "risk" for entrance to the college. Mary Yost indicated that 1,279 essays were "read" the previous year, and 43.8 percent of incoming students received less than the 60 percent recommended for admissions; 56.2 percent of students received above it (Wellesley College 5).

Mary Yost's report on the entrance exams reveals a surprisingly contemporary attitude toward the exams, their evaluation, what they actually measured, and the use of the results. Yost argued that further work needed to be done on this system and criticized colleges that had not given enough thought to the entrance exam. She suggested that the accuracy of the exam could only be determined after students had been in college for a year and told the participants that "[f]or years mens' colleges have had examinations, but no constructive work has been done" (Wellesley College 5). What should be done is a study of the students' records before they came to college, their records in college, and their exam grades. Yost urged that

> [. . .] We should formulate what in our judgment are the qualities which indicate power and ability of the students to do college work, and we should study the records of the students in order to throw light on how nearly our reading was a correct estimate of the power of the students. (5)

Looking closely at the success of students based on entrance exams is a radical approach, suggesting that the colleges, or at least Vassar, did not necessarily place a great deal of faith in a one-time, high-stakes writing test. Overall, the approach to the entrance exam described in the transcript seems to be much less skill oriented than one might expect at this time period.

The rest of the faculty members were concerned about the multiple issues surrounding the entrance exams, including making sure that they were read "fairly" with inter-rater reliability while also maintaining rigorous academic standards. The concern for both the design of the exam itself and the need for evaluating its effectiveness in predicting a student's success at the college suggests that, despite the admissions question, the faculty members saw the entrance exams not as a way to keep people out, but as a way to provide the faculty with information about the students' skill levels and abilities in order to work with them before promoting them; such assessment was, for the most part, used in a positive manner, rather than as a punitive measure.

Class Placement

The conference discussion eventually moved from the entrance exams to placement of students within the writing classes. There was considerable conversation on how to best separate students, as well as the effect of different models. Segregating students according to skill level was problematic for all four of the colleges, and this topic occupied the next part of the conference conversation. Both Vassar and Mount Holyoke separated their students while Smith and Wellesley did not take entrance exam scores into account when they formed their classes. Mount Holyoke, Ada Snell reported, had separated the 1918 students into groups at the end of the first semester, and then into "weak and good sections" (13); the 1919 students, however, had been put into graded sections immediately upon their entrance into college based on their entrance exams. Vassar, on the other hand, separated students after three or four weeks worth of work, dependent on their written work up until that point (14). Additionally, Vassar also attempted to divide students into "a group that would be better for a wide range of reading and another where the students have a real interest in writing" (14).

Separating students is logical activity from a pedagogical and theoretical standpoint, but it violated a traditional belief of women's colleges. Historically, women's colleges had strongly discouraged competition among women for "competition, and its accompanying assertiveness, belonged to the world of men" (Gordon 143); in keeping with that same belief, the colleges downplayed intellectual differences and did not issue grades for fear that it would create unhealthy competition.[7] Teachers instead worked individually with weak students or informed poorly performing students privately that they needed to work harder in order to receive a C (for credit) in the classes. Wellesley students, for example, didn't know their academic standing and whether or not they had received credit for a course until 1897; it was 1912 before they received specific grades in their coursework (Converse). By 1919, however, there was significant discussion about what each grade represented within each department.

Because of the non-competitive tradition, as well as the pedagogical implications, Smith and Wellesley questioned Vassar and Holyoke about the effect of such separation on students, teaching, and the classes as a whole. Neither method, segregated versus nonsegregated, was wholly satisfactory to Agnes Perkins of Wellesley. In separating students into groups there were problems with what she called a loss of "standard"—"in weak divisions we are likely to over-emphasize any gleams of ability; in a strong division the weak students may be underestimated" (Wellesley College 13). Conversely, the mixed group had its own set of problems. Strong students had little incentive to work harder if they were at the top of their particular class, and weak students were deprived of the individual attention that she sensed they needed in order to meet the standards of the rest of the class.

In keeping with the noncompetitive belief, administrators didn't always inform students which sections they were in. Although students often asked if they were in the top, middle or bottom group, Sarah Hincks of Vassar noted that instructors tried to make the change with as little discussion of grading as possible. Both she and Buck suggested that being moved to the poor section could become an empowering moment for the students, as it would "give them a chance to come out to their best advantage" (15). Ada Snell said that "the students did not know they were segregated according to marks, although they sometimes seemed to sense it" (14).

Administratively, the participants were concerned about more than the typical idea of how to place students into classes (in order to balance numbers or meet instructors' needs, for example). Should they place students in segregated classes? How should they place students? Was it dependent on the level of writing expected of students at the institution or their perceived intelligence level?[8] Were groups of incoming students held to standards derived by a particular department—

and what were those standards—or were they simply compared to one another? While the group does not answer these questions, their discussion of them indicates both an awareness of them and a need to address them. Clearly, they understood that the placement of a student in a course could have a direct effect on the student's (and the course's) outcome.

Themes

Part of the conference discussion is listed under the topic of "required course in composition." However, the crux of the conversation quickly turned to the use of theme-writing in the classroom. The participants followed a clear path as they move into the discussion: the course in writing was required for all students and the course used theme-writing in all sections. But if theme-writing was to be used, how could it best be used to achieve course objectives and still provide an interesting and intellectually stimulating experience for the students? As before, the discussion focused on which design and instructional method would result in the best course for the students, rather than what might be administratively most expedient.

The use of themes has been much maligned and vilified in the history of writing instruction. They have come to represent what was bad about the Harvard model, including an obsession with "correcting" the themes in red ink, but the women's colleges typically used themes to get students writing regular essays based on common topics. Theme writing would have been an appropriate and popular model for the four colleges to use in their classrooms. Theme writing, as David Russell notes in *Writing in the Academic Disciplines, 1870-1990*, continued to be a model for required composition courses at small liberal arts colleges much longer than it did in the larger universities, in large part because the universities could no longer keep up with the labor-intensive practice of having students write multiple essays over the course of a semester or year (58). The use of themes in the four colleges reflects this. As a guide for the discussion, the conference program lists three conversation questions for the Friday evening session:

1. What amount of time is given to description, narration, exposition, and argument in the freshman year, and in what sequence are they taken up?

2. What is the relative value of handling material found in assigned books or poorer material based upon student's own experience and immature thought?

3. What is the real purpose or function of a required course in freshman composition? (Mount Holyoke, "The Intercollege Conference" 1)

As part of the discussion on teaching modes, themes inevitably come up. However, their use is not simply accepted; rather, the group questioned how they could best be used to meet course goals. The discussion centered primarily around how best to design themes in order to allow students to write about their own experiences. Thus, they also address question two: there seems to be full consensus that there is value in relating material, even "poorer" material, to students' experiences. As a group, the participants felt that material should not simply be given to a student in order to fill that student with "knowledge." This is an overtly Deweyian concept. In *Experience and Education*, Dewey writes, "the notion that some subjects and methods and that acquaintance with certain facts and truths possess educational value in and of themselves is the reason why traditional education reduced the material of education so largely to a diet of predigested material" (46). That "diet of predigested" material was not present in this discussion. Instead, the work to design theme assignments which interested the student and met the requirements of the course in writing seemed to be of priority. One conference attendee noted her attempts to draw student interest into assignments so that they would be more successful. She noted that

> I began working from the viewpoint of interest and of personality in a larger sense, working in themes on any subject which the girl might think would interest the class. I read aloud papers to test these themes for their interest, and very soon the girls began to try to make them interesting. (18.2)

The connection between the themes and their student participants indicates that the course in required English was not one which denied the student a chance to be an active participant in her own education. While the course in composition may have been required, there was much discussion about how to make it as interesting, and consequentially as productive, as possible.

The use of themes was also recognized as a way to also help create programmatic unity. Amy Kelly of Wellesley requested help in designing work, in particular, themes to be assigned, that would meet her aims for teaching composition, but still be interesting. According to Kelly,

> I should have been helped if the discussion had been about how to achieve the aims of Freshman Composition. I am looking for a little orthodoxy, and I would like to see four people from this conference, one representing each college, who would set up a model program of theme assignments for Freshmen and would indicate what each theme is intended to do. I do not always feel that students are making the steady growth and progress that they should. (Wellesley College 19)

Kelly's request was remarkably close to the questions that Edward Corbett recounts from his own days as a graduate student in the late 1940s. He recalls the desperation of the teaching assistants, and the way "we buttonholed our colleagues, pleading for a topic for next week's theme. We wanted tips about how to occupy the fifty minutes of the class period. Should we use the opaque-projector to display the best and worst themes that we got last week?" (66). However—and this is significant—Kelly appears to be a reflective teacher, attempting to answer metacognitive questions about achieving the aims of the course and her students' progress. Kelly conceptualized the course as a whole and its curriculum as a programmatic issue whereas Corbett's primary concern seems to be filling the next class period.

While Corbett's question and concern reflects the disciplinary isolation writing teachers felt at that time, the conference's response reveals a community interested in the question as a larger pedagogical and disciplinary issue. Kelly's request was considered seriously by the group, and is indeed picked up again at later conferences. Although Gertrude Buck believed it would be impossible to find a singular plan that could be effectively administered to the whole of the freshman class, she added that a list of themes that could be used to certain ends would be "very interesting" (Wellesley College 20). Miss Egan noted that "[t]here is a distinct gain in working out a definite program of subject matter" and "there would be a great advancement if we worked more from definite lists of subject matter" (20).

Kelly's question indicates a larger issue for the colleges: the programmatic need for a cohesive curriculum and pedagogy within each writing department. Without this, the writing program was unable to articulate a philosophy regarding the teaching of writing and what constituted good writing, which would, in turn, help solidify its disciplinary status (or perceived non-status) within the college.

Departmentalization and the Writing Program

Joseph Villiers Denney wrote in 1897 that "composition work is in theory the business of everybody, and in reality the business of nobody" (6), and this attitude is reflected in the often contested location of writing in the courses at the four colleges in 1919. The final topic for the 1919 conference was writing's place within the institution. Departmentalization had only just begun at the turn of the century for many institutions, and the result was that the teaching and administering of writing was placed in an awkward position. Previously, writing and rhetorical instruction was considered more general and thus did not really belong to any department, yet many faculty did not believe that it was enough of its own discipline to have its own department. In many cases, writing was not a separate subject, but was instead integrated as part of other courses, requiring both a flexibility on the part of the instructor to teach multiple subjects, and an overall responsibility on the part of the institution to make sure that writing was attended to by all instructors. Clara Stevens, for example, taught at Mount Holyoke prior to departmentalization, which occurred in 1897. As a result, she taught courses as varied as rhetoric, mathematics and rhetoric, and Latin and modern history (Snell 27). These pairings reflect a diversity of knowledge on the part of the instructor, as well as a looser conception of knowledges than was present after departmentalization. After departmentalization at Mount Holyoke in 1897, Stevens solely taught courses in the English department, which was separate from the department of English literature.

Because departmentalization was still relatively new at the colleges at the time of the 1919 conference, much of the discussion about interdepartmental cooperation centered around the topic of responsibility: who was responsible for work in writing? As Russell notes, "[D]espite pious announcements about every teacher being an English teacher, responsibility gradually shifted from the whole faculty to the English department" (63). This left the writing teachers and administrators with the tremendous responsibility of developing writing skills in their students that would (ideally) carry over to their work in other courses. Mary Augusta Jordan, of Smith, offered an example of Russell's point and echoed Stevens's early experience when she noted that early on Smith did not have any requirements in English, and "the English instructors looked over papers in such subjects as mathematics and Latin or French translations" (Wellesley 22). However, she noted that later changes brought about a required three hours in English (which seems to be the method in use at the time of the conference). Jordan's comments about the results of this are particularly telling and reflect the fact that the group in 1919 keenly felt the difficulties and contradictions caused by the separation:

> In the loss of the interchange of papers between departments we have suffered much in our opportunities to deal with the material of other departments and to correct the emphasis. We have also lost a burden of considerable weight from the point of view of those who considered the work perfunctory. (23)

As Jordan continued, her views reflected the beliefs of other departments about the role and place of English:

> I should say that the English department has found many foes in the other departments. The comment is often made that English is not the main subject of these other departments, and students' notebooks are never conditioned for poor English. Sometimes an instructor is glad to give some credit for good English, but the general feeling is that any form of English is good enough. Therefore, the cooperation which we have been able to establish at present is very incomplete. (23-24)

Jordan's comments reveal common struggles in English departments at that time. How much involvement should English departments have in the writing assignments given elsewhere? How much did they want to have? How much could they depend on other instructors to carry through with the ideas that were presented in the writing classroom? How was writing to be administered with any faith that the lessons that students learned would be required in other courses? What *was* the purpose of the English department, if not a focus on literature?

In addition to this shift in responsibility, the disdain that Jordan reports ("the point of view of those who considered the work perfunctory") was not isolated at Smith and was not particular to this time period. It seems to have been the prevailing attitude both before and after this conference. While modern historians have documented this as a twentieth-century trend (see Holbrook and Miller, for example), late nineteenth-century reports also reflect this attitude. Katherine Lee Bates, who was teaching literature at Wellesley at the time, wrote an article about English studies at Wellesley in 1894 as part of a series published by *The Dial*. Writing about the composition instructors at Wellesley, Bates noted that

> It is unfortunate that they are themselves mortal, and have thus far been unable to accede to the desire of the other Departments that all students whose technical themes and examination papers, while good in substance are bad in statement, shall be conditioned in English and turned over to the Rhetoric Department for reformation. (Qtd. in Brereton 185)

Ironically, one of those instructors to whom Bates refers is her colleague Sophie Chantal Hart, who would later chair the department of composition. Bates's critique was quite scathing and seems to not only attack the poorly prepared students but to wish for the instructors to be more than "mortal" in order to correct grammatical mistakes. In addition, her statement clearly reflects the fact that "remediating" poor writing had become the sole purview and responsibility of the rhetoric department—at least as far as other departments were concerned.

The discussion at the 1919 conference reflects a sense of dismay about the way that English is viewed at the colleges, but it also reflects a sense that something might be done about it. The conversations reflect an overall trend to decide what, really, the responsibilities of the English departments were and what they should be. Should students write papers for other departments within their English class? Should other departments "report" a student to the English department if they were writing papers of poor quality? Sophie Chantal Hart made it clear that the job of the writing administrator and teachers at Wellesley should be to convey the fact that English should be of consequence in all classes. According to Hart,

> Professor Jordan states that some of the other departments announce that they do not care anything about the form of expression. This gives the student an entirely wrong point of view. We must infect the college with the thought that form is not a detachable thing, and if we could make the instructors see this we could make the students see it. (29)

Hart's attitude may well have been the consequence of working with people like Bates, who had left the college by 1919. The discussion of the English department's role within the colleges suggests that the relationship with other departments was questionable at all four colleges. From what we can tell, departmentalization in many cases helped hasten the academy's view of composition as a service course.[9]

It is possible to see that the 1919 conference was not one where instructors and administrators came together and devised easy answers to the questions that they had. They did not leave with a plan for "fixing" all of the problems they discussed, although they attempted, where they could, to leave with concrete plans of action to implement in their home institutions (e.g., the saving of theme paper assignments so that they could be compared later). Instead, the conversations at the 1919 conference reveal an overall understanding, theorizing, and questioning of writing administration at the time. The longitudinal and/or qualitative work that occurred was indicative of their consistent attempts to function as programs, rather than as service departments and disparate organizations. As such, they worked together to consider the questions which were of importance to them at their individual institutions, as well as those of importance to their colleagues. Unfortunately, it is impossible to know if there was a summative conversation at the end of the conference since the transcript ends in the middle of a sentence on page forty-six. However, it is clear that there was a perceived need for further conversations, as the group met again in 1920.

The 1920 and 1922 Conferences

Faculty meeting minutes and administrative correspondence from Mount Holyoke and Vassar indicate that a second conference took place in 1920, at Wellesley College and a third one in 1922 at Vassar.[10] The archival evidence indicates that, in 1920, topics addressing programmatic and pedagogical issues such as the use of periodicals in writing courses, the typical procedure for individual conferences, and the relationship between the English department and college publications were suggested as possible topics (Mount Holyoke College, Meetings of the English Department, May 18 and June 10, 1920). In 1922, topics again included the relation of freshman composition to English work as a whole, the attitude of other departments towards written work, and the relation of the English Department to student publications (Reed).

How other departments viewed composition and written work clearly remained an issue for the colleges. Subheadings for this topic included "In how far do form and precision of expression enter into the estimate of papers in other departments?" and "Should papers notably defective in grammar and spelling be accepted by any departments?" Circumstances had most likely not changed much since 1919, for the final suggestion reads: "In how far is it possible for the English department to be a general clearing house for the maintenance of literacy throughout the college?" (Mount Holyoke College, "English Conference" 1922). The potential "gate-keeping" and literacy function of the freshman composition course, then, continued to be a programmatic question for the 1922 conference participants. It is unfortunate that transcripts do not exist for these conferences, given what they might reveal.

The 1924 Conference

No evidence exists to indicate that a conference took place in 1923, and there is only sketchy evidence that one took place in 1924. The Mount Holyoke College archives contains a document titled "Subjects suggested for the Conference of Teachers of English Composition in the Four Colleges, 1924." The proposed discussion topics indicate some frustration on the part of the conference organizers and a changing sense of what it meant to teach writing in an institution of higher education.

Suggestion A-3, for example, asks if anyone approves of "[t]rying to get something *done*,—even so mild a thing as a letter explaining our views to the high schools" (Mount Holyoke College, "Subjects suggested" 1; emphasis original). This is markedly different from the clear sense in the 1919 transcript that the secondary school teachers should serve the needs of the college instructors during the reading of the exams and in their pedagogy. Additionally, the perceived value of the conference was changing. Item B, titled "Suggestions for topics regarding the conferences themselves," carried the following subheadings:

1. Discussion of the real purpose of these conferences, and of means of increasing their value.

2. Perhaps we shall have thrashed out the subject enough after this next meeting, and might well consider the wisdom of letting the organization drop until some special need may arise. (Mount Holyoke College, "Subjects suggested" 1)

Despite what seemed like complaints about the conference, there was a long list of items for potential discussion. The fourteen subheadings under "Teaching" ranged from the "use and abuse" of the personal conference, to the value of written examinations, to thinking about whether the number of elective courses in writing should be limited. The eleven items under "Preparatory Freshman Work," also seemed to indicate an overall shift in both tone and content. They include "e) The freshman course as a means of developing the artistic faculty, and not merely the reasoning powers and the technique. [. . .]" and "i) How meet the matter of confirmed dislike of writing in the entering class [sic]" (Mount Holyoke College, "Subjects suggested" 3). Discussions of larger theoretical and pedagogical issues seemed to have shifted to a much narrower conception of WPA work. For example, instead of recognizing the impact of textbooks on a program, the 1924 proposed topics asked about the relation of the English departments to book-sellers and publishers, and ways of keeping "in print the works of standard authors in attractive editions" (Mount Holyoke College, "English Conference" 2).

The earlier discussions of the theoretical and pedagogical importance of writing administration and teaching were gone, replaced with conversation about administrative "tasks"—day-to-day duties that writing program administrators must perform but which do not always reflect the theoretical complexity of such a position. Instead, the "Subjects suggested" reflect a trend towards "fixing" the problems inherent in composition classes and promoting literature rather than conceiving of composition instruction as a way of aiding the development of individual writers. Perhaps in part because of the concerns raised in the "Subjects suggested," there do not appear to have been any further meetings of the Intercollege Conference after 1924.

Conclusion

Clearly, we have much to learn from these texts about the teaching of writing at women's colleges at the turn of the century. But there is also much to be learned about the administration of writing. Corbett notes that he suspected that "in the 1920s, the 1930s, and the first half of the 1940s the composition program was such a relatively small operation in our colleges and universities that [. . .] some factotum in the department could run the program out of his or her back pocket" (63). The transcript of the 1919 conference and the very existence of all of the conferences reveals that Corbett's assertion is simply not true. Not only were the programs complex, but the administrators were aware of the issues at their own and other institutions. Their programs were not run as "back-pocket" operations. Rather, they were concerted efforts at teaching and administering composition programs. They were thought out carefully, both pedagogically and theoretically, in the company of others. These women were WPAs, in the truest sense of the job. Their stories offer us historical snapshots for continuing issues in our field. More importantly, they offer us a theoretical framework for thinking about WPA work that has not previously been made available.

While it is impossible to know exactly why the ideological shift in 1924 occurred, a possible explanation is a change in the administrators of these programs from an "old guard" to a "new guard." The four department chairs represented at the 1919 conference were all strong presences at their individual institutions; by 1924, only one remained. Gertrude Buck died rather suddenly in 1921. Clara Stevens retired from the Mount Holyoke English department in 1921 as well, after chairing the department for thirty-seven years. Mary Augusta Jordan, similarly, retired from Smith College in 1921, after teaching there for thirty-seven years (Wagner 197). Thus, of the four very strong and very progressive department chairs, only Sophie Chantal Hart remained by 1924. Hart would not step down from her position as chair until

1935. By then, however, the conferences seem to have long been discontinued. The influence that these women had brought with them, the Dewey- and Scott-based models of teaching composition, disappeared after their departure. These women created these programs, made them work, and their loss—not unlike the loss of Fred Newton Scott at University of Michigan and Theodore Baird at Amherst—radically changed the programs from their Deweyian system to ones that corresponded more with the current-traditional model. The seeming failure, after 1923, of progressive models of administration also loosely corresponds with the end of the Progressive Era. Regardless of its ties to the Progressive Era, the end of the conferences and the end of the administrations of these four women was the end of an era.

Acknowledgments

We would like to acknowledge the many archivists who have played a role in our efforts to locate information about these conferences: Wilma Slaight and Jean Berry at Wellesley, Dean Rogers at Vassar, and Peter Carini at Mount Holyoke. Patricia Albright's knowledge of the Mount Holyoke archives and her familiarity with the English department records have been invaluable; without her, none of this chapter would exist. We would also like to thank them for their willingness to answer repeated emails and to locate "just one more thing." Additionally, we'd like to thank Will Banks for his reading of our draft and his comments, which came at just the right time and were just what we needed.

Notes

1. The other three "sisters" are Bryn Mawr, Radcliffe, and Barnard. Based on the research presented in this volume, we've speculated that Bryn Mawr did not attend due to M. Carey Thomas's attitude toward writing, which did not encourage professional development nor collegial ties. Radcliffe was, of course, Harvard's school for women, and as such, its courses were taught by Harvard faculty; Simmons has documented the attitude towards women's writing taken by Harvard's professors. Records indicate that Mount Holyoke's English department faculty and Barnard's President Virginia Gildersleeve may have known each other; a Miss Gildersleeve was considered as a judge in the 1920 poetry contest. However, we don't know why Barnard did not have a presence at the conference. By 1924 the name

had changed to the Conference of Teachers of English Composition in the Four Colleges.

2. The Fiftieth Anniversary was also MacCracken's inauguration/inaugural ceremony.

3. It should be noted, however, that Vassar implemented this system in stages and didn't move to a completely competitive system until 1928.

4. The different departments at this time operated under different names. Mount Holyoke had a Department of Rhetoric separate from the Department of English Literature. Vassar was always a Department of English, recognizing the interconnection of literature and writing; Laura Wylie in 1900 argued for a new Associate Professor line, writing that "the next professorship created in the department should represent the rhetorical side of English, which maintains in all our courses a relation with the literature at once coequal and complementary" (Campbell 260). By 1889, Wellesley also had two departments: the Department of English Language and Rhetoric and the Department of English Language. By 1906, their department records indicate three divisions: Department of English Literature, Department of English Language, and the Department of Composition, all under a general heading of English. By 1925, English Literature absorbed English Language, and Composition stood alone; by 1947, the remaining two departments were combined into a single English Department.

5. Mary Yost's 1915 dissertation was titled *The Functional Aspects of Argument as Seen in a Collection of Business Letters*. Her later research also focused on writing and argumentation.

6. Ada Snell's 1916 dissertation "Pause" was published in Scott's *Contributions to Rhetorical Theory* in 1918 (Stewart and Stewart 44).

7. The worry about competition seemed limited to grades and intellectual ability. "Grinds," or the women who received top academic honors, were often seen as odd or not considered part of the campus life. However, competition between the classes (e.g. freshman, sophomore, junior, senior) was fierce and so were the athletic competitions. Out-and-out campaigning for something, such as class president or the like, was strongly frowned upon. Students were expected to receive those honors based on their innate abilities, which did not need to be advertised or touted (Gordon; Horowitz; Solomon).

8. Towards the end of the discussion, Miss Egan of Smith stated, "There have been two principles of segregation suggested here today. Do we believe in segregation according to weakness or according to need? I do not object to being told I am limited, but I do object to being told I am dull or stupid" (18.1). As Miss Egan noted, beliefs about students informed the ideology that underlay the segregation discussion. Vassar, for example, segregated so that they could give more attention to the good students, while Miss Hanscom

from Smith (which did not segregate) saw the greatest disadvantage to the poorer students.

9. As a result of the conversation during the conference, some faculty did work to make improvements or to gain a greater understanding of the role of writing instruction at their home institutions. Clara Stevens, for example, issued a survey to the Mount Holyoke College faculty in 1920. It included such questions as "What are the chief complaints you have to make of the papers the students hand in to you?" and "Do you consider matters of English in grading your papers?" Lastly, the questionnaire asked "Have you any suggestions for more effective cooperation between the English department and other departments?" (Mount Holyoke College, untitled document, 1920, 4). The tabulated results offer an interesting and complex picture of the way that writing was viewed by other departments. For example, the results include the following pairs of contradictory statements:

- Students are unable to sustain their thought through a paper of any length.
- Students are unable to condense their thought to a paper of any brevity.

and

- Students cannot write in a logical form with a definite outline.
- Students have been overtrained in the conventional outline form; they warp their material for the sake of neat tabulation. (Mount Holyoke College, untitled document, 1920, 1).

These contradictions make clear the difficulties that the English departments from all four colleges would have had in addressing the use of English with other departments. Unfortunately, the findings presented in the transcript do not include an overview of the "suggestions" that the departments might incorporate in order to help the relationship between departments.

10. Gertrude Buck supposedly published an account of the 1920 conference in the *Journal of Education*. At the time of this writing, we have been unable to locate a copy of that article.

Works Cited

Bates, Katherine Lee. "Wellesley College." *The Origins of Composition Studies in the American College, 1875-1925*. Ed. John Brereton. Pittsburgh: U of Pittsburgh P, 1995. 183-85.

Berlin, James. *Writing Instruction in Nineteenth-Century American Colleges*. Carbondale: Southern Illinois UP, 1984.

Campbell, JoAnn. "Women's Work, Worthy Work: Composition Instruction at Vassar College, 1897-1922." *Constructing Rhetorical Education*. Ed. Marie Secor and Davida Charney. Carbondale: Southern Illinois UP, 1992. 26-42.

Connors, Robert. *Composition-Rhetoric*. Pittsburgh: U of Pittsburgh P, 1997.
—. "Dreams and Play: Historical Method and Methodology." *Methods and Methodology in Composition Research*. Ed. Gesa Kirsch and Patricia Sullivan. Carbondale: Southern Illinois UP, 1992.
Converse, Florence. "The Story of Wellesley: Part II." *The Story of Wellesley*. 3 August 2001. http://www.worldwideschool.org/library/books/hst/northamerican/TheStoryofWellesly/chap4.html (Sept. 2003).
Corbett, Edward. "A History of Writing Program Administration." *Learning from the Histories of Rhetoric*. Ed. Theresa Enos. Carbondale: Southern Illinois UP, 1993.
Daniels, Elizabeth. *Bridges to the World: Henry Noble MacCracken and Vassar College*. Clinton Corners, New York: College Avenue Press, 1994.
—. "Vassar History, 1915-1922." *History of Vassar*. November 1999. http://faculty.vassar.edu/daniels/1915_1922.html (4 Sept. 2003).
Denney, Joseph Villiers. *Two Problems in Composition Teaching*. Ann Arbor: Inland Press, 1897.
Dewey, John. *Experience and Education*. 1938. Kappa Delta Pi. New York: Touchstone, 1997.
Gordon, Lynn D. *Gender and Higher Education in the Progressive Era*. New Haven: Yale UP, 1990.
Griffin, Gail. *Calling: Essays on Teaching in the Mother Tongue*. Pasadena: Trilogy Books, 1992.
Holbrook, Sue Ellen. "Women's Work: The Feminizing of Composition." *Rhetoric Review* 9.2 (Spring 1991): 201-16.
Horowitz, Helen Lefkowitz. *Alma Mater*. 2nd ed. Amherst, MA: U of Massachusetts P, 1993.
Kitzhaber, Albert. *Rhetoric in American Colleges, 1850-1900*. Dallas: Southern Methodist UP, 1990.
L'Eplattenier, Barbara E. "Investigating Institutional Power: Women Administrators During the Progressive Era, 1880-1920." Diss. Purdue U, 1999.
MacCracken, Henry Noble. *The Hickory Limb*. New York: Charles Scribner's Sons, 1950.
Mastrangelo, Lisa. "Learning From the Past: Rhetoric, Composition, and Debate at Mount Holyoke College." *Rhetoric Review* 18.1 (Fall 1999): 46-64.
Miller, Susan. "The Feminization of Composition." *The Politics of Writing Instruction: Postsecondary*. Ed. Richard Bullock, John Trimbur, and Charles Schuster. Portsmouth: Boynton, 1991. 39-53.
Mount Holyoke College. "English Conference, 1922." Mount Holyoke College Archives and Special Collections, English Department Papers. South Hadley, MA.

—. "The Intercollege Conference on English Composition." Mount Holyoke College Archives and Special Collections, English Department Records, Series C, Sub-Series 4, Folder 1, n.d. South Hadley, MA.

—. Meetings of the English Department, May 18, 1920. Mount Holyoke Archives and Special Collections, English Department Papers, Box 5, Folder 1. South Hadley, MA.

—. Meetings of the English Department, June 10, 1920. Mount Holyoke College Archives and Special Collections, English Department Papers, Box 5, Folder 1. South Hadley, MA.

—. "Subjects Suggested for the Conference of Teachers of English Composition in the Four Colleges, 1924." Mount Holyoke College Archives and Special Collections, English Department Papers. South Hadley, MA.

—. Untitled Document, 1920. Mount Holyoke College Archives and Special Collections, English Department Papers. South Hadley, MA.

Reed, Amy. "Department of English Annual Report May, 1923." Vassar College Special Collections, Vassar College. MacCracken Collection. Box 28. Folder 71. Poughkeepsie, NY.

Ricks, Vicki. "'In an Atmosphere of Peril': College Women and Their Writing." *Nineteenth-Century Women Learn to Write*. Ed. Catherine Hobbs. Charlottesville: UP of Virginia, 1995: 59-83.

Russell, David. *Writing in the Academic Disciplines*, 1870-1990. Carbondale: Southern Illinois UP, 1991.

Scott, Joan Wallach. *Only Paradoxes to Offer*. Cambridge, MA: Harvard UP, 1996.

Snell, Ada F. "History of English Studies in Mount Holyoke Seminary and College." Unpublished typescript, 1942. Mount Holyoke College Archives and Special Collections, Mount Holyoke College. English Department Records. South Hadley, MA.

Solomon, Barbara Miller. *In the Company of Educated Women: A History of Women and Higher Education in America*. New Haven: Yale UP, 1985.

Stewart, Donald C., and Patricia L. Stewart. *The Life and Legacy of Fred Newton Scott*. Pittsburgh: U of Pittsburgh P, 1997.

Wagner, Joanne. "'Intelligent Members or Restless Disturbers': Women's Rhetorical Styles, 1880-1920." *Reclaiming Rhetorica: Women in the Rhetorical Tradition*. Ed. Andrea Lunsford. Pittsburgh: U of Pittsburgh P, 1995. 185-202.

Wellesley College. "Intercollege Conference on English Composition." 24 and 25 Oct. 1919. Records of the Department of English Composition. Wellesley Archives and Special Collections. Wellesley College. Wellesley, MA.

Woody, Thomas. *A History of Women's Education in the United States in Two Volumes*. New York: The Science Press, 1929.

7

Sifting Through Fifty Years of Change: Writing Program Administration at an Historically Black University

Deany M. Cheramie

> There is a multitude of Negro children crying out to us for aid, for the education that will help them to live aright as good citizens of our common country, to earn a livelihood, to come to the knowledge of God. Here is a great career.
>
> —*Mother M. Agatha Ryan*

> Composition studies remains one of the few academic disciplines in which outsiders insist on naming and authorizing its activities, without accepting the intellectual responsibility—and the institutional consequences—for doing so.
>
> —*Donald McQuade*

As a historically Black university, Xavier University of Louisiana shares a unique history with a group of colleges and universities that sometimes seem far outside the mainstream of most academic discussions. Like other such universities, Xavier was founded by a group of people who saw a need such as the one described by Mother M. Agatha Ryan. These people were dedicated to educating African-Americans and giving them opportunities denied them by a lack of civil liberties. Yet the educators who had this calling quite often did not understand the needs of the students they were teaching. As W. Ross Winterowd points out in *The English Department: An Institutional and Personal History*, "literarists" in an English department often have no background in the theories of rhetoric or composition, yet compositionists are supposed to be competent in literary theory and genres. It is, however, the literarists who define and make up the majority of the department, despite the fact that most of the instructional work is in freshman composition. This explains why the department of English at Xavier University did not have a writing program administrator for almost the first fifty years of its existence. Overall, archival evidence illustrates that, although there were freshman English writing courses from the inception of the college unit, there was no clearly defined writing program, nor was the university large enough or financially capable of supporting a sufficient staff, much less a writing program administrator, until the 1970s.[1] Additional influences, such as Xavier's Catholic and historically Black college affiliation, have also influenced the administration of composition courses over the five decades before an administrator was appointed.

To understand why Xavier was not capable of supporting a writing program administrator for the first five decades of its existence, we must understand the history of historically black colleges and universities (HBCUs) and Xavier itself. As Evans, Evans, and Evans point out, HBCUs were developed primarily because of racism. During post-Civil War reconstruction and into the early part of the twentieth century, liberal southern whites believed that blacks should have access to postsecondary education, but not at the same level as whites (LeMille). HBCUs were instead intended as "holding areas" for blacks so they would not matriculate into Historically White Colleges and Universities (HWCUs). African-Americans created a few HBCUs themselves; state governments and religious groups created the rest of them. In the first half of the twentieth century, there was the argument as to whether HBCUs should concentrate on classical or industrial-based education. This argument was eventually considered moot as state legislatures were (and in some cases still are) reluctant to adequately fund

HBCUs and the cheaper classical curriculum reflected this. Private HBCUs, like Xavier, have relied on private donations, endowments, grants, and some limited state and federal funding for most of their operating capital. Thus, HBCUs have always been, and continue to be, poorly funded.

In addition to the problems of funding and acceptance, HBCUs have also been plagued by the desire to have their students fit the middle-class mold. Historically, American universities have taught a cultural literacy composed of middle-class American values. As Christopher Schroeder and others have shown, this literacy and value learning is expected to take place in the composition classroom. The plight of HBCUs put a particular twist on this expectation. The language values of the middle class relied, and still rely, on a perceived standard of American English associated primarily with a "white" middle and upper class. This standard was also reflected in the perceived dialect of the educated. In their desire and effort to transform African-Americans into an educated middle class, HBCUs instructed their students in the perceived dialect, often ignoring their students' own culture and dialects. Xavier administrators fell into step with this traditional viewpoint of education. The descriptions of composition and rhetoric courses in the 1926 course bulletin indicate that not only was writing taught, but also speech and dialectic, an endeavor to prepare students to adapt their speech to academic and workplace requirements. This is further supported by the fact that some upper level English courses were titled "Public Speaking" (*Bulletin 1926-27* 15-16). Even in the 1970s, when massive changes were occurring to the freshman English program, students were required to take an introductory speech course, and grammar instruction and literary texts in the freshman English classrooms asserted a continued reliance on current-traditional methods.[2] Models from other universities were clearly influencing the freshman English program, but course descriptions give no concrete clues as to how such courses were taught. Most of the course descriptions give the impression that the freshman English courses were primarily about developing speaking and writing skills to a certain standard, and that the African-American students who were enrolling at Xavier needed additional remediation to meet this standard. Additionally, the standard was set by academics with little regard for the students' African-American culture. Considering the fact that historically black colleges were created from a combination of the progressive movement towards education and "holding spaces" for African-Americans, there seems to be an ambiguous quality to the standards imposed in these schools. On one hand, the freshman English courses at Xavier taught students the writing and speaking skills they needed to be successful in their college courses and their careers. On the other hand, the courses told students that they needed to sound and write "white" to "make it."

The emphasis on middle-class values and literacy for African-Americans was a direct result of the mission of the Catholic order that founded Xavier University. The Sisters of the Blessed Sacrament (SBS), who founded Xavier College for the purpose of educating black Catholics in the city of New Orleans, were dedicated to ministering to Native- and African-Americans. Founding schools like Xavier was part of that mission. In fact, Xavier Preparatory School, a combined middle/high school, and Xavier College served as the capstone schools of a parochial school system the SBS created for Catholic African-Americans in New Orleans (Lynch).[3] Xavier "University," which was really a combined middle/high school and two year Normal School, was opened in 1915; Xavier College, a four-year college, was not opened until 1925.[4] The influence of the SBS stayed with Xavier until 1966 when the corporation founded by the sisters disbanded and the university was handed over to the administration of a lay board and president. However, the SBS remains on campus and continues to play a part in the administration and classrooms of the university. Over the decades, sisters worked as instructors and administrators in the department of English. For most of the time period discussed here, sisters also served as deans and presidents of the university. Their influence on the educational and administrative practices of the university is undeniable.

The Early Years: Governance Through Expedience (1925 to 1940)

Archival evidence describing the first fifteen years of Xavier's existence affirms that the founders of the university were trying to give their students a strong foundation in a classical Catholic education that combined studies of English, math, Latin, religion, and the sciences.[5] Existing correspondence and the *Annals of St. Francis Xavier Convent* indicate that these first years were times of extreme expediency for

Xavier and the writing program. The first principal of Xavier, Mother M. Paul of the Cross, and succeeding deans of the college, seemed desperate for qualified instructors throughout the early years, a need that would continue to plague administrators through the decades (*Annals* 10).[6] This need was especially strong during the first few years of the college. The Dean of the College, Sr. M. Gonzaga, had Miss Margaret Shelly, the high school English teacher, teaching some of the "Composition and Rhetoric I" courses during the first year of the college. Otherwise, composition and rhetoric was taught by sisters; few lay faculty taught writing in the first years of the university.

Of the three composition courses available at this time, only Composition and Rhetoric 3, a remedial course taken *after* students had performed poorly in their other composition and rhetoric courses, had class sizes averaging ten students. Information from the "Schedule of Classes" from 1925 to 1935 indicates that teachers taught the course infrequently. Class sizes for the other composition courses, however, were quite large and could be anywhere from eleven to forty students in a class, depending on the instructor or time of day. In other words, there were no class size limits. During the first decade of Xavier College, it seems that the dean of the college, her secretary, and the other sisters scheduling students—rather than classes—placed students where convenient. Instructors taught as many as eighteen to twenty hours of courses a week. Considering the limited number of faculty, the administration must have considered it expedient. Also, instructors were not teaching a single subject. In 1928, Sr. Consuela Marie taught Composition and Rhetoric 1, Public Speaking, the English Essay, Latin, and Religion, some in multiple sections, for a total of twenty-two hours.[7] Such large classes and faculty course loads became a problem for Xavier when the sisters began applying for accreditations. Arthur D. Wright, chair of the Standing Committee on the Approval of Negro Schools for the Association of Colleges and Secondary Schools of the Southern States, was concerned that English classes were oversized and students poorly distributed in these courses (Wright). This comment suggests both inadequate administration of these courses, as well as a lack of understanding of how to best meet the course objectives. By 1936, this requirement seemed to have been satisfied, as it was no longer listed as a need to be addressed. The "Teachers Schedule" for both 1933-34 and 1934-35 shows first-year English classes with an average of twenty-five students, but with variations as low as sixteen to as high as thirty-four students per class, showing that there was some regularizing of class sizes, albeit inconsistent.

It should be made clear at this point that the deans of the college were performing most of the administrative work of the institution and making the decisions concerning class sizes, faculty, and faculty loads. The college presidents seemed to have little to do with decisions concerning the instructional practices of the university. In 1927, Sr. M. Gonzaga was dean of the college, while Rev. E. G. Brunner was the president. However, Brunner acted in an advisory capacity only; the sisters performed most of the administrative work (*Annals* 54). In 1931, Mother M. Agatha Ryan became president of Xavier and the SBS Corporation, and Sr. M. Frances became dean of the college. Ryan would often be away at the Motherhouse of the SBS in Pennsylvania or traveling to other parochial schools in Louisiana. Thus, the dean of the college performed most of the administrative responsibilities of the college, including course assignments.

Changes appear in the composition offerings in 1932-33 (*Xavier College Bulletin 1932-33*) when Sr. M. Madeline Sophie was named the new dean of the college. Courses at this time were renumbered to follow a more common collegiate style, such as English 101: Composition and Rhetoric and English 102: Composition and Rhetoric. These composition courses were worth three credit hours, with the first instructing the "essentials of rhetoric and the various modes of composition with special emphasis in exposition" (15). The second course was a continuation of the first course with emphasis in narration, description, and argument. Freshman Public Speaking became a separate course from Composition and Rhetoric. A new course, English 101-D: English for Deficient Freshmen, was created, a three-credit course taken over one-and-a-half semesters. Considered supplementary to English 101, it was designed to help students who were doing poorly in 101. The course began after midterms in the fall semester for students who scored less than 70 percent on their midterms. It was a non-credit course, but if students passed it, they received credit for English 101. A replacement for the earlier Composition and Rhetoric 3, the course was designed to help students with language difficulties earlier in their college experience. Instructors who taught this course, however, did so as a course overload, because it was not assigned until the middle of the fall semester.

Another factor influencing change in the curriculum at this time was the construction of buildings for the college at the corner of Pine Street and Washington Avenue in the Carrollton area of New Orleans. These buildings, referred to as the "New Unit" in the Corporate minutes, formed the foundation of what is now Xavier University. This move, the addition of a new building, and the continual, but gradual growth of the student body, further influenced the administration to improve course offerings and pedagogy. This is further evidenced by changes in the department faculty. By 1933, the English faculty was composed of one sister, Consuella Marie (Cunningham), and three lay faculty, Harold Simon, Ellen Cavanaugh, and Marie Young. Cunningham, Simon, and Cavanaugh all had MA degrees, but no PhDs (Corporation of SBS, *Corporate Minutes: Book 1* 168).

The lack of doctorates and advanced graduate work among the Xavier faculty proved a serious hindrance for the college, the English department, and any administration of a writing program. It hindered the accreditation processes for the university. While Xavier received a number of certifications in the 1920s and 1930s from the State of Louisiana, the Sisters had great difficulty getting accreditation from the Association of Colleges and Secondary Schools of the Southern States. In response to the sisters' first petitions in 1928, Arthur D. Wright, chair of the Standing Committee on the Approval of Negro Schools, gave Xavier a Class B rating. He informed the college that in order to achieve Class A status, Xavier would have to improve a number of standards, one of which was that department chairs had at least three years of graduate work and full professors had to have at least two. According to the corporate minutes and corporate president's reports, the sisters and lay faculty were taking leave and summer travel to universities in the East and North to work on graduate degrees, but many did not return, either because of reassignment (for the religious) or because of better job offers.

Changes in the writing courses continue in the 1930s and indicate that the administration was still trying to find ways to improve course offerings. It was in 1935 that the English department finally realized that a remedial English course would better serve students if they took the course before taking English 101. In the 1935-36 *Xavier University Bulletin*, the English 101-D course was listed first in the sequence and was a noncredit course. The intent of the course was to serve as a supplement to English 101 and was "required of students who fail to pass preliminary tests" (21). Who implemented or designed these diagnostic tests is unknown, but in 1938-39 a comprehensive examination at the end of the sophomore year was required for graduation. In response to the competency examination, the 1939-40 catalog indicates that "students who fail in this examination are required to follow non-credit remedial courses for improvement in writing under the Department of English" (*Bulletin 1939-1940* 20). However, English 101-D was soon removed from the offerings of the English department, and no other remedial courses were listed in the bulletin of that year. It is possible, however, that students were tutored privately by members of the English department as needed. James Connolly was "directing" the English department at this time and may have been responsible, along with other members of the department, for these changes. The reason for removing the remedial English courses is unclear, but could be related to the university's push towards a more professional academic standard for students and faculty.

By 1939 the English faculty was composed of Oscar Bouise, a Xavier graduate (Pharmacy, Class of 1930), Ellen Cavanaugh, Alvin H. Jones, Stephen Ryan, J. Henderson Shields, and James Connolly, all of whom were lay persons. Other faculty members are listed, but none remained with the university for more than a year. There were no sisters nor PhDs on the English faculty, which Mother M. Agatha Ryan, President of Xavier University, commented upon in her President's Report. As she stated, "The weakest department in the school, to my mind, is the Department of English" (*President's Report: 1938* 4). Mother Ryan contended that the English faculty were performing to high standards, but insisted that the department needed a department head with a PhD (4). Why Xavier did not have a PhD in the English department may be answered by the fact that it was a small Black and Catholic college. There was little prestige associated with teaching at such institutions, especially since they were often barely supported by grants or endowments to allow for competitive salaries or benefits. Combined with low salaries were the long teaching hours. According to the accreditation report written by D. O'Connell for the National Catholic Education Association, Xavier faculty taught "18 hours of class" per week (Corporation of SBS, *Corporate Minutes: Book 2* 17). Such a large teaching load would have been a serious drawback to a scholar and inhibited the faculty from working on higher degrees during the fall and spring semesters. These conditions were also deterrents when trying to hire faculty with doctorates.

Administration from Within (1940 to 1950)

The decade from 1940 to 1950 saw a shift. More of the administrative practices of the writing program happened from within the English department, despite the fact that at the beginning of the decade, Mother Agatha Ryan continued to be concerned about the quality of the department, still considered the weakest "whereas it should be the best" (*President's Report: 1939* 4). As the department entered the decade, James Connolly continued as the "Director" of English. He had an MA, but could not afford to take a year's leave to pursue a PhD. Members of the SBS did join the faculty with MA degrees from Catholic University of America: Sr. M. Berenice, Sr. M. Anthony Daniel, and Sr. Mary of Nazareth. Stephen Ryan, who joined the faculty in the 1930s, completed a PhD from the University of Ottawa; he was the first in the department with a doctorate. During World War II, however, there were serious changes in the department. Connolly was called to the service in 1942, as was Ryan.[8]

In Connolly's absence, Sr. Mary of Nazareth was named department chair in 1942. During her tenure as chair, and later associate dean under the new dean of the university, Sr. M. Frances, Nazareth initiated changes in the composition courses that seemed in line with the current-traditional model. In the 1943-44 bulletin, descriptions for the composition courses reflect a more general review of the fundamentals of grammar and writing. The description of English 102 included a required research paper (30-31). Other elements of the current-traditional model had already been added to English 101: "regular and systematic practice in writing" and "extensive reading of certain masterpieces of prose and verse" (*Bulletin 1940-41* 27). Also, using literature as a basis for writing, which Berlin describes as an element of current-traditional rhetoric, begins in this decade (71). And while the title of the 101-102 sequence was changed to "Guiding Principles of English" in the 1944-45 catalog, the description "practice in writing, reading, and speaking" implied that speech was still a large component of composition instruction. The fact that a written "theme" was required weekly in 101 at this time further shows that the administration was dedicated to a current-traditional rhetoric.

At the same time that the "Guiding Principles" composition course was developed, Otto Ramsey was hired to teach in the English department. While there is no evidence as to why Sr. Mary of Nazareth hired Ramsey, his short time with Xavier would prove to be boon to the writing program. Ramsey had experience with English and reading remedial programs at Columbia University where he went to graduate school. Ramsey left Xavier after only two years, but he put into place a remedial program that would be the foundation for the University's preparation for an influx of post-World War II veterans. As a result of Ramsey's work, in 1947, the developmental English course reappeared: English 100: Essentials of English. The course was worth two-to-five credit hours and met five days per week. The description indicated remediation in what the catalog calls the "essentials of English" (*Bulletin 1947-48* 40).

The first standardized entrance examinations for freshmen were required in English and reading and were a part of Ramsey's program. According to Mother Ryan in her *Report of the President Concerning Xavier University: 1945*: "Freshmen who give evidence through tests that they are lacking in fundamental knowledge in these subjects [English and reading] are required to pass the remedial course before they are admitted to regular college program of studies in these fields." There are no descriptions available as to the composition of these "placement tests," nor of who designed them or scored them. Ramsey may have had a part in designing them as they were part of his program. Interestingly, the students did not complete the exams once they arrived at Xavier; rather, the tests were given by Xavier recruiting staff during their visits to segregated African-American high schools around the country (Ryan *1947*).

The Literarists (1950 to 1960)

From 1950 to 1960 the writing program moved toward a more literature-based curriculum. The study of literature in both the freshman and sophomore sequences during these ten years shows the influence of literature studies on the department of English. This change is pointed out in James Berlin's discussion of literature and composition when he discusses how English departments following World War II and the advent of New Criticism called for teaching literature in composition classes (107). The idea that literature "makes for 'self-reliant and well-rounded personalities'" (Berlin 110), as well as provides a moral foundation, was in line with the humanistic mission of the university and the Sisters of the Blessed Sacrament. Additionally, Xavier worked to provide its students with the same sort of education as the rest of America: "these course changes are intended to be in line with [. . .] practice in most American colleges and universities" (Josephina, *President's Report 1957*). The movement toward using more literature in the core English courses would also have been in line with the make-up of the faculty in the department of English, most of whom had English/literature degrees. In 1951, Sr. Mary of Nazareth was called to the Motherhouse of the Sisters of the Blessed Sacrament, and Dr. Stephen Ryan was appointed department chair, following the appointment of Sr. M. Helene as the new dean of Xavier University (Ryan, *President's Report 1951*). Throughout the decade of the 1950s, Ryan remained a dynamic force in the department as far as the continued emphasis on literature was concerned. However, despite the changes in the writing curriculum, the continued high turnover of contract instructors indicates continued administrative problems for composition in the area of finances, class loads, class sizes, and the lack of prestige that came from teaching at a Catholic HBCU.

Changes in the philosophy of the department and its writing administration were reflected in the writing courses. In the 1951 *President's Report*, Mother Ryan reports that the department of English changed its standardized testing program. The department had been using standardized testing to determine placement and to evaluate students in the English 100, 101, and 102 courses at the end of each semester. The department reported that it would no longer be using a standardized test to evaluate English 102 students "since this is primarily a course in actual composition." The implication is that the standardized tests used were not testing for writing ability in the students, but for knowledge of grammar. The descriptions of English 100 and 101 do suggest that the courses were heavily weighted in grammar instruction, especially English 100. Yet English 101 was still requiring students to write weekly "themes" and read literature.

Changes in university administration and governance at this time also illustrated that faculty were getting more control of the curriculum. In 1955, Sr. M. Josephina, the new president, reorganized the administration, creating both an administrative council and an academic council. The academic council was composed of the dean of the university and department chairs. Academic issues were now brought before the academic council and decided upon at this level. One such issue was "the problem of student deficiencies in oral and written English" (Josephina, *President's Report 1958-59*). This may have been a response to the fact that English 100: Essentials of English, a five-hour developmental course, was discontinued the previous year (Xavier, *Bulletin 1957-58*, 54). Students needing extra work were placed in special sections of English 101, which met five days per week. This decision by Stephen Ryan and the English department faculty seemed to better motivate students, yet the university faculty did not seemed pleased with the results (*Annual Report 1960-61*).

A Time of Change and Upheaval (1960 to 1970)

The reality of the department during the 1960s is that the university, while private, was in many ways acting like an open admissions university. This was especially evident after the Corporation of the Sisters of the Blessed Sacrament was dissolved, and the university was turned over to the administration of a lay president, Norman C. Francis, and a board consisting of two-thirds lay people and one-third members of the Sisters of the Blessed Sacrament. In the decade of the 1960s, enrollment at Xavier decreased. This was not a new development; enrollment had been steadily declining since the previous decade. It would continue to do so into the 1970s. The general reaction to this decline was to loosen admission requirements in order to increase student enrollment. This resulted in a continued need for remedial English courses. The department of English also had problems with keeping long-term faculty. Stephen Ryan resigned in 1960. Oscar Bouise, who had been with Xavier for thirty years, took a position at Southern University as director of freshman composition, but returned by the end of the decade. New faculty members, mainly graduates of Tulane University, came and went frequently. The position of chair changed hands four times over the decade, with James Connolly as acting chair at Ryan's resignation. Henry Delaune took the position for two years, until Sr. Ancilla Marie Flory was appointed acting chair and then chair for three years. Oscar Bouise rounded out the decade as acting chair for one year. This frequent turnover of positions and faculty, with few senior faculty to lead the program, prevented administrative continuity for the writing program. As their own report to the

Southern Association of Colleges and Schools revealed, there was only one PhD in the department in 1969, and only three members of the faculty had any form of professorial status (Xavier, *Summary* 85). Any administration of the freshman writing program would have been haphazard at best.

The frequent upheavals and inconsistency were also reflected in the course offerings of the decade. Administrators eventually responded to the faculty's concerns about students' writing and oral skills in 1962 and re-introduced a remedial course. English 101: Guiding Principles of English became a three-credit, five-day per week course and was "an application of the fundamentals of English with intensive practice in writing, reading, and speech" (Xavier, *Bulletin 1962-64* 92). This course had to be "satisfactorily completed" before students could take any other English course so that students had the "proper background in the fundamentals of grammar and composition before the completion of the freshman year" (Josephina, *Annual Report 1960-61*). English 102 became an introduction to literature course that covered genres. Thus, while the expressionistic movement of rhetoric became prevalent in the 1960s, it did not make much of an impression on the composition program at Xavier. Despite the surface-level changes in the program during the 1960s, it was still primarily a current-traditionalist model. The advent of honors courses saw them leaning towards an elitist model which supported the literary concerns of the English faculty (Josephina, *Annual Report: 1964-65*). Yet the stated purpose of the department was to develop in students the abilities that would lead them to a liberal education (Xavier, *Summary* 82). This statement helped the department balance the elitism of an honors program with the fact that students from the other side of the spectrum still needed remediation of some form, as seen in the move to a five-hour English 101, a tutorial program, and a return to a remedial English course, now known as English 99. The tutorial program, begun in 1964, was for students who failed the placement test and were judged incapable of doing the work required in English 101 (Josephina, *Annual Report: 1964-65*). These students could not take English 101 until they exhibited the skills necessary to pass the course. In their report to the Southern Association of Colleges and Schools (SACS) in 1969, the department of English recommended that in order to meet the goals of the department, they must continue to evaluate and improve the tutorial and remedial programs (Xavier, *Summary* 84).

Administration by Composition Principles (1970 to 1976)

The department's efforts to meet the goals expressed in the SACS report can be seen in the inception of the Freshman Studies Program (FSP) in 1970, directed by Dr. Joseph Rice, a member of the department of English. Other members of the department, namely Dr. Thomas Bonner, director of freshman composition at the time, and Dr. Ronald Johnson, who would became director of the composition workshop, were instrumental in planning the composition section of the grant that funded the FSP. The Title III Advanced Institutional Development Program grant was a true windfall for the writing program, as it is quite possible that little change in the composition program would have been possible without such funding (Rice 1).[9] As part of the AIDP federal requirements, the FSP was evaluated in each year of the three-year grant by outside evaluators. These evaluators were selected from similar programs at other universities from around the U.S. and had credentials that specialized in each of the specific areas of the AIDP grant. The FSP was divided into five components: math, reading, composition, speech, and freshman counseling. Evaluators assessed the effectiveness of each component in comparison to the stated philosophies and goals of the components, the mission of the FSP, and the mission of the university. The evaluators' comments would ultimately be a boon to the writing program, as they allowed administrators to argue for change using external and professionally developed standards.

The composition program was set up into two main parts: courses and a composition workshop. The courses were further divided into three groups of students: honors, average, and developmental (McFarland 1). The stated goal of the developmental courses was "to produce students who are consistently capable of writing clear, correct standard English prose" (McFarland 1). The developmental courses were organized into English 99, a noncredit summer course which prepared students for regular composition, and English 101-D and 102-D, which were for credit. Both student morale and student and university budgets were helped by the fact that these courses were for credit and counted the same as regular courses. Another change was that the whole department taught developmental courses, which were primarily centered on the idea of grammatical "error," but acknowledged the need for compositions to have clear central ideas that are "reasonably developed."

The FSP was evaluated in its first year, 1974-75, by Dr. Shirley McBay of Spelman College, Rosa Tift of Albany State College, and Edwin Sanders of Fisk University. McBay was chair of Spelman's math department and associate academic dean; Tift chaired Albany State's special services department; and Sanders was director of freshman programs at Fisk. Each was highly qualified to evaluate FSP and gave honest critiques of the program. In a letter to the FSP faculty that accompanied the final report of the evaluators, Joseph Rice expressed discomfort with the required outside evaluations, but only because of the limited time—two days—they had to perform their evaluation. In their reports, the three evaluators themselves express reservations at being able to make adequate assessments in such a short period of time. Yet their reports still manage to point out strengths and weaknesses of the FSP. For the composition program in particular, a number of strengths were mentioned, such as the guidelines for instructing the courses and the goals set, which were detailed yet flexible (McBay and Tift 13). Weaknesses discussed concerned poor facilities, unmet goals, and inadequate textbooks. The evaluators recommended that the director of composition have workshops for the faculty about methodology and be more meticulous about implementing a philosophy that concentrated instruction in teaching writing and usage rather than syntax. An item that concerned one evaluator was the fact that there were few African-American faculty in the English department. He recommended that more funds be found for "black academic professionals," especially for the developmental program, stating that students needed to see positive role models (Sanders 1-2).

In the second year of the evaluations, 1975-76, the evaluators are more specialized in their areas, with each assessing a specific component of the program.[10] The composition program evaluator was Betty McFarland, Writing Workshop Director at Appalachian State University. McFarland went into much greater detail in evaluating the composition program than her predecessors. She noted a number of strengths in the program, many of which were described by the previous evaluators. She also, however, noted discrepancies in the program, stating that the final assessment of students in the course, which was based on evaluation of basic errors, was not supportive of the goals of the course (McFarland 3). McFarland's discussion of the difference of teaching grammar usage versus teaching syntax in writing instruction, as well as recommending more instruction in organization and audience, suggests that the courses still concentrated on teaching grammar rather than rhetorical strategies or writing processes (3b-5). Other recommendations included using textbooks designed for developmental courses (the *Harbrace Handbook* was the text being used at this time), standardizing the theme-writing test used for placement, and lowering class sizes from twenty to fifteen. Another weakness pointed out was the transfer value of the 101-D/102-D sequence (5-10). As the department of English eventually discovered, graduate and professional programs were reluctant to accept credits from a course listed as "developmental" or "remedial." This led to the dissolution of the developmental sequence into a noncredit course again, in the mid-1980s.

The reviewer of the composition program in the final year of the initial AIDP grant was Dr. Harvey Weiner, Coordinator of Composition at Pennsylvania State University. Weiner complemented the faculty for their dedication to teaching composition. He also wrote that Dr. Thomas Bonner, the department chair, and Dr. Ronald Johnson, the director of composition, were both "strong leaders" with a "clear sense of direction" for the program (2). Other strengths of the composition program noted were frequent meetings to discuss pedagogy; instructors conferencing with students; and writing performed in all courses. There were even some attempts to promote a form of writing across the curriculum; writing instructors consulted with other departments about teaching writing and supplied grading sheets to other faculty. Yet there were still some problems with inconsistency in syllabi, especially for English 101, and an overemphasis on the instruction of grammar syntax versus grammar usage in context (Weiner 4-9).

One component of the composition program under that AIDP grant was the "Composition Workshop." Considered the first writing center in Louisiana, it used primarily student tutors to work one-on-one with developmental writing students and other students who wished for writing help (Wilson). While at first it primarily concentrated on helping students alleviate grammar problems using grammar drills, it also used audio tapes and materials developed by the faculty. By the 1976-77 report on the FSP, the evaluator, Betty McFarland, who directed her own writing workshop, was comparing the composition workshop favorably to similar facilities at larger institutions. Yet McFarland also questioned the overemphasis on grammar teaching, drill, and testing, and recommended more attention be paid to students' actual writing (McFarland 12). In 1976-77, Dr. Ronald Johnson would direct both the freshman writing program and the composition workshop. For his work, he received a release from teaching one course.

Conclusion

As the above discussion shows, writing program administration at Xavier University was often based on expedience. In the beginning, the Sisters of the Blessed Sacrament determined which composition courses would be taught, who would teach them, and how many students could be assigned to a course. These women based their work in expediency: Whom could they afford to hire? Where could they fit the students? How many students could be in a single class? How many hours could an instructor teach? Because this decision-making process was the result of a lack of planning, there was never a cohesive vision—let alone a *vision*—for the writing courses. Later, as department chairs became involved in the process, administration of writing courses became more focused on meeting the literacy needs of the academy and the professional wishes of the literarists. The high rate of instructor turnover allowed for little continuity in the program, and while change did take place, it was always in response to university administrative pressures and only rarely from a departmental drive for progress. The 1970s, however, became the time when an effort toward radical change could occur with the advent of a writing program that was led by a writing program administrator and assessed by evaluators experienced in composition.

Berlin states that "the curriculum [. . .] is always responsive to the changing economic, social, and political conditions of the society" (5). Such responsive change may be possible in universities and colleges where faculty and administrators have resources and backgrounds in rhetoric and composition to encourage change. But such transformations come slowly on campuses that were originally designed to limit an entire culture and keep it from transformation, like an HBCU. The original intent of the legislatures that founded and then refused to fund HBCUs was to restrict and slow change for an entire race while appearing to support liberal ideals of education. Yet as Xavier University's history shows, change may come slowly to such institutions, but it does come. Progress may have limits, but as the renaissance that appeared in the freshman English program at Xavier University in the early 1970s demonstrates, responsive change does come.

Acknowledgments

I would like to thank the University Archives and Special Collections Division of the Xavier University of Louisiana Library for access to its collections. I would especially like to thank archivist Lester Sullivan, who seemed to know which dusty box might have documentation I was looking for. I would also like to thank Thomas Bonner, Michele Levy, and Vivian Wilson for their willingness to answer my questions.

Notes

1. Unfortunately, there are no files of memos from the dean's, the president's, or the English chair's offices. There are certainly no private files from or about the key individuals. To maintain such records may have been seen as a violation of the sisters' vows and is a clear aspect of the SBS's influence on the university. The majority of what is available to the historian includes president's reports and corporate minutes.

2. Xavier still requires students to take a speech course and speech competency examination. Part of the examination requires reading aloud a passage that contains words which can have both standard and dialectical pronunciations.

3. The founding of a parochial school system for African-Americans was the idea of Archbishop Blenk, the Archbishop of New Orleans. It was his response to the opening of colleges and trade schools for African-Americans in the city by Protestant sects. Blenk wanted to keep the Catholic African-Americans "in the fold," and asked the SBS to create a school system for this purpose.

4. There is some confusion as to what the schools were called in the beginning. In 1915, the SBS started Xavier University under a charter from the Louisiana state government. The SBS started a middle/high school and two-year Normal School under this name with the intent of eventually starting a four-year college, which they did in 1925. College classes were taught in the same building as the middle/high school until 1933 when the college moved to a new physical location. The original buildings, which continued to house the middle/high school, would eventually be named Xavier Preparatory School, while the new location was Xavier College and eventually Xavier University.

5. Because of its tradition as a Catholic university and its dedication to the liberal arts, Xavier has almost always required six hours each of theology

and philosophy in its core curriculum. This is despite its reputation as a sciences school.

6. At one point, Mother M. Paul asked Drexel to pray for teachers to be found (*Annals* 11).

7. Often, the sisters would carry more classroom hours than the lay instructors. Their vows of obedience and servitude would require them to. Their belief in self-sacrifice made it possible.

8. Stephen Ryan was able to obtain a form of deferral when he joined the Coast Guard Reserves for the Port of New Orleans. As part of his service, he gave fifteen hours per week to patrolling the port and the Mississippi River. Ryan continued to teach at Xavier while performing this service.

9. Freshman Studies was an umbrella program for core freshmen courses in math, English, and reading. These curricular areas were grouped together under this program for two reasons: each had a developmental course element, and each was a core academic skills area.

10. Another bonus that came about during the new emphasis on composition instruction was a one-day "Conference on Freshman Composition" held on Xavier's campus in September 1975. Sponsored by the composition program, Thomas Bonner organized the event. Sheridan Baker and Ray Shepherd were the guest presenters. Over seventy participants attended (Bonner).

Works Cited

Berlin, James A. *Rhetoric and Reality: Writing Instruction in American Colleges, 1900-1985*. Carbondale: Southern Illinois UP, 1987.

Bonner, Thomas. Personal interview. 19 Feb. 2003.

Corporation of the Sisters of the Blessed Sacrament for Indians and Colored People of Louisiana. *Corporate Minutes: Book 1. 1916-1933*. Library Archives. Xavier University of Louisiana, New Orleans.

—. *Corporate Minutes: Book 2. 1934-1939*. Library Archives. Xavier University of Louisiana, New Orleans.

Evans, A. L., V. Evans, and A. M. Evans. "Historically Black Colleges and Universities." *Education* 123 (Fall 2002). Education Full Text. 16 Mar. 2003. Xavier University of Louisiana Library. New Orleans.

Josephina, Sr. Mary. *President's Report of Xavier University of Louisiana: 1957*. Library Archives. Xavier University of Louisiana, New Orleans. n. pag.

—. *Annual Report of the President: 1958-59*. Library Archives. Xavier University of Louisiana, New Orleans. n. pag.

—. *Annual Report of the President: 1960-61*. Library Archives. Xavier University of Louisiana, New Orleans. n. pag.

—. *Annual Report of the President: 1964-65*. Library Archives. Xavier University of Louisiana, New Orleans. n. pag.

LeMille, Tilden. "The HBCU: Yesterday, Today, and Tomorrow." *Education* 123 (Fall 2002). Education Full Text. 16 Mar. 2003. Xavier University of Louisiana Library. New Orleans.

Lombard, J. E. Letter to Sr. Mary Frances, Dean of Xavier University. 19 Mar. 1928. *Corporate Minutes: Book 1. 1916-1933.* Corporation of the Sisters of the Blessed Sacrament for Indians and Colored People of Louisiana. Library Archives. Xavier University of Louisiana, New Orleans.

Lynch, Patricia. *Sharing the Bread in Service: Sisters of the Blessed Sacrament: 1891-1991.* Vol. 1. Bensalem, PA: 1998.

McBay, Shirley, and Rosa Tift. "Evaluation of AIDP Freshman Studies Program at Xavier University." *Freshman Programs Reports: 1974-75.* Library Archives. Xavier University of Louisiana, New Orleans.

McFarland, Betty. "Evaluation: Freshman Studies Program. With Major Emphasis on the Composition Sequence." *Freshman Programs Reports: 1975-76.* Library Archives. Xavier University of Louisiana, New Orleans.

McQuade, Donald. "Composition and Literary Studies." *Redrawing the Boundaries: The Transformation of English and American Literary Studies.* Ed. Stephen Greenblatt and Giles Gunn. New York: MLA, 1992. 482-519.

Rice, Joseph. "Introduction." *Freshman Programs Reports: 1975-76.* Library Archives. Xavier University of Louisiana, New Orleans.

Ryan, Mother M.. Agatha. *Catholic Education and the Negro.* Washington, D.C.; Catholic U of America P, 1942.

—. *Report of the President Concerning Xavier University: 1938.* Library Archives. Xavier University of Louisiana, New Orleans. n. pag.

—. *Report of the President Concerning Xavier University: 1939.* Library Archives. Xavier University of Louisiana, New Orleans. n. pag.

—. *Report of the President Concerning Xavier University: 1945.* Library Archives. Xavier University of Louisiana, New Orleans. n. pag.

—. *Report of the President Concerning Xavier University: 1947.* Library Archives. Xavier University of Louisiana, New Orleans. n. pag.

—. *Report of the President Concerning Xavier University: 1951.* Library Archives. Xavier University of Louisiana, New Orleans. n. pag.

Sanders, Edwin C. [Report on AIDP Program at Xavier University.] *Freshman Programs Reports: 1974-75.* Library Archives. Xavier University of Louisiana, New Orleans.

Sisters of the Blessed Sacrament. *Annals of St. Francis Xavier Convent (Magazine Street): 1915-1920, 1927-1945.* Library Archives. Xavier University of Louisiana, New Orleans.

"Schedule of Classes. First Semester: 1934-35. Xavier University New Unit." M. Agatha Ryan Private Papers. Library Archives. Xavier University of Louisiana, New Orleans.

Schroeder, Christopher. *Reinventing the University: Literacies and Legitimacy in the Postmodern Academy*. Logan: Utah State UP, 2001.

"Teachers Schedule. First Semester: 1933-34. Xavier University New Unit." M. Agatha Ryan Private Papers. Library Archives. Xavier University of Louisiana, New Orleans.

Weiner, Harvey. "Report on Programs: Xavier University." *Freshman Studies Program: 1976-77*. Year End Report. Library Archives. Xavier University of Louisiana, New Orleans.

Wilson, Vivian. Personal interview. 6 May 2002.

Winterowd, W. Ross. *The English Department: A Personal and Institutional History*. Carbondale; Southern Illinois UP, 1998.

Wright, Arthur D. Letter to Sr. M. Madeleine Sophie. 28 Dec. 1931. *Corporate Minutes: Book 1. 1916-1933*. Corporation of the Sisters of the Blessed Sacrament for Indians and Colored People of Louisiana. Library Archives. Xavier University of Louisiana, New Orleans.

Xavier University of Louisiana. *Summary Report of Xavier University of Louisiana Institutional Self Study: Prepared for the Southern Association of Colleges and Schools*. New Orleans; n. p., 1969.

—. *Xavier College Bulletin: 1926-27*. New Orleans; n. p., 1926.

—. *Xavier College Bulletin: 1932-33*. New Orleans; n. p., 1932.

—. *Xavier University Bulletin: 1935-36*. New Orleans; n. p., 1935.

—. *Xavier University Bulletin: 1939-40*. New Orleans; n. p., 1939.

—. *Xavier University Bulletin: 1940-41*. New Orleans; n. p., 1940.

—. *Xavier University Bulletin: 1947-48*. New Orleans; n. p., 1947.

—. *Xavier University Bulletin: 1957-58*. New Orleans; n. p., 1957.

—. *Xavier University Bulletin: 1962-64*. New Orleans; n. p., 1962.

Part III: Discipline

8

A Genesis of Writing Program Administration: George Jardine at the University of Glasgow

Lynée Lewis Gaillet

> Jardine was not important merely as a living embodiment of the Scottish academical inheritance. He was the chief formulator of its educational ideals.
>
> —*George Davie*

The contributions of Scottish rhetorician George Jardine, Professor of Logic and Philosophy at Glasgow University from 1774 to 1824, are often mentioned and footnoted in the unfolding stories of the origins of composition (see Ferreira-Buckley, Horner, Miller, Aley). The field is aware of Jardine's unique pedagogical plan as one that prefigures twentieth-century teaching theories and practices; in his own classes, Jardine sequenced writing assignments, established a detailed plan for peer review, stressed the role community plays in writing instruction, adopted nurturing attitudes toward beginning writers, and clearly outlined the duties of effective teachers. Composition scholars and historians are still realizing the far-reaching implications of Jardine's work—efforts that extend far beyond the parameters of his own moral philosophy classroom. Works by Scottish scholars such as Davie recognize Jardine as representative of the best Scottish education had to offer during the nineteenth-century, but as a field we are just now examining ways in which Jardine not only prefigured but also influenced North American educational practices, especially in composition studies.

Jardine, himself a student of Adam Smith, taught at the University of Glasgow for over fifty years. In his tenure there, Jardine—an extremely popular and influential educator—taught many students who would later immigrate to North America. Several of Jardine's students, in turn, became influential educators in North America. For example, both Alexander Campbell—religious reformer and founder of Bethany College in West Virginia—and his father, Thomas, were Jardine's students at Glasgow before immigrating to America. Carisse Berryhill's dissertation *Sense, Expression, and Purpose: Alexander Campbell's Natural Philosophy of Rhetoric* denotes Jardine's extensive influence on Alexander Campbell's rhetorical theory (64-72). Reflective of Jardine's direct influence on American educators, Bethany College Library holds a large collection of manuscripts pertaining to Alexander Campbell's life and work, which includes Campbell's notes from Jardine's lectures (Berryhill, "A Descriptive Guide"). Five years before his death, Campbell commented that Jardine's discussion of the faculty of attention was "the most useful series of college lectures of which I have any recollection" (Berryhill, *Sense* 20). Campbell's sphere of educational influence continues to be enormous, particularly within the Disciples of Christ religion. The Disciples of Christ's westward migration was led in part by Thomas and Alexander Campbell between 1809 and 1823. Under the guidance of Alexander Campbell, many universities and colleges, including Texas Christian University, were formed in the wake of this westward expansion. Through interdisciplinary studies, we are only now recognizing and discovering the extent of Jardine's influence on educational theories, practices, and administration.

This chapter offers an analysis of Jardine's plan for including writing instruction in courses across the higher education curriculum and examines ways in which Jardine prefigured modern WPA work. Jardine's major treatise, *Outlines of Philosophical Education, Illustrated by the Method of Teaching the Logic, or, First Class of Philosophy in the University of Glasgow* (1825), can easily be read as a precursor of modern WPA manuals. In this work, Jardine provides a theory for how composition should be taught, detailed commentary on the role of the teacher, curriculum development guidelines, and specific pedagogical advice for implementing composition instruction in humanities courses. Let me be clear. George Jardine did not direct a writing program at the University of Glasgow, but he did offer theoretical and practical models, as well as encouragement, to other teachers and administrators who wished to adapt their courses to include writing instruction and assessment. His nineteenth-century text prefigures much current work in writing program administration.

Scholarship tells us that Jardine not only made unprecedented contributions to rhetorical theory and practice but also influenced the establishment of composition as an integral component of Scottish instruction and assessment across the disciplines:

> The essay was, so far as we can gather, the chief means of testing the students' powers in all subjects. We even hear of them as being set in the mathematical classes, and in the class of physics, and we may infer from what Kelland says in the small volume of Edinburgh lectures he published in 1843 that the theme of these scientific essays would be chiefly the philosophy of the subject. (Davie 17)

Linda Ferreira-Buckley credits Jardine for providing "the philosophical underpinnings of the curriculums and many of the concrete exercises" found in classes taught at English universities founded in the first half of the nineteenth century ("'Scotch' Knowledge" 174). Winifred Bryan Horner explains how Jardine's teaching plan "was ideal in serving the needs of a democratic nation" because "it furnished a broad liberal arts education for all the citizens" ("Rhetoric in the Liberal Arts: Nineteenth-Century Scottish Universities" 93). And Davie labels Jardine "one of the most significant figures—at any rate, from the purely pedagogical point of view—in [the] Scottish academical tradition" (9).

Jardine's composition practices were enormously successful and were not only continued by his successor at the University of Glasgow, Reverend Robert Buchanan (*Evidence* 38) but also adopted by professors at other Scottish and English universities from a wide range of disciplines. According to Davie, "Jardine found imitators everywhere; at St. Andrews, the Professor of Logic, Spalding, gained fame as a second Jardine for his ability to work the students hard, and to inspire them with a serious interest in writing essays on cultural subjects" (19). Years after his death, proponents of a philosophical education as described by

Jardine echoed his thoughts on educational practices: William Hamilton's attack on Cambridge mathematical philosophy and Alexander Fraser's defense of the Scottish educational system against "anglicizing encroachment." Davie credits Jardine, the champion of a Scottish philosophical education based on written exercises and frequent oral and written examinations, as one of the "conscious exponents of this educational method" and for perfecting "its tuitional techniques" and extending the components of philosophical education "to subjects outside the philosophical group" (25).

The Scottish educational climate, Davie suggests, ultimately would have given rise to similar educational practices and theories "even if Jardine had never existed" (25). Perhaps he is right, but Jardine's comprehensive writing program plan mingled with his fierce advocacy of both students' rights and teacher responsibilities is worthy of admiration. Recent comments on historiography in the field suggest (rightfully so) that composition researchers have focused too much on hero-villain dichotomies, engaged in a rhetoric of victimization, and adopted backward looking/"presentism" methodologies for critiquing past pedagogical practices. I agree with Charles Paine that historiography must be "complicated" by paying "closer attention to the individuals—their lives, their work, their ideas about what they were creating—who helped create the institution of composition" (36). For fifteen years, I've been researching works by and about Jardine through a variety of methodological lenses and, based on existing evidence and extant documents, find him to be a professional "hero" any way you look at him. Jardine was a "good man speaking well" (in a civic-minded, non-agonistic sense of that phrase) on educational topics and devoted his entire professional life to promoting them. For over fifty years, he strived to improve educational practices at Glasgow and to export his pedagogical theories/practices both to other disciplines and other universities in an effort to serve the students themselves, not to highlight or further his personal interests. In fact, he devotes the last three pages of *Outlines* to a vehement censure of those high-profile educators who do not use their positions to improve education. In this interesting conclusion to his treatise, Jardine offers a lengthy description of the cushy life afforded teachers and administrators in the Scottish universities during his time. Citing the "magnificent and venerable mansions which they inhabit," the enormous privilege and legislative representation they enjoy, and "marks of the bounty of public and private" donations, "bestowed upon them as the guardians of public education—as the directors of teachers and students," Jardine finds it to be

> impossible to suppose, that all this has been done to place the teachers of youth in so respectable and enviable a situation, without the well founded hopes of a suitable return, in the shape of activity and zeal directed to the education of youth. It cannot be imagined even by the most presumptuous, that its object was to promote the self-confidence, the interest, or the ease of a few individuals. On the contrary, the members of such institutions must be convinced, that a sacred trust has been committed to them by the public—the education of youth, which involves in it the hopes and affections of parents, the respectability and happiness of an efficient part of the community, and the best interests of their country. (*Outlines* 526-27)

Jardine exemplifies the model educator he describes in the preceding sentence. By augmenting the existing curriculum to include what we label a writing across the curriculum approach to composition instruction, Jardine fulfilled his obligation to improve his students, their communities, and Scotland at large. In addition, Jardine provides us with a nuanced model of WPA authority worthy of emulation.

In "Politics and the WPA: Through and Past Realms of Expertise," Doug Hesse tells us that whether we like it or not, WPAs must be both politicians and rhetoricians (41). Citing debates in WPA scholarship over the roles WPA authority should take, Hesse explains that WPAs must adopt both the perspective of "having considerable authority and decision-making power (White)" *and* "more overtly democratic or collaborative arrangements (Gunner)" because of the many spheres in which WPAs work (43). Within departments, Hesse encourages a collaborative model of WPA authority. If teachers are enlisted in decisions, they are then invested in writing policies and practices; however, when working within administrative structures outside the department, Hesse suggests WPAs must "act with a decisiveness that may exceed their democratic sensibilities" (43). Working from the stance of politician, civic rhetorician, moral philosophy teacher, administrator, collaborator, educational reformer, promoter of WAC, historian, and believer in the power of writing instruction and assessment, George

Jardine's plan for instituting composition instruction in the Scottish universities embodies Hesse's advice and offers an early model/foreshadowing of thoughtful and successful WPA work.

Substantive (and Insubstantive?) Characteristics of Jardine as a WPA

In 1989, in an attempt to investigate the actual authority of composition directors within the power structures of their departments, Gary Olson and Joseph Moxley surveyed 250 English department chairs. Of the twenty-one WPA tasks Olson and Moxley asked chairs to rank, the substantive activities defining WPAs as directors—establishing liaisons with the community, promoting curricular reform, determining program policy in written documents, maintaining his/her own scholarship—reflect the work of George Jardine during his fifty-year tenure at the University of Glasgow. Jardine certainly did not hire, train, and supervise a composition staff. Rather he provided a rhetorical model for the establishment of composition instruction in a variety of disciplines at the other major Scottish universities (and subsequently, English universities as well). Jardine envisioned a comprehensive educational reform based on the inclusion of composition instruction and assessment, and in his treatise on education, Jardine addresses a wide range of topics we commonly associate with substantive (and insubstantive) WPA work: text/curriculum selection, composition theory/pedagogy, teacher mentoring, writing across the curriculum initiatives, collaborating with other university administrators, budgetary issues, establishing community relationships.

Olson and Moxley characterize an effective WPA as one who has power to reform, asserting that "the future of any composition program depends on the quality of its leadership" (56). The following examination of Jardine's leadership and career accomplishments proves undeniably that he possessed attributes of a powerful WPA as defined by Olson and Moxley. Even more noteworthy, however, is that Jardine's administrative "style" and "authority" (remember, over two hundred years ago) also resembles modern characteristics of a feminist administrative structure. Let me explain. Marcia Dickson, critiquing Olson and Moxley's list of substantive and insubstantive WPA duties from a feminist perspective, claims that the two researchers ignore the reality of most WPA work. She finds their model to be "patriarchal/bureaucratic" because it "emphasizes control rather than collaboration" (143). Reacting against their model Dickson lists the following attributes of feminist administrative structures:

1. a willingness on the part of the WPA to relinquish control over the word—dictating official policy;

2. a heavy emphasis on collaboration;

3. an agreement to assign duties according to ability rather than according to title or rank—diversifying rather than delegating authority;

4. an ongoing conversation about the projects in which the faculty is engaged: teaching, research, and administration;

5. a workshop and a forum atmosphere that allows for experimentation in teaching and research;

6. a commitment to provide ample support and mentoring services for all levels of participants; and

7. a constant and steady system of rewarding excellence and effort. (152)

Dickson suggests these program characteristics facilitate trust among program members, stress "moral and ethical issues" as well as "rational and logical" ones, and allow for "freedom to act upon good ideas" (152). Finally, she asserts that it isn't "power a WPA needs to control a writing program" but rather "the ability to step back and let the program grow through the concerted efforts of the members of the community rather than by insisting that it conform to rigid and cripp[l]ing policy" (153). I don't want to overstate my point; Jardine *was* teaching in an all-male institution and did not officially hold an administrative position, but his philosophy of education (described below) shares many characteristics with Dickson's feminist WPA model. He repeatedly stresses that changes to the educational system must come from the teachers themselves, and he criticizes teachers/administrators/legislators in educational positions who take advantage of their rank and privilege without improving the status of education and answering the needs of students, community, and nation. Throughout *Outlines*, Jardine critiques the existing educational system in Scotland, which he clearly finds to be rigid and crippling. In addressing budgetary concerns associated with implementing his teaching plan, Jardine suggests that although taxpayers certainly would not withhold "pecuniary aid" to put his novel teaching plan into place, additional funds were not necessary to make the educational changes he suggested. Jardine explains that limited funds present "no bar to improvement" and suggests that "could we secure a hearty co-operation on the part of the professors in all our universities, the work of reform would proceed with the greatest ease" (*Outlines* 525). Jardine's philosophical plan for reforming Scottish education is collaborative, innovative, non-"patriarchal/bureaucratic," and de-centered.

Locating Jardine[1]

In *The Democratic Intellect*, George Davie explains why Jardine is important to Scottish education:

> Jardine was respected throughout Scotland as an influential link in the great chain of national educators. He was one of Adam Smith's favourite pupils, and, through Smith's offices, had gone off to Paris with a set of introductions given by David Hume himself; in his prime he became the friend and close colleague of Thomas Reid and John Millar in Glasgow College; and in his old age he had the satisfaction of seeing his own pupils become the most famous writers and critics in the Scottish capital—men such as Francis Jeffrey, Sir William Hamilton, 'Christopher North' and J. G. Lockhart. (99-100)

As stated in the opening of this chapter, Davie believed "Jardine was not important merely as a living embodiment of the Scottish academical inheritance. He was the chief formulator of its educational ideals" (100). Although Hugh Blair and George Campbell, Smith's famous successors, would turn Smith's "interests into the key components of rhetoric for the succeeding century" (Bizzell and Herzberg 651), it is Jardine who codified Smith's rhetorical theory in his detailed description of a unified teaching plan based on reading and producing English texts. Like Smith, Campbell, and Blair, Jardine also advocated the study of literary works, but Jardine put forth a teaching plan that fully integrated the study of *belle lettres* and the study of the rhetoric of composition. Jardine's conception of education was utilitarian: to prepare young men for careers in business and science. Jardine was teaching communicative skills to his students to enable them to break class bonds and become competitive in British society. He was attempting to improve the quality of education for his students in the larger interest of creating a more just, radically democratic society. Instruction in written composition became a means to this end. As a result, his pedagogy, although based on a curriculum associated with enlightenment rhetoric, closely resembles our own.

Jardine was an outspoken champion of Scotland's democratic philosophy of education and realized that, unlike Oxford and Cambridge, the Scottish universities were designed to train young men for careers in business and science. He radically altered the traditional method of instructing the philosophy and logic class to meet the changing academic, economic, and social needs of his students. During Jardine's tenure at the University of Glasgow, the students were often as young as fourteen and drawn primarily from the working classes. Jardine supported discussion and writing as a way of learning in conjunction with lectures for these nontraditional students. His carefully outlined method for teaching philosophy reveals his intense concern about the integrity of language, the separation of writing and speaking from communication, the preparation of students to function in and contribute to society, and methodologies that concentrated simply on correctness rather than on the social nature of writing. Jardine envisioned a comprehensive rhetoric, stressing that the abilities to reason, to investigate, to judge, to write, and to speak are crucial components of a liberal arts education.

From Jardine's letters preserved in the manuscript library at the University of Glasgow and the testimony of his colleagues found in the Royal Commission Reports, it is evident that he was highly regarded by both his students and colleagues. After his retirement, they carried on the method of instruction Jardine initiated. He organized his research and disseminated his findings to other practitioners and researchers in his major work, *Outlines of Philosophical Education,* first published in 1818. In addition to the published *Outlines*, two preserved sets of students' notes and two collections of letters exist in which he discusses his teaching theories and practices. Jardine describes *Outlines* as "having been found by experience to answer at least some of the most important purposes of a first philosophical education [. . .] combining elementary instruction with active habits on the part of the student" (*Outlines* 42). Additionally, Jardine advocates the work of teachers. In fact, he states that "whatever changes for the better shall be made on our system of education, it must begin with the teachers themselves" (*Outlines* 524). Jardine believed teachers must take on the role of "companion or friend," stimulating and cultivating the student's natural abilities "when his difficulties are most formidable" (*Outlines* 315). Jardine encouraged teachers to closely analyze the needs of their students and to abandon prescriptive texts in favor of picking and choosing appropriate subject matter for the student from all the arts and sciences (*Outlines* 51). Through his published treatise, he took upon himself the task of training teachers and spreading his plan for putting a democratic philosophy of education into practice at other universities.

In the preface to *Outlines*, Jardine, speaking as the author of this treatise, states:

> He is fully sensible of the genius, the knowledge, and the eloquence, which have been displayed in the public lectures delivered by many professors in our universities,—some of whom, during the last century, have attained to the highest rank in their respective departments; but still he cannot help thinking that little has been done to generate, in the student, that activity of mind, and that facility of applying his intellectual powers, which ought to be the great object of all education. [. . .] It has been the object of the author, who has been employed for the long period of fifty years in the department of the first philosophy class in University of Glasgow, to endeavor, as much as possible, to remedy this defect; and while he has, in the course of his public lectures explained the first principles of the philosophy of the human mind, he has uniformly accompanied these lectures with a system of active discipline on the part of his students, with a view to invigorate, and improve, the important habits of inquiry and of communication. (v-vii)

Jardine explains that "changes which were taking place in society required a more miscellaneous and practical kind of instruction in the first philosophy class" (*Outlines* 28-29).

Jardine's Plan for Educational Reform

The syllabus for the logic and philosophy class prior to Jardine's appointment as professor of logic was as follows:

- October 10 (Commencement of the term) to November 1—the students read and analyzed portions of memorabilia of Socrates.

- November 1 to February 1—the instructor explained Aristotle's logic.

- February 1 to April 15—the instructor lectured on metaphysics.

- April 15 to the end of the term—the instructor lectured specifically on ontology "or that branch of metaphysical science which comprehends the various doctrines on the general attributes of, existence, essence, unity, bonity, truth, relations, modes of possibility, impossibility, necessity, contingency, and other similar abstract conceptions of pure intellect" (*Outlines* 23).

The lectures were delivered early in the morning and were followed by an oral one-hour examination in the afternoon. At intervals throughout the term, the instructor assigned two or three compositions loosely connected to the subjects discussed in class (*Outlines* 23-24). From his experiences as both a student in and later professor of the philosophy class at Glasgow, Jardine found that this method of teaching failed because the class was both boring and useless. In fact, the class was routinely known as "the drowsy shop of logic and metaphysics" among the students (*Outlines* 24). He claims that traditional education failed to prepare the students "to adorn conversation, or to qualify the student for the concern of active life" (*Outlines* 26). Jardine knew that knowledge alone was not enough for the Scottish students to succeed in business and, therefore, advocated that the Scottish Arts program depend upon writing and rhetoric in its fullest sense.[2]

Citizens of Glasgow, a growing commercial city at the time, echoed Jardine's thoughts on the unsuitableness of the class of philosophy. In an undocumented reference, Jardine quotes a published opinion of higher education:

> Some of the classes in universities bear evident marks of their original design; being either totally, or in

> part, intended for the disputes or wranglings of divines, and of little use to the lawyer or physician, and still less to the merchant and the gentleman. Of this sort we reckon logic and metaphysics. These arts or sciences (for it is not agreed yet which of them they are) to the greatest part of students, are quite unintelligible; and, if they could be understood, we cannot for our life discover their use. (qtd. in *Outlines* 26-27)

Students, the teacher, and the public shared the "conviction of the general uselessness, and even positively hurtful consequences, of spending six or seven months in the study of logic and metaphysics" (*Outlines* 25). The successful merchants, who financially supported the university, called for a liberal arts education suitable for students going into business. Jardine agreed and called for an alteration and expansion of the class in logic and philosophy:

> It ought therefore to be the great object of a first philosophy class to supply the means of cultivation, [. . .] to present appropriate subjects for their exercise; to watch over their movements, and to direct their expanding energies. [. . .] To secure a suitable education for young men destined to fill various and very different situations in life, the course of instruction ought not certainly to be limited to the narrow range of logic and metaphysics; but, on the contrary, should be made to comprehend the elements of those other branches of knowledge, upon which the investigation of science, and the successful despatch [sic] of business, are found chiefly to depend. (*Outlines* 31)

Jardine supported discussion and writing as a way of learning in conjunction with lectures. He knew that adopting his plan would mean more work for the teacher than simply composing lectures, but he thought his system was necessary in the Scottish universities where there were many students who were "not qualified, either in respect of age or of previous acquirements" (*Outlines* 427). Jardine used writing as a means of encouraging students to be their own best teachers and as a way of tracking their development. For example, he discouraged the traditional practice of taking down verbatim the teacher's lectures and instead advised students to "commit to writing, in their own composition, whatever they judge[d] to be of leading importance" (*Outlines* 279). He encouraged his students to write down the most interesting important thoughts they encountered as they read for pleasure (*Correspondence* 282). And he promoted a method of revision by suggesting that students keep a journal of all the letters they both received and wrote, encouraging them to write several drafts in order to teach themselves "accuracy and exactness" (*Correspondence* 284). His more formal assignments included daily writing exercises, which he too wrote and then shared with his students; a lecture review through discussion and writing; and a hierarchy of four levels of sequenced writing assignments spaced throughout the course. Jardine stressed the concept of writing as process and recognized the value of prewriting and revision: "In all cases, perfect specimens must be preceded by many unsuccessful efforts." Imperfect early drafts are the "natural and indispensable steps which lead to higher degrees of perfection" (*Outlines* 313).

In an effort to shorten the time needed to evaluate essays and to shift responsibility for learning back to the student, Jardine encouraged teachers to abandon the practice of "exposing" every error on a paper and instead to direct the student "to those parts of his theme which require farther attention, and to the general nature of the defects which have been noted" (364). He explains that not only does this method of correcting themes decrease grading time but also encourages the students to improve and revise. In addition, the students gain confidence in their ability to write:

> [Y]oung persons may be readily excused for thinking too highly of their own performances, and they are apt to be disappointed and discouraged upon discovering imperfections, where they were not expected. In such circumstances, the professor must touch their failings with a gentle hand. [. . .] The earliest buds of spring are easily affected by the inclemency of the atmosphere, and harsh remarks, particularly when delivered in a forbidding and authoritative manner, might prevent altogether the farther effects of such useful exercises. (365)

Although he admits that teachers "cannot possibly accomplish the examination of all the themes" (*Outlines* 367), Jardine stresses the fact that students can learn by writing only if all of their papers are closely examined. He warns that the "attention of those students whose exercises are overlooked will soon become relaxed, their spirits depressed, and their feelings irritated. If our essays pass without notice, they naturally ask, why need we give ourselves so much trouble in composing them?" (367). So to ensure that all student writing is not only evaluated but also written for a specific audience, Jardine developed a method of peer review. He asserted that it brought about "incalculable advantages which cannot be obtained in any other way" (367). He explains that peer review allows all students to receive individual attention, weaker students to learn from stronger ones, and all students to improve their own writing by increasing their powers of criticism (366, 371). In *Outlines*, Jardine carefully explains each fact of his peer review plan, stipulating: 1) the advantages of such a system of examination; 2) the rules to be followed by peer editors, whom he labels "examinators"; 3) the method of reporting criticism to the author and the other class members; 4) the ways to solve differences of opinion between critic and author; and 5) the role of the teacher in the peer-review process.[3]

Although he did not use our terminology, Jardine created an extensive practical plan for using modern concepts, such as free writing, sequenced essay assignments, writing as discovery, writing across the curriculum, and peer review, as well as traditional lectures, to teach philosophy to under-prepared students and to train them for careers in business and science—and he disseminated his ideas to other teachers at other universities. Jardine firmly believed that improvements in education must be initiated by experienced teachers and not by "legislators and politicians, who have many other objects to engage their attention; not even from men of science, unless they have had experience in the business of education" (*Outlines* 524). Jardine wouldn't have supported the educational "reform" that followed the Harvard Committee Reports in the United States. The actual changes in educational policies and curriculum, according to Jardine, should not be made by public officials, local businessmen, or public outcry—although local concerns and opinions may/should influence the need for changes. Rather, it is "the duty of every one engaged in teaching philosophy, to collect facts,—to record observations,—to watch under the influence of education;—and thus to unite their efforts for the general improvement of our academical establishments" (*Outlines*

524). Jardine's insightful teaching philosophies and practical plan did not directly affect composition instruction in North America, yet the work of his fellow Scotsman Alexander Bain—often labeled the bane of modern composition instruction—was widely (mis)appropriated and influential in the development of North American composition practices. Why?

Bain and Jardine

Both Jardine at the University of Glasgow and Alexander Bain at the University of Aberdeen adapted their teaching practices to accommodate poorly prepared students. In fact, in an inaugural address to his 1860 logic class, Bain applauds Jardine's contributions to education. He quotes William Hamilton's *Lectures on Metaphysics,* who credits Jardine for doing

> more for the intellectual improvement of his pupils than any other public instructor in the country [Scotland] within the memory of man [. . .] not by great erudition or great philosophical talent though he was both a learned and able thinker, but by the application of that primary principle of education which wherever employed has been employed with success. I mean the determination of the pupil to self activity, doing nothing for him which he is able to do for himself. ("The Position and Province of Logic" 6)

In this address, Bain goes on to quote extensively from Jardine's *Outlines* concerning the practical education of students. Although Bain admittedly builds on Jardine's earlier theories of education, he specifically excludes essay writing from his classroom. Bain says that assigning essay assignments excuses the teacher from actively instructing the students and "ranks among the crude devices of the infancy of the education art" *(On Teaching English* 24). In critiquing the practice of essay writing, Bain says that "under some of the most celebrated and successful teachers, as Jardine, of Glasgow, the pupils were kept incessantly at work in Composition" (*English Composition* 24). Ironically, Bain's critical reading text *English Composition and Rhetoric, A Manual* (1866) was widely adopted as a composition textbook in this country following the 1890s Harvard Report rather than Jardine's enlightened theories of using writing to teach both subject matter and social responsibility described in *Outlines*. Why?

First, Bain's work is accessible for classroom use. The text is written in an abbreviated form intended to be used by the students; Bain numbers and states his principles outright and then adds brief explanations. He also includes excerpts from contemporary English authors upon which the students can apply the principles in the textbook. Jardine's *Outlines*, on the other hand, is a philosophical treatise written primarily for teachers.

Second, Bain's prescriptive delivery is convincing. Bain's authoritative tone in *English Composition* contributes to the success and acceptance of the work as "Truth" by the keepers of the language who found Bain engaging during the period following the Harvard Commission Reports. Because of its format, the work was easily translated into a writing text, although Bain designed the work as a critical reading text. Then, as now, busy practitioners were often drawn to clear-cut handbooks for teaching subject matter and rules, not philosophical treatises. Jardine's theoretical discussion, although accessible and punctuated with practical teaching advice, was not as immediately employable as Bain's *English Composition*. Unfortunately, Bain's systematic, matter-of-fact manner probably encouraged the misappropriation of much of his work. His teaching approach is currently regarded as product-oriented and usage-obsessed, although a closer examination of his primary works, rather than appropriations of it, don't fully support that reputation. As Andrea Lunsford explains, "Alexander Bain, the master of analytic and inferential thought, perhaps did the wrong thing in excluding essay writing from his classroom—but for the right reasons" (441). Bain believed rote essay assignments were divorced from real teaching and that asking all students to write essays in response to the same prompt divorced writing from learning. Instead, Bain believed students shouldn't write essays for the class but should write on their own with advice from their elders, from members of their clubs and societies, and their peers. In essence, he advocated a writing across the curriculum, collaborative approach to essay writing that fell outside the domain of his rhetoric and composition course.

Finally, Bain delivered many public lectures and published extensively, not primarily in the field of logic and rhetoric but natural philosophy and psychology—popular subjects of his day. Jardine was not self-promoting, nor did he publish a great deal. He theorized about how students learned from his own classroom experiences, and he shared those experiences with other teachers/administrators who wished to adopt epistemic models of writing instruction.

Conclusion

Ten years ago, Edward P. J. Corbett claimed, "The history of writing program administration has all to be recovered, for a complete history of that aspect of collegiate activity does not now exist" (60). This lamentation is still valid. Ten years after the publication of Corbett's brief history of the establishment of the WPA in a festschrift honoring Winifred Horner, the field still lacks sustained examinations of WPA work or figures in the field. Certainly this volume goes a long way toward addressing that void. Although the field has many commendable historiographies/examinations of the origins of English Studies and practices in higher education,[4] the development of composition studies has yet to be fully viewed through the lens of writing program administration. As this volume illustrates, however, alternate histories of the origins of composition theory and practice exist. The earlier model of writing instruction and administration presented in this chapter, unfortunately, neither survived in Scotland nor influenced mainstream writing instruction in North America following the Harvard Commission Reports.[5] Unlike the work of fellow Scotsman Bain, Jardine offers a rhetorical theory for incorporating composition instruction in existing courses across the disciplines. Additionally, he describes a concrete plan directed to teachers and administrators for implementing composition instruction. Scholars have certainly examined the relationship between Scotland/other British cultural provinces and American education,[6] but George Jardine's plan for teaching communicative competence in the Scottish universities, although often briefly identified and heralded in the field's histories, is neither widely recognized nor fully understood in the development of composition theory, practice, and administration. Jardine's work merits further attention.

Notes

1. I have previously published portions of this essay, in particular the "identification" of Jardine and his teaching plan segments: see "George Jardine: The Champion of the Scottish Commonsense School of Philosophy";

"George Jardine's Outlines of Philosophical Education: Prefiguring Twentieth-Century Composition Theory and Practice"; "An Historical Perspective on Collaborative Learning"; "A Legacy of Basic Writing Instruction"; and "George Jardine."

2. See Appendix A: Jardine's principles and views guiding the restructuring of the logic and moral philosophy class.

3. For a thorough discussion of the details of Jardine's collaborative learning/peer editing plan, see Gaillet, "An Historical Perspective on Collaborative Learning."

4. See works by Berlin, Brereton, Crowley, Dickson, Horner, Kitzhaber, Thomas Miller, Susan Miller, Rosner et al., and Russell.

5. Reminiscent of the fate of Fred Newton Scott's Rhetoric/Composition program at Michigan.

6. See in particular Winifred Horner's *Nineteenth-Century Rhetoric: The American Connection* and Thomas Miller's *The Formation of College English.*

Works Cited

Aley, Shelley. "The Impact of Science on Rhetoric Through the Contributions of the University of Aberdeen's Alexander Bain." *Scottish Rhetoric and Its Influences.* Ed. Lynée Lewis Gaillet. Mahwah, NJ: Lawrence Erlbaum, 1998: 209-17.

Bain, Alexander. *English Composition and Rhetoric: A Manual.* London: Longsmans, Green, and Co., 1866.

—. *On Teaching English.* London: Longmans, 1887.

—. "The Position and Province of Logic." *Aberdeen Free Press and Buchan News* 9 Nov. 1860: 6.

Berlin, James. *Writing Instruction in Nineteenth-Century American Colleges.* Carbondale: Southern Illinois UP, 1984.

Berryhill, Carisse. "A Descriptive Guide to Eight Early Alexander Campbell Manuscripts." December 2000. http://www.mun.ca/rels/restmov/texts/acampbell/acm/ACM00A.HTM (16 Feb. 2004).

—. "Sense, Expression, and Purpose: Alexander Campbell's Natural Philosophy of Rhetoric." Diss. Florida State U, 1982.

Bizzell, Patricia, and Bruce Herzberg. *The Rhetorical Tradition.* New York: Bedford/St. Martin's, 1990.

Brereton, John, ed. *The Origins of Composition Studies in the American College, 1875-1925: A Documentary History.* Pittsburgh: U of Pittsburgh P, 1995.

Corbett, Edward P. J. "A History of Writing Program Administration." *Learning from the Histories of Rhetoric*: *Essays in Honor of Winifred Bryan Horner.* Ed. Theresa Enos. Carbondale: Southern Illinois UP, 1993: 60-71.

Crowley, Sharon. *Composition in the University: Historical and Polemical Essays.* Pittsburgh: U of Pittsburgh P, 1998.
Davie, George. *The Democratic Intellect.* Edinburgh: Edinburgh UP, 1982.
Dickson, Marcia. "Directing Without Power: Adventures In Constructing a Model of Feminist Writing Programs Administration." *Writing Ourselves into the Story: Unheard Voices from Composition Studies.* Ed. Sheryl I. Fontaine and Susan Hunter. Carbondale: Southern Illinois UP, 1993. 140-53.
Evidence, Oral and Documentary, Taken and Received by the Commissioners Appointed by His Majesty George IV, July 23rd, 1826; and Re-Appointed by His Majesty William IV, October 12th, 1830; for Visiting the Universities of Scotland. Volume II, University of Glasgow. London: Clowes, 1837.
Ferreira-Buckley, Linda. "'Scotch' Knowledge and the Formation of Rhetorical Studies." *Scottish Rhetoric and Its Influence.* Ed. Lynée Lewis Gaillet. Mahwah, NJ: Lawrence Erlbaum, 1998. 163-75.
Gaillet, Lynée Lewis. "George Jardine." *The Encyclopedia of Rhetoric.* Ed. Theresa Enos. Garland, 1996.
—. "George Jardine: The Champion of the Scottish Commonsense School of Philosophy." *Rhetoric Society Quarterly* 28.2 (1998). 37-53.
—. "George Jardine's Outlines of Philosophical Education: Prefiguring Twentieth-Century Composition Theory and Practice." *Scottish Rhetoric and Its Influences.* Ed. Lynée Lewis Gaillet. Mahwah, NJ: Lawrence Erlbaum, 1998. 193-208.
—. "An Historical Perspective on Collaborative Learning." *The Journal of Advanced Composition* 14.1 (1994): 93-110.
—. "A Legacy of Basic Writing Instruction." *The Journal of Basic Writing* 12.2 (Fall 1993): 86-99.
Hesse, Douglas D. "Politics and the WPA: Through and Past Realms of Expertise." *The Writing Program Administrator's Resource.* Ed. Stuart C. Brown and Theresa Enos. Mahwah, NJ: Lawrence Erlbaum, 2002. 41-58.
Horner, Winifred Bryan. *Nineteenth-Century Scottish Rhetoric: The American Connection.* Carbondale: Southern Illinois UP, 1993.
—. "Rhetoric in the Liberal Arts: Nineteenth-Century Scottish Universities." *The Rhetorical Tradition and Modern Writing.* Ed. James J. Murphy. New York: MLA, 1982. 85-95.
Jardine, George. "Correspondence of Professor Jardine with Baron Mure." *Selections from the Family Papers Preserved at Caldwell.* Ed. William Mure. Paisley: A. Gardner, 1883.
—. *Outlines of Philosophical Education, Illustrated by the Method of Teaching the Logic, or, First Class of Philosophy in the University of Glasgow.* Oliver and Boyd, 1825.

Kitzhaber, Albert R. *Rhetoric in American Colleges, 1850-1900*. Dallas: Southern Methodist UP, 1990.

Lunsford, Andrea A. "Essay Writing and Teachers' Responses in Nineteenth-Century Scottish Universities." *College Composition and Communication* 32 (1981): 434-43.

Miller, Susan. *Textual Carnivals: The Politics of Composition*. Carbondale: Southern Illinois UP, 1991.

Miller, Thomas. *The Formation of College English: Rhetoric and Belles Lettres in the British Cultural Provinces*. Pittsburgh: U of Pittsburgh P, 1997.

—. "Where Did English Studies Come From?" *Rhetoric Review* 9 (1990): 50-68.

Olson, Gary A., and Joseph M. Moxley. "Directing Freshman Composition: The Limits of Authority." *College Composition and Communication* (1989): 51-60.

Paine, Charles. *The Resistant Writer: Rhetoric as Immunity, 1850 to the Present*. Albany: SUNY P, 1999.

Rosner, Mary, Beth Boehm, and Debra Journet. *History, Reflection and Narrative: The Professionalization of Composition, 1963-1983*. Stamford, CT: Ablex, 1999.

Russell, David R. *Writing in the Academic Disciplines, 1870-1990: A Curricular History*. Southern Illinois UP, 1991.

Appendix A: Jardine's Introduction to His Published *Synopsis of the Lectures on Logic and Belles Lettres*, Dated Glasgow College, 1805*

The Logic, or First Philosophy Course, in the Academical *Curriculum* of the University of Glasgow, is placed immediately after the study of the LATIN and GREEK languages; and the Lectures are generally delivered to student, from fourteen or fifteen, to eighteen years of age.

During the reign of the Scholastic Philosophy, the prelections delivered to students of Logic, were chiefly occupied with an explanation of the Analytics and Metaphysics of Aristotle. But the change of public opinion on subjects of Literature, and the progress of liberal science in this country, have occasioned a corresponding change in the manner of conducting this branch of the Academical Course. While the useful and curious parts of the ancient Logic still occupy their proper place, the business of the class has been extended to the elements of other branches of knowledge; which, though not immediately connected with the former, are thought subservient to the great ends of general education, in this first department of philosophical study.

Only the out-lines of the Lectures referred to are now published; and, though the whole subjects of the course, comprehending several different branches of literature, have certainly not all the *unity* of system, they will yet be found closely related in another point of view—namely, in their fitness and tendency to unfold progressively the powers of knowledge—to begin and to establish that habitual exercise in the minds of young persons, upon which the active business of life, as well as that of science, depend. The Lectures delivered in the Class, which are accompanied with copious illustration, and great variety of examples, are composed and adjusted upon the following principles and views.

That the powers of Knowledge, of Taste, and Communication, can only be improved by exercise.

That the exercise of these powers is called forth, by proposing or presenting such objects as are best suited to promote it—by arranging and disposing them in such a manner as may best facilitate that exercise—by suggesting and impressing the student with such motives and inducements as may best support and encourage a regular plan of industry and exertion.

That lectures, or prelections, delivered to young persons in the circumstances above stated, however ingenious they may be, cannot reach the great end of education, unless they shall be aided by a strict and regular examination, followed up with a system of essays, or specimens of compositions, required from the students, on the most useful and important parts of the lectures.

That the first essays or specimens should be accommodated to the previous attainments and habits of those who enter the class and the subjects of them be such as to accustom the students—to distinguish—to divide—to define—to analyze—to select and arrange in a clear and luminous manner—to express with plainness and perspicuity.

That after the method of Analysis and Synthesis, and the rules of conducting simple and complex Themes, shall be explained in the course of the lectures—Subjects of Reasoning, of Taste, and Composition, should be prescribed; to which the rules of Criticism, as they respect different kinds of composition, may be applied.

That the method of conducting and reviewing such specimens publicly in the class, should be such as to give the Teacher an opportunity of pointing our defects or successful efforts, in the matter, method, or style of such compositions; and, by judicious approbations or censure, to encourage and promote higher and more spirited exertions. In a word, the Professor, in the discharge of the duties of his office, must descend to the humble occupation of the *master* in the common arts; and, in the *work done*, or specimens *given*, point out to the young artist wherein the *essay* is defective, and in what respects it may be improved.

Finally, the author of these out-lines, conceiving that every part of the Academical Course should be adjusted in such a manner as to fit men, not only for the pursuits of Science, but of Business and of Active Life, has endeavored, for many years, to promote in his particular department, those fundamental habits upon which both Science and Business depend—habits of Thinking, of Reasoning, and of Communication by Speech or Writing.

If there be any thing suitable or useful in the plan or study adopted in the First Philosophy Class here, the merit of it belongs, in a particular manner, to those youth who have studied in this Class; for it has been suggested by the experience of the industrious and spirited efforts of many young adventurers in Science, who have left deep impressions on the mind of the teacher, and have enabled him to mark, with some accuracy, the natural steps and progresses in the acquisition of Knowledge, in the habits of Communication, and in the cultivation even of the more delicate powers of Taste.

* I have modernized orthographical usage in this transcription.

9

Moving Toward a Group Identity: WPA Professionalization from the 1940s to the 1970s

Amy Heckathorn

> In 1976, when the National Council of Writing Program Administrators was organized, WPAs were largely divided, exploited, politically weak, an unsophisticated lot. Three years later, when *WPA* first appeared as a journal, our situation looked a little brighter. We had begun to identify ourselves professionally. We had begun to identify our needs and the nature of the particular skills we needed to acquire in order to do our jobs adequately. Most important of all, perhaps, we had begun to identify each other.
>
> —*Kenneth Bruffee*

Few written documents exist to chronicle the evolution of writing program administration—certainly no unified and coherent accounting of their historical work. While many of the chapters of this book sketch individual portraits of early WPAs, this one outlines how these individuals began to come together to create a group identity, an evolution glimpsed through primary research in journals, books, and direct interviews which demonstrate that WPAs have struggled to transform themselves, and others' impressions of them, from bureaucratic managers of an undervalued discipline to dynamic administrators and theorists of their work and their field. The formation of a group identity is not the only story in this evolution—WPAs also struggled to gain training and power to better meet their challenges—but a professionalized identity was a critical first step toward achieving other goals. Although much administrative work began prior to 1940, I use this date as the starting point for group identity-crafting as it marks the emergence of professional literature dedicated to the study of English (e.g. the founding of *College English* in 1939, which included discussions of composition and its administration). Similarly, although much was in flux before 1964, this date marks the emergence of specialized composition journals and a general trend in published sources to acknowledge the evolving roles of WPAs. I examine the struggle toward a professional group identity in two time periods: an Early Era (1940 to 1963), when WPAs began to publicly identify the individual problems confronting professionalization as writing program administration surfaced in relation to discussions of teaching composition, and a Transitional Era (1964 to 1979), when WPAs gained more public responsibility and acknowledgment and began to form a group identity to address the problems hindering professionalization.

Analyzing WPAs' evolutionary struggle through distinct eras is, to some extent, artificial, but it provides a heuristic for understanding how administrative work changed to meet the challenges of an evolving discipline. The position did not begin in one specific year and uniformly transform in another year. Writing program administration has grown intermittently, sooner in some areas and universities than in others, along a continuum of sometimes gradual, sometimes dramatic change and evolution. These two eras, however, do help to identify the larger public and publishing trends in the evolutionary continuum. These timeframes mark periods in which enough consistency exists in the professional literature to draw clearer images and conclusions about a group identity than would be possible from any one program or year.

Similarly, individual administrative positions may not always fall neatly into this overview of the struggle toward professionalization. WPAs' work and status vary from program to program—several universities appointed and cultivated professional WPAs prior to the 1940s while many universities still do not. In spite of this variation, however, a distinct pattern emerges for the evolving professionalization of the

Moving Toward a Group Identity 193

position in general. Even though exceptions arise outside of this general trend, this study documents the general growth and turning points in WPAs' struggle for a professional group identity.

Because WPAs' duties vary widely, the challenge of locating documentary evidence might appear more difficult than in a closely unified field; however, in early writing program administration, the challenge is to find any information at all. Two major factors appear to account for this lack of early publication. First, scholars traditionally saw administrative positions as service functions that one did in addition to, but not as the subject of, teaching and research. Second, instruction in composition—the foundation for writing program administration—was a fledgling field, often viewed in service to other disciplines and student needs and, consequently, not worthy of senior professors or published research. However, as composition courses expanded, interest in their purpose, development, teaching, and administration also expanded.

A limited number of published sources for discovering and documenting WPAs' struggle toward professionalization exist in the Early Era. No books focus exclusively on writing program administration issues, and only two journals address the topic during this time-frame: *College English*, begun in 1939, and *College Composition and Communication*, begun in 1950. Occasionally articles in these journals address the work of WPAs directly, but more often administrative issues must be gleaned from the articles' discussions and descriptions of writing courses and the teaching of writing. Thus, the challenge in this era is to interpret insights into writing program administration buried in discussions of English in general and composition in particular.

A larger number of sources for discovering and documenting WPAs' struggle for professionalization surface in the Transitional Era. Although no entire books specifically address writing program administration, a growing number of journals begin to address composition and, consequently, the administration of the writing programs in this growing field. In addition to the Early Era journals, three more journals begin to address writing: *Research in the Teaching of English* in 1970, *Freshman English News* in 1972, and *Journal of Basic Writing* in 1975. In addition to these writing-focused journals, a publication emerges in 1977 dealing exclusively with the administration of writing programs—*WPA: Writing Program Administration*. Although many administrative insights continue to lie buried in other discussions, articles dealing exclusively and specifically with writing program administration and WPAs begin to surface.

In addition to journal articles, another publication emerged in the Transitional Era that offers unique insights into WPAs and their work. The *MLA Job Information List* is a unique source for defining the conceptions of and possibilities for WPAs and their work. The job list began as an effort to organize a growing job market and to make that market more open to all—identifying employer needs to streamline the application process. In this discussion of employer needs, however, lie insights into the work and worth of the positions being advertised. WPAs' evolutionary changes are visible in these job descriptions—from early, undefined attempts to articulate the work of WPAs to later, more specific and complex descriptions of the roles WPAs would fill. Finally, interviews with experienced WPAs afford insights not included in published materials. Case studies can serve as unique and dynamic primary sources, reflecting the growth of the position, filling in insights not captured in print sources, and providing concrete, specific accounts of the macrocosmic evolution of WPAs.

Through these sources, we can witness the emergence of a professional WPA identity and the factors that contributed to the evolutionary journey. One of the markers is the position's designation within the department. Is the job a service post that counts as a general professional duty, or is the job given an administrative designation that indicates greater professional responsibility? How is the job described in employment announcements? Along with questions of position designation come questions of recognition and compensation. Are WPAs credited for their work, and if so, how? In addition, questions of professional status relate to WPAs' subject matter as well. Whether WPAs conduct and receive departmental acknowledgment for research and publication within their administrative position speaks to the level of professionalization of the position. Finally, the professional status of WPAs and their issues—not just on an individual basis but also within larger social institutional contexts—is also an important measure. Is there a developed writing program administration community beyond individual WPAs? Often a clear reference for the growth and acceptance of the administrative job as an academically sound field, professional status is a critical marker within the history of writing program administration. Each of these markers helps delineate the growing professionalization of WPAs—from early, individual needs identification to group generation and problem-solving.

The Struggle for Professional Identification and Recognition

The work of WPAs grew out of departmental need. The ability to successfully address these needs, however, relied in great part on WPAs' ability to craft a professional identity and have that identity recognized by others. To define and articulate one's work in a way that is both personally meaningful and professionally acknowledged marks the legitimacy of a field. For WPAs, the development of a professional identity, and its subsequent recognition, has been an uphill battle. Glimpses into this identity formation and recognition are seen in studies of job descriptions, professional compensation, research and publication, and professional organizations.

Early Era—1940 to 1963: Identifying the Problems

For WPAs, the realization of a professional identity, much less its widespread recognition, was elusive. Although administrators held what were clearly writing program positions, actual job descriptions reflecting these responsibilities did not exist. There was not even a call for clarification or articulation of a professional identity for WPAs in the Early Era. WPAs placed much emphasis on the function and status of composition and its instructors, but there was no mention of clarifying the work or status of WPAs themselves. This lack of formal job articulation implied that the administrative position was not one that required specific training or skills. It appeared not to be a job people were hired specifically to do; writing program administration was essentially a service appointment taken on or assigned as one's contribution to the running of the English department, just as one might be appointed director of undergraduates or graduate studies. This glaring absence of self-identification through job description illustrates the lack of professional status for Early Era WPAs.

Self-identification of WPAs did emerge, however, in discussions of their administrative work. Although direct references to administrative work are rare, some allusions are evident in articles on writing. The actual identification of an administrative title began to appear in the Early Era. Only a small number of WPAs wrote articles on composition and administration and identified themselves with a special title—most authors identified themselves as "professors" or "instructors" of English. A few authors, however, took on an administrative designation: George Wykoff, Assistant Professor and Chairman of English I; Theodore Morrison, Lecturer and Director of English A; John S. Bowman, Chairman of English Composition; and Frank Moake, Director of Freshman Rhetoric. WPAs began to use administrative titles within journal articles as well. Adolphus Bryan was "Chairman of Freshman English" at Louisiana State University (6); Charles Roberts of the University of Illinois noted, "The head of our Department. . . . told me, as Chairman of Freshman Rhetoric, to initiate action" (96); Samuel Hazo explained that in the graduate program at Duquesne University "classes of the graduate assistants are visited by representatives of an evaluating committee, of which the Chairman of the English Department and the Director of Freshman English are members" (120); and E. W. Gray noted that the program at the University of New Mexico "includes a director and an assistant director of composition" (146). These early attempts at self-identification point out both the possibility for and general lack of titular identification and recognition of the work of WPAs.

WPAs also raised the question of compensation as recognition for administrative duties in the Early Era. Published articles noted the workload of these administrators and argued, "With reference to the improvement of the situation, it is recommended [. . .] that the administrator of the course receive some compensation" (Leyden 24). In addition to monetary compensation, the issue of released time for administrative work also surfaced: "Sixteen [of eighteen] of the institutions have a permanent or rotating Director of Freshman English who is released an average of 33% from his other duties; however, two institutions have no relief from other duties for the Director while two others give as much as 66% relief" (Noonan 175). Moake explained how the University of Illinois addressed compensating the administrative work of WPAs: "Funds were made available to give one-third released-time to ten ranking members of the Department of English to act as teaching advisors to the rhetoric staff" (82). Finally, a very few articles began to address compensation for administrative work in relation to promotion and tenure:

> Institutional activity in the form of leadership or other effective performance in departmental, college, or university committees, curriculum or course

> planning, moderatorships, special lectures, is generally significant for promotion, though often less significant generally for promotion to the higher ranks. Effective directorship of the freshman English program and staff, and effective chairmanship of a department may also be considered, though promotion to the higher ranks will often also require some other distinctions. (NCTE, "Professional" 460)

Thus, although very limited, WPAs' Early Era articles began to identify the problems associated with acknowledgment of and compensation for writing program administration.

In addition to issues of personal identification and recognition, WPAs questioned the possibility for broader professional identification in the form of research and publication. Although there were more calls for research and publication than actual studies and articles, the foundation for a scholarly position had begun. Occasionally, WPAs published a study by or about composition and writing program administration. Lennox Grey of Columbia University Teachers College noted the beginning of a survey on composition and its administration when he offered a "summary of a first report of the committee of inquiry into required English courses in American colleges, the report covering the organization of composition courses" (584). Grey's 1942 study surveyed 450 colleges and universities, gathering information on composition requirements, class sizes, conferences, proficiency testing, remediation efforts, writing centers, and teacher motivation (584-86). Another fleeting reference to research and publication in administration appeared when Edna Hays of the State Teachers College of Indiana summarized the year's publications: "Interest in curriculum revision has grown. The number of articles dealing with the subject has doubled since 1945. Composition, how to teach it, and even whether or not it should be included in the program have provoked lively debate" (430).

More common than actual articles, however, were WPAs' requests for research and publication on all facets of writing program administration. Early calls looked to clarify composition and its goals: "Perhaps it is even more important for the composition teacher than for the routine literary research scholar to do original thinking, and to communicate its results to the profession" (Griggs 11). Similarly, Albert Kitzhaber noted that

> in view of the vast amount of time, money, and effort that is annually invested in the teaching of English composition in this country, it is striking that so few English teachers have felt impelled to do research on the writing process and the teaching of writing. ("New" 444)

Gradually, however, the focus of these calls for research turned from composition in general to the administration of composition specifically. James Mason of Arkansas State College noted, "One way to improve both the administration and organization of the freshman courses is to write reports on successful experiments for publication in the many relevant journals, *College English, College Composition and Communication*, etc." (13). Mason added that, not only should administrators publish in these journals, they and their departments should also subscribe to and read them for administrative ideas and insights (13). In the same vein, Eugene Grewe of the University of Detroit stated that "there is thus still an urgent need for a comprehensive national survey of factors relevant to teaching and administering the multiple-section English courses and programs, including the matter of professional status" (214).

One of the few attempts to formalize and address questions of composition and its administration was Erwin Steinberg's discussion of his Project English conference: "To start Project English under way, fifty teachers of English and other educators met at Carnegie Institute of Technology on May 5-7, 1962, as participants in an invitational conference to determine the research needed to improve the teaching of English" (149). Conference participants posed several questions that research and analysis could answer: how do high school and college writing demands differ? What is the best content for a writing course? How is writing best taught? How should teachers of writing be taught (both pedagogically and as writers themselves)? How can administrators articulate criteria for evaluating writing? (150). Steinberg noted, "In its final report the group recommended a series of what it felt to be important projects and research studies on writing" (151). The proposed research projects aimed at resolving many of the untheorized aspects of composition instruction and administration: developing courses for future writing teachers to learn their craft; asking professional writers to advise composition teachers and administrators on course and program design; testing the effectiveness of structured versus relaxed writing courses; comparing students who write frequently in other classes with those in composition classes; evaluating the effectiveness of student-teacher conferences; and exploring the usefulness of different content areas for composition classes (151-52). According to Steinberg, the group "urged that organizations sponsoring research and development find competent people and relieve them of the routine of much of what they are doing so that they may undertake the needed research and the development of useful, imaginative teaching materials" (152). Thus, although not many WPAs published articles addressing administrative research, their many calls for study brought the scholarly issues of professional identity and recognition to the forefront.

In addition to the professionalization afforded through research and publication, such reaching across communities from individual WPA to individual WPA sparked the beginnings of a larger WPA community—the struggle for a national identity. Some WPAs hoped for just such a collection of ideas and resources early in the era, as seen when Wykoff described a utopian university: "In Utopia, the teacher of composition has time and money to belong to, read the publications of, and take part in the affairs of, certain national and state organizations" (436). One of the first manifestations of this larger WPA community was the first Conference on College Composition and Communication in 1949. One of the workshops at this first conference was titled "Administration of the Composition Course." With this session, the social networking of individuals had begun to form a larger collective. This workshop group continued to meet and to make decisions that would affect all WPAs. By 1955, in the workshop "Administering the Freshman Course," which had forty-five participants, the chair noted that the group reached consensus on the following issues: administrators needed to 1) stress "the vital importance of reduced class size, reduced total student load, and reduced total credit-hour load, if reasonable success in the achievement of goals is to be expected;" 2) eliminate theme readers as a solution to understaffing problems; 3) keep enrollments down, and, finally, the chair noted, 4) "Another workshop on administering the freshman course should be requested for the 1956 meeting. [. . .] A questionnaire concerning certain basic administrative matters should be drawn up and circulated among CCCC members" (Qtd. in Kitzhaber "Administering" 160). Subsequent workshops called for broadening the national identity of

WPAs through greater national study and standardization. "The participants expressed strong interest in the establishment of a national accrediting agency for composition/communication courses" (Houp 157). And H. J. Sachs of Louisiana Polytechnic Institute called for national standards:

> (1) to spell out standards as to teaching conditions and as to course aims and content, (2) to evaluate programs, (3) to study and cite good programs, (4) to disseminate information about poor courses and departments, (5) to seek the aid of existing accrediting agencies, (6) to call a special meeting on the subject, (7) to foster research in this area, (8) to maintain an advisory service for directors of courses. (193)

Thus, although no national agreements joined WPAs and their work, the beginning need for such unification blossomed in the Early Era.

Key in laying the foundation for a national identity for WPAs was a seminar for English department chairs in 1963. This collection of administrators validated the concept of administration as an intellectual endeavor; the meeting also called for larger national interest in and action for writing programs and WPAs:

> The chairmen of college and university English departments should organize at the state or regional, and national levels for the purpose of (a) formulating policy as to the conduct of English departments; (b) disseminating information on the teaching of English through conferences, meetings, journals, and special publications; and (c) undertaking concerted action to insure that the views of official representatives of college and university departments of English are effectively presented to the leaders in education and public affairs who make decisions affecting the teaching of English. [. . .] The chairmen of college and university English departments organized in a permanent national association, though autonomous and independent, should work, where this is an appropriate way of achieving professional ends, with such existing organizations as the Modern Language Association, the National Council of Teachers of English,

the College English Association, the Conference on College Composition and Communication, and the American Studies Association. (Rogers 473-74)

This organization of English department chairs paved the way for other administrators to organize to discuss administrative issues as valued intellectual work. Thus, although not formally organized into a national organization, WPAs began to assert a national identity through their own informal conference workshops and the advancement of other administrative groups—laying the foundation for professionalized identity crafting and recognition in the Transitional Era.

Transitional Era—1964 to 1979: Proposing Some Solutions

Similar to the Early Era, the Transitional Era began with no formal identification of the job description of WPAs. Although the duties involved in writing program administration had begun to circulate, formal position announcements had yet to surface. By 1971, however, the Modern Language Association (MLA) published the first MLA Job Information List. In an effort to coordinate and disseminate teaching positions, the MLA began to print a quarterly report describing openings at various colleges and universities. In these formal job descriptions, the professional identity of WPAs began to form and circulate.

Early job descriptions were few, vague, and often reflected the schizophrenic combination of literary training and composition practice. In the first year of the MLA Job List (1971-72), ten listings mentioned some degree of writing program administration. Kansas State College noted, "We are interested in receiving applications from individuals qualified to direct a freshman composition program, especially with a concentration in English or comparative literature, preferably with the PhD" (64). The vague description seemed to assert that it was common knowledge as to what "qualified" one to direct a writing program, but the literary emphasis implied that administration was more a duty than a scholarly field. After this first year of publication, job descriptions for WPAs subtly changed and professionalized throughout the Transitional Era. Although most ads still catered to linguists and literary specialists, by 1973, Kansas State University advertised for a "Director of Freshman English [. . .] Administrative experience in large program desirable [. . .] primary commitment to English composition" (63). By 1974, composition as a discipline rather than an avocation began to appear in ads for WPAs. The State University of New York at Stony Brook advertised a "projected vacancy for assoc. prof. in composition & rhetoric to serve as Director of Composition. Minimum 5 yrs. full-time college teaching plus publications in fields related to college composition" (9). And an Ohio State University job advertisement noted

> Applications are invited for a senior appointment as director of our large freshman-writing program (with some teaching responsibility). Applicants must have considerable experience in the administration of a college-level writing program (preferably as director) and must be committed to writing and rhetoric as a discipline (as evidenced by publications and professional activity). (25)

Although rare, by 1975, some elaboration of the professional duties of WPAs began to appear in job descriptions. Whitworth College advertised that it was "looking for a Director of Writing Programs. Must have PhD in Rhetoric, Comp, Grammar, or Linguistics. [. . .] Duties: beg. & adv. comp; Intro to Linguistics; Structure of English; design competency-based writing programs; hire staff" (43). By 1976-77, the majority of ads (sixteen of twenty) specified that WPAs should have composition as a primary area of study. Thus, although still rarely detailing the complexity of administrative duties, the actual job descriptions for WPAs reflected the growing professional identity of composition scholarship and writing program administration.

In addition to job descriptions, WPAs advanced the forging of a professional identity through other outlets. While job descriptions highlighted the beginning of and greater need for a clearer professional identity, more WPAs began to personally assert their administrative affiliations. Whereas in the Early Era administrative self-designation through titles was rare, by the Transitional Era it was more common to see such titles in print. Only four authors of journal articles identified themselves through administrative titles in the Early Era, but nearly half of the authors publishing in composition and its administration in the Transitional Era referred to themselves as either "Administrator," "Coordinator," "Director," or "Chair" of some aspect of the composition program. In addition to this self-reference, it was commonplace to refer to administrative titles within the body of the articles themselves. Such visible self-identification helped to move WPAs toward more professional recognition.

While identification of WPAs became more common in this era, compensation for these emerging administrators was still a rarely discussed subject. The few references to supplemental pay, released time, and promotion and tenure in the Early Era were equally limited, in frequency and force, in the Transitional Era. When examining released time for oversight of composition instructors, John Jordan of the University of California at Berkeley noted

> Only 81 colleges reported that student teachers in composition courses were supervised by a single faculty member who is relieved of part of his teaching load in order to care for these duties. [. . .] In 37 schools the supervision falls to a single faculty member who does not have course relief. (110)

Others seemed not only aware of this situation but also frustrated with the limited professional recognition of writing program administration. Kenneth Bruffee complained that "most writing program administrators are untenured, and, therefore, vulnerable" ("Editorial," 1978 9). Similarly, Marion Coulson of Kansas State College explained, "Generally, the chairman is given fewer classes; occasionally, perhaps, extra financial compensation. Too often, he has too much to do and too little time" (196). The National Council of Teachers of English (NCTE) took issue with this lack of professional recognition and compensation. In 1966, NCTE released its preliminary recommendations on college teaching and noted that "professional, scholarly, and institutional activities should be taken into account in determining teaching loads" ("Workload" 57). By 1976, NCTE expanded this position to help explain and articulate the value of administrative work: "The time and responsibility required for administrative, professional, scholarly, and institutional activities should be considered in determining teaching loads and schedules for English teachers" ("Guidelines," 1976 874). Because these activities often required large time commitments in addition to one's teaching, NCTE proposed that such work should garner professional recognition. Thus, although no in-depth discussions of the recognition and compensation of WPAs and their work existed, this era marks the beginning of some possible solutions for developing a professional identity for WPAs and recognition of their administrative work.

Efforts at individual identification and recognition were not the only goals of WPAs in the Transitional Era. The struggle for professionalization required broader professional identity crafting and recognition through research and publication. While Early Era WPAs called for more research and writing on program administration, Transitional Era WPAs began to answer the challenge. More research projects and publications focused on writing program administration, and by 1964, the opening of the Transitional Era, *College English* actually provided a forum specifically for publication of these types of articles:

> 'Departmental Memo' welcomes brief, concise articles or notes treating subjects of departmental interest such as: [. . .] new programs or curricula [. . .] staffing [. . .] use and training of graduate assistants; teaching schedules or loads; appointments, promotions. (Archer 620)

The acknowledgment of the need for such research and a forum for sharing it marked the possibility for, if not realization of, large-scale professional identity crafting and recognition in the Transitional Era.

Much early research began at conferences. Gordon Wilson of Miami University explained:

> The Executive Committee recommended the following matters for consideration: the professional status of the composition and communication teacher; the teaching load; the problem of diagnostic and achievement tests; teacher training; and articulation with the high school. None of this sounds very exciting; but it was. For the first time, those of us engaged in teaching and directing freshman composition were able to meet and discuss our common problems. We had a sense of a common enterprise and mutual discovery. The workshops and general sessions focused on the matters of our immediate concern. [. . .] Aggrieved by the discrepancy between our status and our function, and impelled by our interests, we set out to change things: to shape programs and textbooks, to lighten

> loads and to make the budgets heavier. For many of us the conferences gave us the first sense of being professionals. (128)

By the early 1970s, WPAs strongly felt the need to move beyond conference presentations and discussions into the larger community. Some WPAs gathered regionally to discuss administrative matters—"Harvey Wiener started CAWS, the precursor to WPA, a city group" that brought together New York area WPAs to discuss emerging issues (Bruffee interview). Other WPAs, however, realized that the larger WPA community would only be reachable by publication. Gary Tate noted, "There was general agreement that directors of freshman English needed a means of communicating their problems and solutions" (315). And by 1973, the desire for published information was so great that a workshop of first-year English administrators recommended an administrative task force be established to compile a directory of English requirements and exception policies, course descriptions, and testing procedures at different colleges and universities (Hitchcock 326).

In response to these calls for research and publication, not only did *College English* and *College Composition and Communication* print articles on writing program administration, new journals surfaced as outlets for WPAs and their work. *Freshman English News* began in 1972, and its editor explained that composition and its administration would be the publication's main focus: "*What* has been tried and *how* it has been tried will be the central concerns of the newsletter" (Tate 1). Tate went on to encourage submission of formal and informal discussions of freshman writing courses, their requirements, teacher training, experimental programs, duties of the program director, course evaluation procedures, writing labs, and any other topics which relate to the business of freshman writing (1). This new journal published the results of a growing number of administratively focused articles. Richard Gebhardt used the journal for professional exploration—surveying directors of freshman writing programs—to compile what was happening in programs around the country "to uncover information about the contents, instructional approaches, and the academic and administrative conditions surrounding composition teaching in liberal arts colleges" (12). And Ron Smith used the journal to call for greater self-identification and recognition. Believing that WPAs could benefit greatly from the experiences of others, and believing that not enough WPAs wrote about or discussed these experiences, Smith urged that journals could provide an outlet for collecting and disseminating information about composition and its instruction: "What we can learn from the experiences of others is the need, especially at *this* time, for a heightened awareness of what is going on, what has gone on, and, as best we can, what will go on elsewhere that involves the composition requirement and programs" (12). Because pressure from external sources often drove administrative decisions, Smith argued, it is "[o]nly through the efficiency of rapid input and dissemination of information that we will *know* when to fight and *know* when to give in" (12). Thus research and publication on freshman composition and its administration could not only help to unite WPAs in their work, it could also help forge the professional identity that would give WPAs more power to shape their programs in theoretically productive ways.

By 1977, WPAs began a publication to deal exclusively with the work and ideas of writing program administration. Begun as *WPA: A Newsletter for Writing Program Administrators* in 1977, the informal publication became a refereed journal, *WPA: Writing Program Administration*, by 1979—ending the Transitional Era with a formal outlet for professional dialogue through publication:

> With this issue, the *WPA Newsletter* becomes a full-fledged journal. [. . .] We will continue to be a refereed publication whose purpose is to focus thought, information, and expertise relevant to the teaching-administrative function of writing program administration and to explain to educators and the general public the special needs, values, and aims of writing program administrators. [. . .] *WPA* is necessary to writing program administrators and to the larger educational community, we believe, because it helps define an important field within our profession. Although many of us do most of the other things that college and university administrators do—hire and fire, tinker with budgets, schedule classes, and keep our programs running from day to day—WPAs also serve an institutional function quite distinct from that served by presidents, deans, chairs, provosts, and the like. Most writing program administrators continue to be writing teachers, differing from other writing teachers only in the nature of the people we

> teach. We teach not only college and university students, but often other college and university teachers as well. We are called upon sometimes to teach other administrators, trustees, and legislators, and even the general public. As a result, WPAs are not just teachers who also administrate, or administrators who also teach. We administrate in part *by* teaching. We teach in part *through* administration. (Bruffee "Editorial," Fall 1979 7-8)

Not only did the journal itself help to professionalize WPAs by valuing and publishing articles on composition and its administration, such explanations of the work and worth of WPAs (as described by the journal's editor) helped to explain the importance and uniqueness of the position. Bruffee described the value of such focused research, publication, and identity crafting:

> The newsletter of an organization such as ours, as I see it, is one method of "bonding" this nationwide group of people with common interests. It can help to establish a new synthesis of thought, information, and expertise relevant to our unique teaching-administrative function. The *Newsletter* can help us understand our own professional role better, and can explain to educators generally the special needs, aims, and values shared by writing program administrators. [. . .] In focusing on these and other such topics, we are literally creating a new field of interest, expertise, and value. ("Editorial," March 1979 4-5)

Thus, research and publication by and about WPAs grew dramatically in the Transitional Era—opening many possibilities for professional growth and group identity formation.

The final factor that played a role in the crafting and recognition of a professional identity for WPAs in the Transitional Era was the growth of professional organizations. Because English department chairs had laid the foundation for professional administrative organizations in the Early Era, the Transitional Era opened with the formation of a national identity and community for WPAs. This community was seen when *College Composition and Communication* put out a special edition in 1964 that included a "Directory of Chairmen of

Freshman Composition." Listing the names and addresses of WPAs—some department chairs, some instructors, some coordinators, some directors—the directory itemized 772 WPAs distributed through all fifty states of the United States. Thus, the opening of the Transitional Era set the stage for the development of a meaningful and possibly powerful national grouping of WPAs. Each year this directory grew in size and scope until discontinued in 1975. Larger professional affiliation was not, however, limited to print listings—conferences and workshops provided opportunities for WPAs to develop professional connections with other WPAs. A conference announcement noted the importance of such community-building: "Those interested in composition and rhetoric will find the MLA meeting in San Francisco this December a far more attractive meeting to attend than it has been in years past" ("Freshman English" 3). WPAs attributed the meeting's attractiveness to the inclusion of a forum on first-year English. Several speakers led workshops on the content, practice, and administration of writing—a first for MLA meetings. By 1975, several English-affiliated organizations opened their doors to compositionists in general and WPAs in particular:

> The literature-oriented Modern Language Association established in 1975 a Division on the Teaching of Writing, which has become the fastest growing of MLA's seventy-three divisions. A Rhetoric Society has been formed, and [. . .] the thirty-year-old Conference on College Composition and Communication is booming. (Hook 270)

Most importantly, however, the end of the Transitional Era was witness to a national professional organization devoted entirely to WPAs and their work. Bruffee noted:

> Last September a notice in the MLA Teaching of Writing Division Newsletter announced a new organization loosely associated with the division, called the Council of Writing Program Administrators. This new organization of writing program administrators, along with such programs as the new institute for writing program administration being planned at the University of Iowa, is important not just to our colleagues who do jobs variously called Director of

> Freshman Comp, Chairman of Rhetoric, Supervisor of Freshman Comp, Chairman of the Comp Committee, and so on. In my judgment, efforts to improve writing program administration are important also to all of us who work as classroom teachers under the guidance and protection of writing program administrators. Today, especially, and increasingly in the future, successful writing program administration in our colleges and universities is essential to our own success as writing teachers. ("Editorial," 1978 6-7)

Although seeming to be the culmination of professional identity crafting and recognition, the Transitional Era ended with the Council of Writing Program Administrators pointing out the long road ahead in the struggle for professionalization. The Council outlined nine goals in their bylaws to address in order to professionalize both WPAs and their work:

1. identify the needs of good writing programs,
2. share information among writing programs,
3. outline the requirements for good writing instruction,
4. support and disseminate research on writing instruction and administration,
5. improve writing competence,
6. publish newsletters to support the work of the Council,
7. help primary and secondary schools develop good writing programs,
8. develop productive writing assessment tools, and
9. help fund exemplary writing programs as models for other schools (14).

By March 1979, *WPA* reported on three conferences devoted entirely to WPAs (6-7) and listed a membership of 179 ("WPA Membership" 13-17). This growing group membership and the activities it sponsored laid the foundation for the future professionalization of WPAs and their work on a national level.

Although publications give some insight into the work and worth of WPAs, many individual acts and concerns go unpublished. Through discussions with participants in the struggle toward group identification, we can arrive at a deeper understanding of the position's evolution—putting individual faces on some of the problems of the Early Era and the possibilities of the Transitional Era. In addition to the chapters in this collection, included in Appendix A are two such examples that speak to the emerging professional identity of WPAs. In brief excerpts from longer interviews, Kenneth Bruffee and Erika Lindemann discuss their inadequate introduction to writing instruction and administration in the Early Era and their growth as writing instructors and WPAs in the Transitional Era, both mirroring and, at points, actually shaping the professional group identity of WPAs.

Conclusion—Toward a Modern Era

Since WPAs filled diverse and evolving positions, it is not easily apparent why a history of the struggle to create a professional identity would be valuable, but the drive for professional recognition is crucial in the evolutionary story of WPAs. Only when departments and universities were forced to confront the work and power of unified WPAs could writing program administration advance as a scholastically important field of study. As the number of writing programs and administrators grew, WPAs questioned and theorized the value and function of composition and its administration, and the outcome was a more professionalized field. The excavated primary sources which discuss WPAs and their work from the 1940s to the 1970s paint a vivid picture of this remarkable evolution which holds meaning for current and future WPAs.

The lack of a group identity for WPAs is clear in the Early Era. With English departments steeped in a literary tradition, composition instruction and administration were marginalized. Notable in this era was WPAs' first step toward professionalization—the recognition of individual circumstances and issues. WPAs were most often reacting to their unique surroundings rather than theorizing and shaping the larger environment. It is clear from the language of this era that WPAs were trying to find one another and their place in colleges and universities which undervalued composition and writing program administration—referring to their largely managerial status and the untheorized

Moving Toward a Group Identity

nature of the discipline. Early Era WPAs focused more bureaucratically on identifying the issues involved in writing program administration and other WPAs interested in dealing with these issues.

If the Early Era marked the identification of the problem in combination with individual solutions, WPAs in the Transitional Era took a professional step forward. In this era, WPAs began forming a group identity and a dynamic understanding of the discipline. WPAs recognized that the constraints faced in the Early Era were not solved by the individual remedies they had proposed. At this time, WPAs began to look for new ways to approach their difficulties; they began re-envisioning the position and its theoretical base as a discipline. Such a theorizing of writing program administration allowed WPAs to propose newer, more substantial solutions to their problems. Although WPAs were still reacting to their surroundings, these reactions began to come from disciplinary strength rather than weakness, from a theorizing of the discipline and its place in higher education. It is clear from the language of the Transitional Era that multiple approaches to writing program administration were being created. Through greater awareness and publication, WPAs were focusing less on finding one another and focusing more on working together to shape composition and its administration as scholarly endeavors.

Other than documenting and legitimizing the work of former WPAs, a history can and should inform current and future practices. Modern WPAs benefit greatly from the theorizing and evolution of a disciplinary identity. Although there is always work to be done to disseminate the valuable contributions of WPAs, current and future administrators do not have to begin the fight for professional recognition at ground zero. The theorizing of the discipline in earlier eras laid the foundation for the work of WPAs to be seen as scholarly. Another benefit of professional evolution is the diversity of opportunities for WPAs. No longer are WPAs limited to oversight of first-year writing. Administrators can pursue any number of areas—writing centers, WAC, program design, outcomes assessment, etc.—because of the inroads made in earlier eras. Finally, when working in these diverse capacities, current and future WPAs have the resource of already developed forums for intellectual support and advancement. Pioneers no longer work in isolation when tackling new problems; they can consult the numerous journals, conferences, and organizations for WPAs to find similarly interested or similarly challenged people. This developed community is an invaluable resource for WPAs, providing a living reference of the advancements in training, power, and identity for current and future WPAs. To be trapped in a paradigm that views writing programs and their administrators as unscholarly overseers is devastating. The intellectual theorizing of composition and its administration has made it possible for those working in writing programs to be valued as intellectual contributors to colleges and universities. The challenge then becomes for current and future WPAs to learn about the discipline's historical evolution so that they can proceed armed with the knowledge of the possibilities and pitfalls of writing program administration and continue the individual and disciplinary struggle for professionalization.

Works Cited

Archer, Jerome W., ed. "Departmental Memo." *College English* 25.8 (May 1964): 620.
Bruffee, Kenneth A. "Editorial." *WPA Newsletter* 1.3 (March 1978): 6-12.
—. "Editorial." *WPA Newsletter* 2.3 (March 1979): 3-5.
—. "Editorial." *WPA: Writing Program Administration* 3.1 (Fall 1979): 7-8.
—. "Editorial." *WPA: Writing Program Administration* 7.1/2 (Fall-Winter 1983): 11-12.
—. Personal interview. 18 July 1998.
Bryan, Adolphus J. "The Problem of Freshman English in the University." *College Composition and Communication* 2.2 (May 1951): 6-8.
Coulson, Marion F. "Workshop Reports: 10. Administration of Freshman English, Small College." *College Composition and Communication* 18.3 (October 1967): 196-97.
Council of Writing Program Administrators. "Council of Writing Program Administrators By Laws." *WPA Newsletter* 1.3 (March 1978): 13-15.
"Freshman English at MLA." *Freshman English News* 4.2 (Fall 1975): 3.
Gebhardt, Richard C. "Freshman Writing Programs in Liberal Arts Colleges." *Freshman English News* 3.2 (Fall 1974): 12-15.
Gray, E. W. "Panels: VII. Determining the Quality of Composition/Communication Teaching." *College Composition and Communication* 10.3 (October 1959): 146-48.
Grewe, Eugene. "A Teacher Looks at His Professional Status." *College Composition and Communication* 8.4 (December 1957): 214-20.
Grey, Lennox. "Round Table: National Council of Teachers of English College Section." *College English* 3.6 (March 1942): 584-86.
Griggs, Irwin. "The Professional Status of the Composition Teacher." *College Composition and Communication* 3.3 (October 1952): 10-12.

Hays, Edna. "The College Teaching of English: A Bibliography, 1946." *College English* 9.8 (May 1948): 430-53.

Hazo, Samuel J. "The Graduate Assistant Program at Duquesne University." *College Composition and Communication* 8.2 (May 1957): 119-21.

Hitchcock, Bert. "Workshop Reports: 119. Administering Freshman English Programs: Continuing Problems and New Problems." *College Composition and Communication* 24.3 (October 1973): 325-27.

Hook, J. N. "College English Departments: We May Be Present at Their Birth." *College English* 40.3 (November 1978): 269-73.

Houp, Kenneth W. "Workshop 5. Administering the Freshman Course." *College Composition and Communication* 8.3 (October 1957): 157-59.

Jordan, John E. "What We Are Doing to Train College Teachers of English." *College English* 27.2 (November 1965): 109-13.

"Kansas State College." *MLA Job Information List*. October 1971: 64.

"Kansas SU." *MLA Job Information List*. May 1973: 63.

Kitzhaber, Albert R. "Administering the Freshman Course: The Report of Workshop No. 17." *College Composition and Communication* 6.3 (October 1955): 160-61.

——. "New Perspectives on Teaching Composition." *College English* 23.6 (March 1962): 440-44.

Leyden, Ralph. "Construction and Use of Objective Tests: The Report of Workshop No. 8." *College Composition and Communication* 2.4 (December 1951): 16.

Lindemann, Erika. Personal interview. 3 April 1998.

Mason, James Hocker. "Organization and Administration of the Freshman Composition Course: The Report of Workshop No. 4, Section B." *College Composition and Communication* 3.4 (December 1952): 11-14.

Moake, Frank B. "Training Graduate Students as Teachers: At the University of Illinois." *College Composition and Communication* 14.2 (May 1963): 81-84.

NCTE. "Guidelines for the Workload of the College English Teacher." *College English* 38.8 (April 1976): 873-75.

——. "Professional Career of the College English Teacher." *College English* 23.6 (March 1962): 445-69.

——. "The Workload of a College English Teacher." *College English* 28.1 (October 1966): 55-57.

Noonan, John P. "Two Session Workshops: 1. Administering the Large Freshman Program." *College Composition and Communication* 9.3 (October 1958): 174-76.

"Ohio SU." *MLA Job Information List*. October 1974: 25.

Roberts, Charles W. "The Unprepared Student at the University of Illinois." *College Composition and Communication* 8.2 (May 1957): 95-100.

Rogers, Robert W. "Departmental Memo: Resolutions Adopted at a Seminar of English Department Chairmen." *College English* 24.6 (March 1963): 473-75.

Sachs, H. J. "Workshop 17b. Problems of National Standards and National Accreditation." *College Composition and Communication* 8.3 (October 1957): 192-93.

Smith, Ron. "A Further Look Into the Fall 1973 Survey." *Freshman English News* 3.3 (Winter 1975): 1-12.

Steinberg, Erwin R. "Departmental Memo: Needed Research in the Teaching of College English." *College English* 24.2 (November 1962): 149-52.

"SU of NY." *MLA Job Information List*. October 1974: 9.

Tate, Gary. "From the Editor." *Freshman English News* 1.1 (March 1972): 1.

—. "Workshop Reports: 50. The Director of Freshman English: His Role." *College Composition and Communication* 23.3 (October 1972): 314-15.

"Whitworth C." *MLA Job Information List*. February 1975: 43.

Wilson, Gordon. "CCCC in Retrospect." *College Composition and Communication* 18.3 (October 1967): 127-34.

"WPA Membership." *WPA Newsletter* 2.3 (March 1979): 13-17.

Wykoff, George S. "Teaching Composition as a Career." *College English* 1.5 (February 1940): 426-37.

Appendix A: Administrators Who Span the Eras

Kenneth Bruffee

Q: Could you talk about how you got into writing programs—teaching writing and writing program administration—what drew you into this work and how your involvement evolved?

A: I got to Brooklyn in 1966 and experienced a series of riots [. . .] The City University was creeping very slowly toward some kind of Open Admissions, and then there was another riot. That was the last riot—the riot which precipitated Open Admissions. A friend of mine had been elected chairman of the English department, and in May, before anything happened, he asked me if I would run freshman English. He said it was an easy thing, a piece of cake. Then in June, the City University became an Open Admissions place. We didn't know what that meant, we hadn't the slightest idea. Suddenly I became the de facto first Director of Freshman English at Brooklyn College—the Open Admissions Director. I have always been associated with that—I was "Mr. Open Admissions." I have always been pegged as the person who brought down the university, or for that matter, western society and all that's good and true. [. . .] But you wanted to know something about the job, what happened there. The job differs from institution to institution, as you know. Some people have obvious budgets, have control over scheduling, hiring, and so on. At my institution the chair controlled the budget and scheduled the courses; my job was more of a teaching job, which was much more appropriate to me in any case. It had to be a kind of large persuasive role—an organizational role. Suddenly we had enormous numbers of students that we hadn't had before. When I went into the job, the assumption was there would be some twenty-five to thirty sections of freshman English. [. . .] Within a year or two, I had 110 sections of freshman English. I had sixty to seventy adjuncts teaching—people who were graduate students and some not much more than undergraduates. There were a lot of people like that around New York because there were a lot of schools, but they didn't know how to teach the people who were coming into the university, and I was supposed to teach them how to do it. And, of course, I didn't know either. I called up people in the other City University schools, and we got together and went off to NCTE and CCCC to find out how to do it and to ask people. We found out they didn't even know the questions; they'd never heard of them. We were asking questions they had never heard of. It eventually spread from New York all over the country. What I did in that job, again the job did not require in that particular instance bean counting or scheduling—neither the task nor the pressures of that—I had to teach. I organized workshops. I talked to faculty, talked to faculty [at] meetings, outreach to other departments trying to explain what to expect and how they could contribute, how the situation had changed. And I published a newsletter which I called *Cadre*. [. . .] That went on for a number of years. [. . .] But in the course of it, the relationships I formed with other people at the other schools developed and were very helpful because it gave you a sense that there was another world out there. In the course of that Mina [Shaughnessy] became quite well known, and her work helped to focus the work a bit. And then Harvey Wiener started CAWS [CUNY Association of Writing Supervisors], the precursor to WPA, a city group, and that focused it in another way—brought people together out of the woodwork. It was quite a productive thing. One of the things that was disappointing was that we realized there was a tremendous amount of talent emerging from this practical conundrum that we were faced with which was not being recognized nationally. [.

. .]1976 was the first major fiscal cutback in CUNY funds, and it was the beginning of the end of Open Admissions. Overnight, or literally over a summer, a whole bunch of people—we must have had 40-50 full-time, reasonably-paid adjunct lecturers—they just disappeared. So it was like there was a kind of mass mourning when we showed back up in the fall, and all these people that we had seen every day and worked with and had lunch with and laughed with were gone. That brought people down a lot—it was very hard. And there has been a series of these radical financial cuts every couple of years ever since then. In terms of the organization, it was at MLA in Chicago in 1976 in a session in which Mina gave that "Diving In" speech, and Ed Corbett was elected to head it up, but he didn't want to do it, so I did it. We organized this thing and blackmailed them into giving us more sections. Harvey and I conspired to set up WPA. To some extent WPA was started as a subversive organization.

Q: Do you feel you got to affect the culture of the institution in your time?

A: Well, in my time, things were moving so rapidly we were just coping—just coping from day to day to week to week—and we knew so little. I mean we didn't know much. We didn't call ourselves WPAs; we didn't have that title. We weren't organized at all; we were trying to get together to cry in our beer once in a while. And the changes to size and colleges, everything was changing so rapidly that we just didn't know from day to day what was going to happen. Whereas now there are serious problems, but they're not all-encompassing problems—they are namable. [. . .] WPA was formed at the time as a matter of survival—and that's an important distinction. Nothing about it is going to be quite like it was because the issue is not survival. And by survival I don't mean the institution doesn't survive or you don't survive, but survival in the sense of keeping from drowning. Writing is now part of the college/university structure in a way that it simply wasn't then. It was just a course in the English department, and because it was just a course in the English department, it remained without much of a support base.

Q: Were there things you would like to have accomplished administratively that you weren't able to do?

A: I was disappointed when I was fired, but probably only for about twenty minutes. I got over it pretty quickly. I continued to be in touch with people at CCCC, NCTE, and MLA. [. . .] I guess I was more interested by that time in the national organization and the CUNY organization. I was quite active with Harvey Wiener. He was the real energy behind WPA. We thought we should write some kind of statement—what it was we thought the organization ought to be doing—and pull together some people who were around, mainly at that point New Yorkers who could just get on a subway and get together and figure out how to present it to the rest of the profession and to our people. At one point we met—in those days we met, I guess they're still doing it, both at MLA and at CCCC—we being just a handful of people, not many people showed up. We just sort of got together and sat down and asked what was the next step. [. . .] Then the journal lent the other dimension of visibility. I made it a refereed journal because I found out by going to a meeting of journal editors at MLA that they were talking about the difference between refereed and non-refereed journals—one counted and the other one didn't. I said, "OK, if we want to count, we'll make it refereed." And we put on people from Yale and Harvard so that we had some fancy names on there, and it looked good. The whole idea was to give it that quality so that people who were publishing in it could say, "This goes on—this refereed journal goes on the resume." So it's legitimized in that way.

Erika Lindemann

Q: Could you walk me through your experiences with writing program administration and how you perceive the position has evolved over the years?

A: My first teaching job was at the University of South Carolina in Columbia. The first year I didn't have any administrative responsibilities; I was just a professor like every other professor, teaching sophomore survey courses, freshman composition, history of the language, courses that my medieval major had prepared me for. Everybody in that department did some service work, so I chose to work in the departmental reading room, which meant working with two graduate students who were sort of like attendants, ordering subscriptions to things, keeping the place cleaned up, etc. I don't remember who was director of the writing program at that time, but by the end of my first year, that person had stepped down. The department chair had wanted a new person, so I got asked. I always tell the story in terms that I administered a departmental reading room and then they thought I was qualified to administer the writing program. And I thought, well, sure, that would be interesting work to do. I had what I thought at the time was very good training at UNC—I didn't understand it then in ways that I do now because I was pretty much a grammarian. I thought teaching writing meant teaching grammar, correcting papers, and making students write to some sort of ideal model that I had in my head, but, of course, I hadn't clued them in on any of it. [. . .] The department chair and I talked about the fact that I didn't know anything. He had heard about the Conference on College Composition and Communication, and he said, "If you want us to send you there, we could maybe do that." So he was willing to spring for my travel expenses to come to this meeting. So the first CCCC meeting I attended was in Spring 1973. [. . .] That CCCC was the "Students' Rights to Their Own Language" CCCC, which was a very untypical CCCC but very exciting because people were talking about linguistic issues I already knew a good bit about. I thought, "Well, this is the group for me." So, I began attending CCCC routinely then. I don't think I've missed one since 1973. Early on the CCCC meetings were sort of my second education. I hadn't had any training in the field, so I would come, and I would hook up with people. I met Gary Tate at the first CCCC meeting. Susan Miller introduced us; Susan had been a UNC PhD. I got to start knowing people, and we would sit around in the bar and all go to breakfast, and they'd be talking about, "Have you read Kinneavy's new book?" or Frank D'Angelo was working on a book. We would talk and I would say, "Oh, yes, that's an interesting book." Of course, I hadn't read it at all. I would go back to Columbia, then, with my year's reading list. The books people were talking about, were mentioning in sessions, that I had not a clue about, became my homework for the next year. Gradually, then, CCCC became my course—my course in rhetoric and composition and literature, and at that time, as many people my age will tell you, it was a manageable bibliography. There weren't that many people in the field. It was an exciting time, and you could pretty much keep up with it year by year. Back home in Columbia, though, I was very much interested in curriculum revision, in training graduate students—many of whom, like me, didn't have a clue about what to do in the classroom—and I began doing workshops with our graduate students. [. . .] Then it seemed to me that I needed to begin writing it down. I had done a lot of reading by that time; it was sort of like graduate school: you do a lot of studying and reading and talking, and you even try to teach some of it, but at some point you have to write a dissertation. So my second dissertation then became *A Rhetoric for Writing Teachers*.

Q: Other than word-of-mouth, where did you learn about ideas that you were interested in pursuing, especially in the early years?

A: Word-of-mouth would lead me to important books, and then the footnotes of the books would lead me to other materials. Word-of-mouth was really important to me. There was no WPA when I first got started. I was a founding member of WPA. There were no NEH grants for writing teachers. That's what I particularly enjoyed or gravitated to as an administrator or as a person in the field. There was no bibliography of composition and rhetoric, so I thought, "Well, there's an interesting project; I'll try to put one of those together." There were a few—William Irmscher had a teaching book out—but there weren't very many, and I thought, "Well *A Rhetoric for Writing Teachers* is a book for teachers." There weren't very many of those, so I thought, "Well, which one of those do you like? What do teachers need to know?"

10

Representing the Intellectual Work of Writing Program Administration: Professional Narratives of George Wykoff at Purdue, 1933-1967

Shirley K Rose

Identifying Narratives of WPA Work

The ongoing project of identifying and developing narratives of writing program administrators' work has helped WPAs and our colleagues and coworkers to better understand the nature of this work, which takes place in what might be viewed as a subculture of the academy. Writing program administration is deeply embedded in and dependent upon the cultures of the particular institutions in which individual writing programs are located, the disciplinary cultures of composition studies and English studies more generally, and the broader culture of faculty life and work in higher education. Yet WPA work differs from other faculty work in significant ways. To understand these differences, which can be intellectually puzzling at best and emotionally wrenching at worst, WPAs frequently turn to narrative as a way to impose order, meaning, and value on their experience.

Narratives can help to provide this understanding in several ways. They impose order and coherence by sequencing and suggesting cause-effect relationships, making experience predictable by fitting it into familiar patterns and making it make sense by transforming it into stories with recognizable characters, conflicts, and resolutions. These stories allow their narrators to integrate the experiences of the individual agent into the broader social experience by naming them, describing them, and contextualizing them. In this way, they can give meaning and value in a broader culture to what might otherwise seem to be singular, inexplicable experiences without significance, representing them in terms of familiar shared metanarratives.

We already have a number of WPA narratives in our WPA literature—those collected by Diana George in *Kitchen Cooks, Plate Twirlers, and Troubadours* and other recent narratives like Wendy Bishop and Gay Lynn Crossley's will probably be known to most readers. The stories their authors tell, though each is unique and compelling, are familiar and conventional—indeed it is their conventionality as stories that make them compelling. The authors have transformed their inchoate experience into coherent action, with themselves as agents deriving meaning from the events in which they have willingly or unwillingly participated. We like to read these narratives—we know we benefit from reading these narratives—because they help us understand our own work and lives as writing program administrators. They help us understand how writing programs evolve—what and how events and circumstances lead to change, how various writing program participants can affect and effect change. They also help us understand how WPAs' professional careers develop. As these stories accumulate in our professional literature over time, we can begin to see patterns, to generalize about the kinds of work that are characteristic of successful and effective WPAs at various stages of their careers and about the ways local and professional circumstances affect and effect WPAs' development. We can begin to speculate about how particular kinds of professional activities lead to particular paths of professional development for writing program administrators. We read these stories with the expectation that they will help us better understand our work, be better at it, derive greater joy from it.

Both as writers and as readers, WPAs may resort to these stories because other, more conventional genres for representing faculty work, such as the *curriculum vita*, have been unwieldy, if not inadequate, for describing WPA experience, expertise, and achievement. In this chapter, I address some of the methodological issues in constructing narratives of WPAs' work, using records from the archive of George Wykoff papers (the "Wykoff File") at Purdue University as a focus for discussion and exploration. I discuss ways of reading two of the genres for representing academic experience included in the file—a *curriculum vita (c.v.)* and a "Personnel Record"—as lenses for examining other relevant archival records and documents. The focus of the chapter, however, will be on working in the reverse direction, reading the records in the file as they are illuminated by the documents and events to which they refer. The primary purpose of the chapter will be an examination of the ways these records can be read as autobiographical narratives (see Phelps) of writing program administration constructed by Wykoff himself. I will argue that, despite the generic constraints imposed by these records types, this analytical and interpretive methodology acknowledges the agency of their creator. Because records such as these are more likely than the elaborate stories of *Kitchen Cooks, Plate Twirlers, and Troubadours* to constitute writing program administration archives, it is important for historians of writing program administration to develop strategies for reading them and for all WPAs to develop strategies for writing them.

George Wykoff

The narratives George Wykoff wrote about his work as a writing program administrator merit our attention because that work was both ordinary and extraordinary. Wykoff's work as a writing program administrator was ordinary in the way most WPAs' work is ordinary: his attention directed to the administrative details that made it possible for him to see how closely the reality of his writing program matched his vision for it; his time given over to a routine of interruptions; his energies spent in work that would have to be done over again the next term. He was, as an editor's footnote described him, "in charge of [. . .] first-year composition" at Purdue (Wykoff, "Toward" 10).

Wykoff was Chair of English I (a position now titled "Director of Composition") at Purdue University from 1933 until 1967. During his tenure as a WPA, the Purdue student body went from 3,699 to 20,176; the English department faculty increased from twenty-one to seventy-six; and the university grew from its land-grant roots into a major public research institution. Throughout this period, first-year composition was required in most of the Purdue schools' curricula. The course was staffed by both junior and senior professorial faculty—more junior than senior—and a few part-time lecturers in the English department.

These characteristics of Wykoff's institutional situation are probably quite ordinary for their time, though Wykoff's longevity as a WPA is probably relatively unusual. This ordinariness is part of what makes this glimpse into the everyday details of his WPA work provided by the documents in the Wykoff file especially interesting to us now, more than forty years later.

But Wykoff's work as a WPA is also extraordinary because it was the ground for his participation in the establishment and early development of the Conference on College Composition and Communication, which has become the chief professional organization for college-level scholars, researchers, and teachers in composition studies. It was George Wykoff who, at a session of the 1948 NCTE convention, issued the "clarion call to the profession to alert itself to 'improve the climate' for the teaching of freshman English" ("Chicago" 286) that led to the creation of the CCCC. His remarks at that session in November, which were published in *College English* the following February and will be discussed at some length later in this chapter, have been credited with moving those in attendance to request and receive permission and support for organizing a follow-up conference on freshman English to be held in the Spring of 1949. That conference was the origin of the CCCC.

As a founding officer—Secretary in 1950 and Chairman in 1951—of the newly organized Conference on College Composition and Communication, Wykoff participated in defining the need for and purpose of the organization and in establishing the ways in which it would operate. He also played an active role in making its initial events a reality and a success. He was responsible for handling the "hotel arrangements" for the first conference meeting—a task that, for a new organization, might well have covered everything except the selection of the speakers for the program. As the third editor of *CCC*, the young organization's quarterly journal and the first scholarly journal to be devoted exclusively to the concerns of college composition teachers and administrators, Wykoff played a significant part in defining the kind of scholarship that would represent the work of the organization's members. His view of the nature and significance of his work as a WPA is reflected in his selection of material to publish—most notably the bibliographies of relevant work in linguistics, education research, communication, and rhetoric that appeared in the issues he edited from 1953 to 1955.

The "Wykoff File"

The "Wykoff File" held in the archives of the English department of Purdue University is quite literally a file folder containing roughly one linear inch of documents, most of which are dated from 1948 to 1954. The institutional circumstance that led to the department's retention of these particular materials for this particular period are impossible to reconstruct, and I can only speculate that they might have included the tenure of a department head or head's secretary with an idiosyncratic approach to records management. Whatever the circumstances and reasons that determined the collection and preservation of these materials, they have proven to be a rich source for insight into the connections between Wykoff's local institutional work as a writing program administrator and his contributions as a participant in a national movement toward professionalization of composition teachers and administrators. Most of the records in the file were created during a period in Wykoff's professional career that is of special significance to scholars of writing program administration and others in rhetoric and composition studies. It coincides with the beginnings of the major professional scholarly organization for composition studies professionals, and with a time of profound change at Purdue and other higher education institutions, particularly public universities after World War II.

The file includes Wykoff's *curriculum vita*; notes and memos exchanged between Wykoff and English department head Barriss Mills; reports on research Wykoff conducted within the writing program and the English department; descriptions of his professional activities included in annual activity reports submitted for merit-raise reviews; and reports on attendance at professional conferences. These records have served as a starting point for my archival investigation and analysis—that is, as they lead to other archival records, such as Wykoff's other publications in scholarly journals and records of professional organizations in which he was active, as well as institutional records at Purdue University. I have been able to locate and read most of the more than eighty publications listed on Wykoff's *c.v.*, including the issues of *CCC* published during his editorship. Though many of the CCCC's organizational records, and those of its parent organization NCTE, have been lost, minutes of the annual CCCC business meeting and early histories of the organization are accessible because they were published in *CCC*. For additional information about the contexts for Wykoff's work, I have examined institutional records at Purdue, including annual university budgets, curriculum bulletins, yearbooks, and annual reports from the department of English. Though all of these records are inherently interesting, my discussion here will be limited to one published document, "Toward Achieving the Objectives of Freshman Composition," and two of the records in the "Wykoff File" created by Wykoff himself: a *c.v.* and a "Personnel Record."

"Toward Achieving the Objectives of Freshman Composition" is described in a footnote to the article as "A paper read at the meeting of the National Council of Teachers of English held at Chicago, November 25-27, 1948" (319). According to an outline of the program for the 1948 NCTE convention published in the October 1948 issue of *College English*, that paper was one of three presented at a ninety-minute "Friday Afternoon Conference" on college undergraduate teaching titled "Required Freshman English." Though accounts of that session describe Wykoff's remarks as extemporaneous (see Bartholomae), it seems likely that they were at least partially planned in advance. Accounts of the session published shortly after agree with Bartholomae's belief that Wykoff's remarks were among the events that inspired those attending that convention session to call for a conference devoted to the concerns of teachers and administrators in college writing programs (see Gerber's "CCCC Facts" and "Three Year History of the CCCC"). The conference was organized and took place in Chicago several months later, in March of 1949, and accounts published shortly thereafter indicate that the "Conference" in the Spring of 1949 was such a success that those who attended received approval for their request that a permanent conference be established, with an executive committee to organize its activities and a journal to publish its proceedings and other scholarship relevant to its members.

"Toward Achieving the Objectives of Freshman Composition" ("TAO") is a significant document in the history of contemporary composition studies because of the role Wykoff's remarks played at the 1948 NCTE convention. But it is also of interest because it describes the professional context of composition teachers and program administrators at the time, and it is of particular interest for the ways in which Wykoff constructs an implicit narrative of his own professional career as a composition scholar, teacher, and program administrator. In this paper, Wykoff called his audience to "begin or continue or emphasize a process of education of ourselves, of our colleagues in composition, of our high-school people, of our colleagues in literature, of our heads of departments, deans, and other administrators, and, oh, yes, even of the students themselves" (319).

Wykoff accounted for the relative lack of contemporary knowledge about composition by locating it in institutional labor issues and the politics of promotion, asserting that the successful achievement of the objectives of freshman composition "depends upon the milieu or climate or environment in which the composition teacher works" (319). The remedy to this situation, he suggested, should begin with composition teachers themselves, who should "aim at a better understanding of the field, with our eventual goal scholarship in composition comparable to scholarship in any literature field" (319). He recommended they become familiar with work in "linguistics, semantics, general educational theory, and the like" (319) and develop a "reading acquaintance" with journals such as "*College English*, the *English Journal*, the *CEA Critic* and some of the state or regional publications" (320).

In addition to identifying resources for learning what was already known, Wykoff called for research on the effectiveness of current practices, suggesting areas of needed study and recommending methodologies for study, urging his audience to "adopt a more scientific attitude toward the details of our work and apply, in addition to our objective tests, much more of the experimental method, either formally or informally." He also called for research on not only the "conventional areas" but "new areas opening up—like audiovisual aids" and replication of others' experiments "until the mass of information is sufficient to justify indisputable conclusions, upon which recommendations for action can be based." If this were to be achieved, composition teachers would have to write "accounts of research and experiments" and "accounts of courses and interesting procedures being tried." These accounts were needed because "we can improve our own programs by knowing what is being tried and accomplished in other places" (320). Furthermore, he argued, "pioneers" were needed who would explore new kinds of courses and new ways of teaching writing. Though this is an incomplete explication and analysis of Wykoff's remarks, it is enough to demonstrate that he was quite conscious of a need to develop a number of ways of adequately representing WPAs' work to their institutional colleagues and to one another across institutions.

This archival document—the convention paper published in *College English*—is accessible because of its publication circumstances. Because it was published in a professional scholarly journal, it was widely disseminated to college and university libraries at the time of its publication and has been more or less carefully preserved in these institutions over the last half-century. Because they are archived and available, such records can be precisely and unambiguously described in documents such as the *c.v.* and "Personnel Record," documents which are used as the primary data source for informing decisions about promotion within the academic ranks and merit raises.

"Toward Achieving the Objectives of Freshman Composition" is especially interesting as documentation of an otherwise ephemeral event. As I mentioned previously, Wykoff's remarks at the convention session have been characterized as extemporaneous, yet a footnote to the publication describes it as "a paper read at the meeting." Regardless of how spontaneous or planned-ahead Wykoff's remarks were during the convention session, through the venue of *College English*, an established scholarly journal with a wide circulation, they were transformed into a print "publication." As an item in a print journal published by an established national professional scholarly association, this publication was, like others in scholarly journals with large library subscription bases, effectively selected for preservation and archived using the media technology of the time. Thanks to this, "TAO" remains widely accessible more than half a century later.

The transformation of the convention paper into a scholarly journal publication also gained "TAO" a more privileged position on Wykoff's *c.v.* On his *c.v.*, Wykoff listed only selected convention papers, without titles, under the category of "Miscellaneous," where he also listed offices he had held and committees he had been elected or appointed to in professional organizations and talks he had given to local clubs. "TAO," the paper delivered at the November 1948 NCTE convention in Chicago is not included. However, "TAO," the article published in the March 1949 issue of *College English*, is listed as one of seventy-eight entries under the category of "Publications."[1]

Reading the Wykoff File in Light of the Published Archive

Though none of the documents in the Wykoff File takes the form of a conventional autobiography, reading them as autobiographical narratives recognizes the agency of their creator at the same time it highlights the ways in which these academic genres constrained Wykoff's discursive self-construction and self-representation as an academic professional, particularly as a writing program administrator.

The format for the version of Wykoff's *c.v.*, included in the Wykoff File, is a numbered list of items in six categories:

- "Personal," in which Wykoff's birthdate and place, citizenship, and marital status are provided;
- "Education," in which dates of attendance and degrees earned are indicated;
- "Experience," in which work experience, including nonacademic work, is indicated by institution, dates, and job title;
- "Publications," which includes seventy-eight items that are not further classified into subcategories and are listed beginning with the earliest in 1926 and ending with items published in 1963;
- "Miscellaneous," which begins with an entry for Wykoff's WPA position at Purdue and includes thirty other items arranged in roughly chronological order from 1949 to 1964, listing offices held in regional and national professional organizations, committee service to professional organizations, editorship of a scholarly journal, papers presented at professional conferences, talks given to local clubs, travel, consultant work, and membership in a scholarship fraternity; and
- "Organizations," which lists eight professional organizations and what appears to be the most recent year of membership (all are either "1964" or "1965" and Wykoff retired in 1967).

The brief entries for each of these items are typed onto 4" x 6" index cards (see Figures 1, 2, and 3), with each category beginning on a new card—a format which would have made periodic updating of the *c.v.* possible without requiring retyping all the entries.

Though the entries describing the publications do not follow precisely any conventional documentation style (such as MLA or APA), bibliographic information for all items is sufficiently detailed to allow even a casual reader to identify the range of interests and the recurring themes in Wykoff's publications. The information has also been sufficient to allow me to locate and review nearly all of the items. The brief information the *c.v.* provides about Wykoff's work for regional and national professional organizations has been enough to enable me to identify and examine published records of these organizations that provide additional information about Wykoff's contributions to the development of the composition studies profession.

```
WYKOFF, GEORGE STEWARD

I.  PERSONAL:

    b. June 28, 1899 - New Columbia, Pa.
    U. S. citizen
    Married

II. EDUCATION:

    Pennsylvania St. College, 1916-20 - A. B. 1920
    Columbia Univ., 1921-22 - A. M. 1922
    Columbia Univ., summer, 1925.
    Univ. of Chicago, 1932-33, 1937-38, and most summers from
                                                1926 to 1938.
```

Figure 1. Wykoff's *c.v.* card page 1

```
                                              Wykoff  -     2
III. EXPERIENCE:

     New York Univ., 1920-21 - Sec'y, YMCA
     Northwestern Univ., summer, 1923 - Instr.
     Purdue, 1922-28 - Instr.
     Purdue, 1928-40 - Asst. Prof.
     Purdue, 1940-45 - Assoc. Prof.
     Purdue, 1945 - Prof.

IV.  PUBLICATIONS:

1. "Morgan Robertson, The Rejected," New York Herald Tribune Books,
    II (1926), 10.
2. "Trusting to Luck" (short story), Blue Book Magazine, (Sept.,
    1920), 93-97.
3. "Charles Mackay: England's Forgotten Civil War Correspondent,"
    S. At. Q., XXVI (1927), 50-62.
4. "The University in Its Relation to Culture and the Engineer,"
    Prof. Eng., XIII (1928), 11-12.
5. "On the Revision of Ph.D. Requirements in English," Eng. Jour.
    (College Edition), XVII (1928), 213-220.
```

Figure 2. Wykoff's *c.v.* card page 2

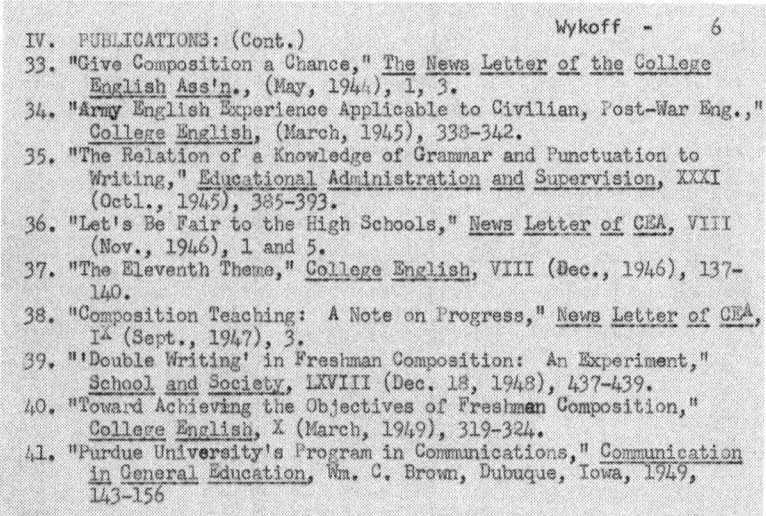

Figure 3. Wykoff's *c.v.* card page 6

However, the information provided about Wykoff's work as chair of freshman English at Purdue University leads only to several of the other records that happen to have been preserved in the Wykoff file itself—several memos exchanged with the English department head, a report on writing program hiring and staffing practices, and university business documents. Because few other records of Wykoff's local WPA work have been retained, reconstructing more than the barest outlines of it is possible only through readings of his publications and organizational records.

Read from the perspective of more than a half-century, the discrepancies between long-term significance of various aspects of Wykoff's professional work at the mid-twentieth century and his representation of them in his *c.v.* are striking. These discrepancies give us some insights into not only the generic constraints of the conventional *c.v.*—especially for representing writing program administration and "service" to professional organizations—but also the ways in which prevailing hierarchies can radically underestimate the long-term value or significance of various professional achievements. The *c.v.* with its list-based design and chronological organization, is particularly well-suited to providing information about publications—information for which highly standardized formats have been developed—making it relatively easy to read, interpret, and evaluate. Teaching, professional and institutional service, and writing program administration, however, are difficult to adequately describe within the constraints of the chronological list. The nature of these achievements and contributions in these areas can vary widely and their cause-and-effect interrelationships cannot be represented well by a list. Reading Wykoff's *c.v.* half a century later, we would find his description of his role in founding the CCCC with the brief itemization "Secretary (1950), Chairman (1951), Director (1952), CCCC" and placement of it in a subordinate position to the publication entry for "A Possible Source of Browning's 'Saul,'" incomprehensible to us if we weren't acculturated to the pre-

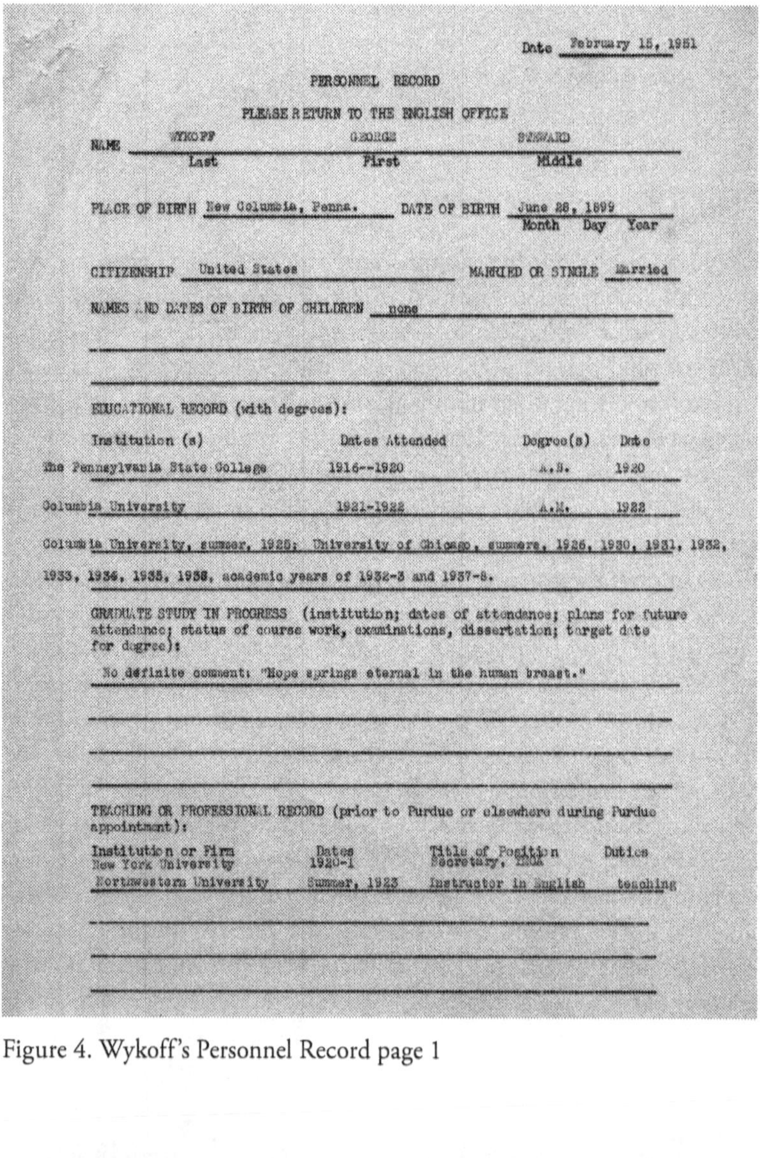

Date February 15, 1951

PERSONNEL RECORD

PLEASE RETURN TO THE ENGLISH OFFICE

NAME WYKOFF (Last) GEORGE (First) SEWARD (Middle)

PLACE OF BIRTH New Columbia, Penna. DATE OF BIRTH June 28, 1899 (Month Day Year)

CITIZENSHIP United States MARRIED OR SINGLE Married

NAMES AND DATES OF BIRTH OF CHILDREN none

EDUCATIONAL RECORD (with degrees):

Institution (s)	Dates Attended	Degree(s)	Date
The Pennsylvania State College	1916--1920	A.B.	1920
Columbia University	1921-1922	A.M.	1922

Columbia University, summer, 1925; University of Chicago, summers, 1926, 1930, 1931, 1932, 1933, 1934, 1935, 1938, academic years of 1932-3 and 1937-8.

GRADUATE STUDY IN PROGRESS (institution; dates of attendance; plans for future attendance; status of course work, examinations, dissertation; target date for degree):

No definite comment: "Hope springs eternal in the human breast."

TEACHING OR PROFESSIONAL RECORD (prior to Purdue or elsewhere during Purdue appointment):

Institution or Firm	Dates	Title of Position	Duties
New York University	1920-1	Secretary, [illegible]	
Northwestern University	Summer, 1923	Instructor in English	teaching

Figure 4. Wykoff's Personnel Record page 1

vailing values of the academy, which privilege publishing over all other academic work.

Similar issues are suggested by examining another autobiographical record created by Wykoff, but substantively shaped by the document's design and the generic constraints it imposes or implies. The Wykoff File includes a copy of a "Personnel Record" dated February 15, 1951 (see Figures 4, 5, and 6).[2] This document is a mimeographed three-page form with prompts and lines which have been filled in with typed responses that have subsequently (no earlier than 1954) been amended and supplemented with information entered in handwriting.

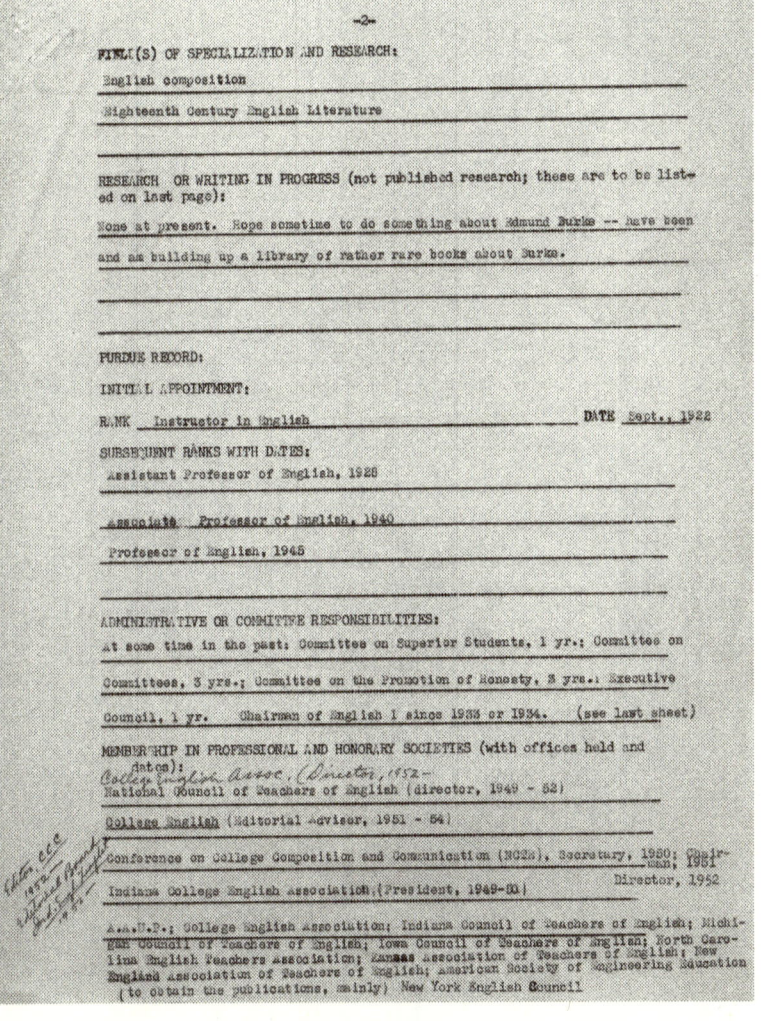

Figure 5. Wykoff's Personnel Record page 2

-3-

RECENT ATTENDANCE AT PROFESSIONAL MEETINGS (if on program, state capacity):

Indiana College English Association (annually, missed two or three meetings since 1935, have given three papers before it (Convention Com., 1951).

National Council of Teachers of English: Chicago, 1949, gave a paper; Buffalo, 1959, on a panel discussion on thinking and writing; Milwaukee, 1950 (Oriental Com., Language Writing, 1st 2 year College Curric Study of NCTE, Cincinnati, 1951

American Society of Engineering Education -- Illinois-Indiana Branch. Terre Haute, 1948; Purdue, 1950

CCCC — March 1951 — Chairman of Conference, presiding (CCCC Subcommittee, Indianapolis, Nov. 28, 1950) officer, Nov.
ABWA, April 26, 1952   CCCC Steer. Com. Mar 28, 1952   1951

CCCC (Board of Directors) Indianapolis, Jan 20, 1951; Turkey Run, May 5, 52

NCTE N.D. Ind. 1953
CCCC Ch. 1953
ICTE Ind. 1953
ICEA, BuPur, 1953
CCCC St. Louis, Mp, May 1, 1954
CTE, Ind Com. C. Sta, May 1, 1954

OTHER EXTRA-CURRICULAR ACTIVITIES (speaking engagements, non-professional organizations, sponsoring of student groups, etc.):

Presbyterian Church; Central Players of Presbyterian Church, vice-president or Executive Board; Purdue University Staff Bowling League

"Practical Method of Teaching Written Composition." ISTA, Oct 25, 1951
"Common Errors in Freshman Themes." Tippecanoe English Club, April 4, 1952
Seminar Participation in Light of action, ISTA   B.L., Oct. 23, 1952
Panel on Pathology, Bates v Coffee, 1954

RECORD OF PUBLICATION (be complete, use additional sheets if necessary):

Title of Book   Publisher   Volume   Date
or   or
Article   Title of Journal   Page

(NOTE: At the time of my last advancement, a full list of publications was prepared (which should be in the office files): poetry, placement tests, essays, short stories, professional articles, book reviews, and three books (editions) of readings for freshmen.)

Freshman Prose Annual, Number Four   Houghton Mifflin Co.   1945
(Ed. with R. M. Gay & M. C. Boatright)
"Army English Experiences Applicable to Civilian   College English   VI:338-42 March, 1945
Post-War English"
"The Relation of a Knowledge of Grammar and   Educational Administra-
Punctuation to Writing"   tion and Supervision   31:385-93 Oct., 1945
"Let's Be Fair to the High Schools"   The News Letter of CEA   VIII:1 and 5 Nov., 1946
"The Eleventh Theme"   College English   VIII:137-40 Dec. 1946
"Composition Teaching: A Note on
Progress"   IX:3   Sept. 1947
"'Double Writing' in Freshman
Composition: An Experiment"   The News Letter of CEA   Dec. 18, 1948
"Toward Achieving the Objectives of
Freshman Composition"   School and Society   68:457-9   March, 1949
"Purdue University's Program in   College English   I:319-24
Communications"   Communication in General Education,   pp. 143-
   ed. by Earl J. McGrath, U. S. Com-   156   1949
   missioner of Education, Wm. C. Brown
   Company, Dubuque, Iowa
"Suggestions for the Reading of Themes"   College English   XI:210-4   Jan. 1950
"American College English" (book review)   College English   XI:227,8   Jan., 1950
"Freshman Composition -- a Definition"   CEA Critic   XII, 1, 8   March, 1950
 ̲ ̲ ̲ ̲ ̲ ̲ ̲ & Harry Shaw, A Complete Course in Freshman
   Composition, Harper & Bros.   1951
Editorial Consultant,   The English Journal   XLI, 3:10-3:12 May, 1952

"Practical Helps for Teaching
Written Composition"

Figure 6. Wykoff's Personnel Record page 3

Three things are immediately striking about this document. First, it makes abundantly clear the ways in which digitized word-processing, which was not widely available until more than thirty years later, has made the creation and use of document templates easier and has resulted in more attractive and readable documents. Second, the format and design of the document, because of its inflexibility, provides some indication of the expectations for faculty lives and work at the time of its creation. The categories and their accompanying prompts provide us with some information about what kinds of work counted and what the expectations were for how extensive the work would be in each category. This is perhaps made most obvious by the inclusion of categories and information that are less likely to be included in similar records today, such as the three lines set aside for indicating names and dates of birth of children (see Figure 4), or four lines for describing graduate study in progress, or the four lines for listing dates of appointment to ranks subsequent to the rank of initial appointment at Purdue (see Figure 5).

Third, the way in which Wykoff's work is represented on this form allows us to see quite vividly the extent to which these expectations were inconsistent with Wykoff's record of achievement. For example, the five lines available for listing offices held and dates for "Membership in Professional and Honorary Societies" (see Figure 5) are wholly inadequate for listing the seventeen entries squeezed onto them, as are the five lines available for describing his participation in the nine meetings he lists having attended between 1948 and 1951 (see Figure 6). The inadequacy of the "Personnel Record" as a genre for conveying the significance of Wykoff's work to the composition studies profession is, however, perhaps most apparent in the entry for his remarks at the 1948 NCTE Convention session on "Required Freshman English," which are described simply as "National Council of Teachers of English: Chicago, 1948, gave a paper" (see Figure 6). Similarly, the form's design forces Wykoff's intellectual work as a writing program administrator to be reduced to the brief entry "Chairman of English I since 1933 or 1934" (eighteen or nineteen years), a characterization that would be no more elaborate or explanatory than the companion entry "Committee on Superior Students, 1 yr." (see Figure 5) if he had not added parenthetically "(see last sheet)." The "last sheet" to which he refers (see Figure 6) lists Wykoff's attendance and presentations at professional meetings and his publications since 1945 (he refers his reader to another document listing publications previous to 1945, the year of his promotion to full professor). With this gesture, Wykoff indicates that an account of his record of achievement as Chairman of English I can be read in his participation in and leadership of state and national professional organizations and in his publications, in which he describes writing program-based research, argues for various pedagogical approaches, and addresses intra-institutional and cross-institutional issues in teaching writing.

I have focused here on the description of two of Wykoff's professional achievements in two document genres intended to allow academic professionals to represent their professional life's work. Both achievements are exceptionally significant, though different: one is a speech (conference presentation) that took perhaps only twenty minutes to make, the other is an effort expended over two decades; one took place in the context of a national organization, the other evolved in the context of the local institution; one is well-documented in easily accessible and widely disseminated records, the other is left to speculation. Both genres—the *c.v.* and the personnel record—radically constrained Wykoff's representation of his achievements.

Representing WPA Work

Half a century later, writing program administrators face many of the same difficulties Wykoff faced in representing their intellectual work in the genres available to them. Thanks to digitized word-processing, we no longer need to use index cards to be able to periodically update our *c.v.*'s, and templates for the local institution's personnel records can be considerably more flexible. However, we are still hampered in our attempts to accurately and adequately and rhetorically describe our administrative work in the conventional genres for academic self-representation. Like George Wykoff a half-century ago, we have to devise and develop every available means of presenting, representing, and documenting the outcomes of our intellectual work as WPAs.

Several new means for doing so have been or are being developed. Christine Hult has offered WPAs some recommendations for preparing administrative portfolios in her chapter "The Scholarship of Administration" (128-29). Jeanne Gunner has discussed ways she found to break free of some of these limits in preparing her materials for consideration for tenure and promotion in her chapter "Professional

Advancement of the WPA: Rhetoric and Politics in Tenure and Promotion" in Irene Ward and William Carpenter's *Allyn and Bacon Sourcebook for Writing Program Administrators*. Jeanne Gunner and Irwin Weiser also presented a workshop, "The Intellectual Work of the WPA: A Workshop on Publication, Professional Issues, and Self-Representation," that addressed these issues at the 2002 CCCC in Chicago. The next step for WPAs must be to develop a shared set of conventions for describing various aspects of their work so that its character and qualities can be more accurately and extensively distinguished by creators of academic autobiographies and more easily interpreted by their readers.

These efforts must be supported by attention to documenting and archiving WPA work. Additional venues for publishing accounts of writing-program-based inquiry are needed. Individual writing programs can create websites that describe their programs; but they also need to establish more conventional program archives in which the work described can be documented. Collectively, WPAs need to develop databases in which this documentation can be stored for access by users outside the local institution. To some extent, the archives of the WPA listserv already provide an easily accessible repository of information about writing program administrators' work, but this information has not been collected systematically, nor has it been provided in a standardized format. If we recognize the agency we exercise each time we document our programs and the range of choices open to us on each occasion when we describe our administrative work in them, we can craft WPA narratives that represent the complexity and significance of writing program administrators' intellectual work.

Addendum: When I began teaching in the English Department at Purdue in August of 1994, George Wykoff, who had by then been retired from the department for 27 years, was still living in West Lafayette. He died in December of 1994, and his papers were destroyed. When, in 1995, I became director of the first-year composition program he had directed for 34 years, the traces of his work as a WPA in that program were invisible to me, and I didn't learn of his work at Purdue or for NCTE and CCCC until I began a historical research project on *CCC* in 1997. If he had never documented his intellectual work as a WPA in published essays and reports, it would have remained invisible and lost to our discipline's history.

Notes

1. One of the individual entries includes more than one publication, providing a catch-all descriptor: "Other contributions to *School and Soc[iety], The Nation, Survey-Graphic, Engineers and Engineering*; and about twenty in some of the smaller poetry magazines."

2. Since this was a full six years after Wykoff's promotion to full professor, this document is clearly not a confidential record created for consideration for a personnel action. It is more likely to be a record created for the information of the new department head, Bariss Mills, who had been at the University of Denver before being appointed English department head at Purdue in 1950.

Works Cited

Bartholomae, David. "Freshman English, Composition, and CCCC." *CCC* 40.1 (Feb 1989): 38-50.

Bishop, Wendy, and Gay Lynn Crossley. "How to Tell a Story of Stopping: The Complexities of Narrating a WPA's Experience." *WPA: Writing Program Administration* 19.3 (1996): 70-79.

"The Chicago Convention." *College English* (Feb 1949): 283-87.

George, Diana, ed. *Kitchen Cooks, Plate Twirlers and Troubadours: Writing Program Administrators Tell Their Stories*. Portsmouth, NH: Heinemann-Boynton/Cook, 1999.

Gerber, John. "CCCC Facts—1956." *CCC* 7.3 (Oct. 1956): 117-20.

—. "Three Year History of the CCCC." *CCC* (Oct. 1952): 17-18.

Gunner, Jeanne. "Professional Advancement of the WPA: Rhetoric and Politics in Tenure and Promotion." *Allyn and Bacon Sourcebook for Writing Program Administrators*. Ed. Irene Ward and William Carpenter. New York: Longman, 2002. 315-30.

Hult, Christine A. "The Scholarship of Administration." *Resituating Writing: Constructing and Administering Writing Programs*. Ed. Joseph Janangelo and Kristine Hansen. Portsmouth, NH: Boynton/Cook, 1995. 119-31.

Phelps, Louise Wetherbee. "Intersubjective Autobiography: Form(ulat)ing Professional Identity in Institutional and Research Writing." Conference on Writing as a Human Activity, University of California, Santa Barbara, Oct. 2001.

Weiser, Irwin, and Jeanne Gunner. "The Intellectual Work of the WPA: A Workshop on Publication, Professional Issues, and Self-Representation." Workshop presented at CCCC, Chicago, March 20-23, 2002.

Wykoff, George. "A Possible Source of Browning's 'Saul.'" *Philological Q.*, 7 (1928): 311-14.

—. "Wykoff File." Purdue University English Department Archives.

—. "Toward Achieving the Objectives of Freshman Composition." *College English* 10.6 (March 1949): 319-23.

11

Industrial-Strength Composition and the Impact of Load on Teaching

John Heyda

Imagine this scenario. You are a veteran compositionist, well versed in the succession of curricular changes that have transformed the first-year course over the last quarter century. You have been asked by your department chair to take on the responsibility of directing first-year writing at your university and have agreed to do so, though you suspect that the pressing problems facing your program may be all but impossible to solve. A recent university review of the program has exposed a startling lack of uniformity in course content across sections, potentially rancorous conflict over curricular aims, and a growing sense of faculty alienation from the program itself. Views on how the composition program could have hit such a rough patch have run the gamut, but have a predictability about them all the same. For some, the problems are due to spending too much time on readings and discussion at the expense of writing instruction. For others, the lack of consensus on required types of writing have produced a hodgepodge of approaches, making coherent presentation of course objectives impossible. Other predictable views blame everything from the abandonment of grammar instruction to permitting students to revise their papers.

Your own experience with first-year writing has led you to another, more radical view. For you, problems with the first-year course stem from adding too much new work to the course while leaving unexamined the definitions of load regulating such work. Too often, you have seen new classroom activities and teaching tasks only partially supplant those they have replaced, so that teachers find themselves with more tasks and less time to do any of them well. You began teaching the course when it was better known as freshman English, at a time when the five-paragraph theme, the modes of discourse, and "writing with a thesis" reigned supreme. This version of the course had its own tightly regulated economy and, while time consuming enough to teach, was sufficiently insulated from the rest of the curriculum that the workload involved had become both manageable and predictable. When writing-as-process and "write to learn" pedagogies emerged in the 1970s and 1980s, however, the first of a series of new demands began to crowd first-year writing's already well-packed curricular space. Teachers scrambled to make room for workshops, for reading and discussing student writing, for working on prewriting and revision. By the early 1990s, new emphases on reading and responding to difficult texts (and not just other students' writing) built new layers of work into the course. More recently, university-wide initiatives have made their own demands. At your school, for instance, the first-year course now has to serve not only as the university-wide required writing course, but also as the foundation course for liberal education, as a seminar showcasing active learning, critical thinking, and group work. In short, while much more has come to be expected of composition instructors, little if any consideration has been given to whether their load assignments could support the additional work expected of them. Instead, thinking about load has remained locked in an inflexible, industrial-era mindset, seemingly impervious to change.

In your first weeks as director of the first-year program, you meet with the department chair, the dean, even the provost. At these sessions you zero in on the workload issue in presenting your analysis of composition's problems. You argue that the program cannot hope to tackle its many problems without restructuring first-year writing and that such changes must address the load issue in teaching first-year writing. You recommend either increasing student credit hours for the course from three hours to four or redesigning the course's structure so that more than one teacher is involved in the delivery of instruction. As you envision it, your latter recommendation would entail one teacher preparing course materials, organizing lessons plans, and leading class discussions, while the other would preside over in-class workshops, read and respond to student writing, and conduct individual student conferences. The administrators you talk to are quick to rule out any

Industrial-Strength Composition

such changes. Adding a credit hour to the course would involve increasing adjunct faculty pay by 33 percent and might also mean reducing the number of courses faculty would have to teach per semester or year. A redesign of the course to include more than one instructor per section would require a comparable outlay of funds, with the additional problem that graduate student instructors would lose the classroom autonomy they have with the long-standing one-instructor-per-section system.

In the end, the administrators are impressed by both your analysis and your recommendations, but find no pressing need to act in response to them. At no point in these meetings do you sense that your way of defining load, in terms of manifold and increasing numbers of tasks, has carried any weight whatever. Instead, the administrators return, again and again, to far simpler definitions of load, chief among them students taught per section, sections taught per semester. In the end, you realize that you will find no traction on the workload issue by pushing for a more complex understanding of load. Only later do you realize that the simpler definitions with which you were bombarded have held sway in composition for nearly a hundred years.

Massive "Delivery Systems"

In "Around 1971: Current-Traditional Rhetoric and Process Models of Composing," Sharon Crowley argues that, contrary to claims made in popular histories of writing instruction, "composition teachers' adoption of process-oriented teaching strategies did not amount to a paradigm shift." She contends that adopting "a process orientation did not challenge us to alter the epistemological and rhetorical assumptions we bring to our teaching." Furthermore, the advent of process models did not, as she puts it, "stimulate us to rethink the huge institutional apparatus within which composition instruction is delivered" (65).

Crowley's essay focuses, for the most part, on the first of these concerns, the failure of process pedagogies to put much of a dent in the epistemological and rhetorical assumptions of current-traditional teaching. She does have this to say, however, regarding the concomitant failure to re-examine the workings of composition's massive "delivery systems":

> As it was conceived during the 1950s, process-oriented instruction was to be adapted to the compos-

> ing needs of individuals or small groups of students working in laboratory settings. Its more widespread advocacy during the 1960s and 1970s, then, presented teachers with a clear opportunity to rethink what one of its early proponents called "mass methods" of instruction. By 1967, however, process-oriented techniques had already been appropriated into new editions of current-traditional textbooks prepared for the mass market. (65)

What might account for this failure to rethink "mass methods" of instruction at so crucial a juncture in composition's postwar history? If process pedagogies required "small groups [. . .] working in laboratory settings," why didn't this spur more of a push for an overhaul of composition's massive "delivery systems"? One explanation for such setbacks resides in the untold story of composition's failing, for decades, to rethink teaching load issues. This failure all but eliminated hopes of significant curricular reform long before the establishment of fully professionalized administration of writing programs. Composition had been losing ground on teaching load issues for years in ways that made such concerns nearly invisible by the 1960s and forgotten by the time of the formation of the Council of Writing Program Administrators in the mid 1970s. The impact of load on teaching had become harder to determine as well, as the gap widened between the institutional support that maturing composition programs needed and the actual support they received. By the 1960s, this gap had widened to the point that first-year writing had become something more like "industrial-strength" composition, designed for heavy teaching loads and in ways that made it all but invulnerable to pedagogical rethinking from within or institutional reform from without.

To address the question of why composition has failed to "rethink the huge institutional apparatus within which composition instruction is delivered," histories of the administration of first-year writing programs need to relate the untold stories of long lost teaching-load battles and the subsequent emergence of an industrialized composition impervious to any further attempts to revive load as an issue. To do so will require extended consideration of the role definitions of load have played in the establishment of an all but impregnable Fortress Composition, a bastion that remains largely intact today. To tell this untold story of wrangles over load and the long-term consequences of such battles for teaching, I must begin with Crowley's charge that "adoption of process-oriented teaching strategies did not amount to a paradigm shift." I begin there in order to suggest that the defeat of the laboratory-course concept early in the twentieth century proved crucial in thwarting later efforts at putting composition loads on a more equitable footing with other courses. While composition's place within the academy may be ever changing, definitions of the workload involved in teaching the course have proved quite resistant to change. Contemporary writing program administration has yet to challenge this legacy of defeat bequeathed to program directors by composition's pre-WPA history. My hope is that the tale I relate here will help in mounting a much-needed challenge to the status quo.

A Laboratory Model for Composition

Industrial-Strength Composition was a long time in the making. In the early years of the last century, when the matter of working conditions for writing teachers first reached critical mass, composition was far more susceptible to challenge on load issues. Teaching loads were outrageous, "hells of overwork" to borrow Robert Connors's phrase. So exposed was composition in the matter of teaching loads that early complaints could take on, as their main concern, the damage heavy loads could do to the individual teacher, with the harm done ranging from lowered morale to physical breakdown. Leonard Greenbaum's memorable late 1960s *College English* broadside, "The Tradition of Complaint," catalogs some of these early studies of the workload issue. He cites, for instance, NCTE's "Preliminary Report on English Composition Teaching," published in 1911, which offers the following "summary points":

> Summary Point 7—"Long continued criticism and correcting of manuscript is one of the *severest tests of physical endurance* to be found in any teaching, and the limit of full and continued efficiency in it is about two hours a day or ten hours a week. Much more than this results sooner or later in the *physical collapse of the teacher*."
>
> Summary Point 9—"To train this number of pupils" [in colleges at this time about 105, the average

number assigned to a single teacher] "according to a proper standard of efficiency would require of each teacher, for manuscript reading alone [. . .] in colleges 31 hours weekly; or *two and one-half times the safe limit of physical endurance*."

Summary Point 11—"Under the average of existing conditions it is a physical impossibility, by any 'method' whatever, for any English composition teacher to bring his work to a proper standard of efficiency." (176)

Greenbaum's catalog also refers to the very first issue of *English Journal*, published a year later in 1912, which featured as its lead article E. M. Hopkins's "Can Good Composition Teaching Be Done Under Present Conditions?" Hopkins's answer is a resounding "no." He writes that, "Every year teachers resign, break down, perhaps become permanently invalided, having sacrificed ambition, health, and in not a few instances even *life*, in the struggle to do all the work expected of them" (176).

Greenbaum's essay presents his "tradition of complaint" in a way that isolates the issue of load. To do so serves his purpose, which is to show that freshman English has been far more trouble than it has been worth, "a luxury that consumes time, money, and [. . .] intelligence" (187). Had he been more sympathetic to the plight of composition teachers, however, he might have presented the work of these early "complainers" in a fairer light. In the case of Hopkins, for instance, he might have included the following, which puts the issue of load in a more compelling context. Hopkins writes,

> Not very many years ago, when effort was made to apply the principle that pupils should learn to write by writing, English composition, previously known as rhetoric, became ostensibly a laboratory subject, but without any material addition to the personnel of its teaching force; there was merely a gratuitous increase in the labor of teachers who were already doing full duty.

Hopkins adds:

> Probably no other laboratory subject has ever been introduced into any school till space enough and apparatus enough and teachers enough had been provided to insure each pupil that degree of individual attention necessary to his individual development. But the laboratory teaching of English during all these years has had so little provision made for it that it has been, for the most part, little more than a travesty. (2)

Hopkins hoped to show that composition teachers needed both reduced teaching loads and additional institutional support for the laboratory teaching expected of them. In order to provide the needed support, reform would have to acknowledge that matters of load involved more than just too many students per class. It also involved teachers having taken on, as an extra unpaid burden, the provision of a laboratory teaching of writing made all the worse for its going on unacknowledged.

Hopkins hoped, too, to employ his expanded definition of load to win support for laboratory teaching based on an analysis of labor and equipment costs for a range of subjects. In a questionnaire accompanying the *English Journal* article, Hopkins asks readers to help him determine the cost of English work by providing information on "total weekly labor of teachers [. . .] in hours" for subjects such as English, math, physics, chemistry, even domestic science and manual training. Labor is broken down into categories such as recitations, laboratory, consultation, themes and exercises, exams and reports, and preparation for classes. It is not difficult to see where Hopkins was going with this questionnaire. His aim had to be to win statistical support for what he already knew, namely that load had to be defined as a good bit more than just students per teacher or sections per semester if composition were to do the job the public expected of it.

Now known as the Hopkins Report, Hopkins's findings provide, as Connors describes it, "a shocking indictment of the conditions and labor involved in teaching college composition" ("Rhetoric" 71). His study did not succeed, though, in redefining definitions of load. Nor did it give rise to the development of alternate models for organizing composition's delivery systems. One might imagine, for instance, a minimal reform in response to Hopkins's work, whereby one teacher would have the responsibility of preparing and presenting class lessons, writing assignments and exercises, and another teacher the tasks of handling recitation and consultation sessions, and reading and grading themes and exams. Even so rudimentary a division of labor as this could make no system-wide headway, however, given the overriding preoccupation with making the delivery system for first-year writing as efficient and cost-effective as possible.

J. R. Rutland's "Tendencies in the Administration of Freshman English," published in *English Journal* in 1923, offers ample evidence of how obdurate the thinking on delivery-system issues had become and would remain. It shows, too, how little impact Hopkins's study had had on administrators' thinking in the decade following his report's appearance in *English Journal*. Citing evidence of "great progress," Rutland writes that

> Slowly, in the face of financial stringency and sometimes administrative neglect, the size of Freshman English sections is becoming what it should be. Most teachers agree that sections should be small enough for the instructor to read all papers assigned and to confer personally with his students at regular intervals. (6)

Reporting on the results of a questionnaire sent out during the 1920-21 school year, Rutland notes that

> One university [. . .] reports that instructors have an average of 300 clock-hours weekly, including conference periods, not more than four sections of from twenty to thirty students, and never more than a total of one hundred students. A technical institution reports that four or five sections of from twenty to twenty-five students are assigned to each instructor. Such is the efficiency of the better organized departments of English. (6-7)

If Rutland had any interest in rethinking load issues, given the manifold instructional tasks Hopkins had identified, it does not show here. Instead, Rutland is content to define load in terms of the industrial categories of hours per week, students per section and per semester. Rutland is not interested in thinking about composition in terms of the very different type of load its teaching entails. For this, Hopkins might be held partly responsible. Hopkins had thought that a laboratory teaching of freshman English should require a delivery system comparable to those already developed for other laboratory-based courses of study. Sadly, though, his *English Journal* study makes the case for the laboratory model he envisions, without advocating, at the same time, for the new pedagogy requiring added support. He had hoped, instead, to rely on feedback collected from composition teachers regarding the many tasks that made up their loads in order to show that these tasks covered much the same territory as the many other laboratory courses across the curriculum. Hopkins hoped data from his questionnaire would demonstrate empirically what had yet to be established politically, namely that first-year writing instruction involved enough work for its teachers, and in sufficiently varied forms, to warrant backing it as a laboratory course. What he failed to recognize was that, in pursuing such a course of action, he was bound to play up similarities between teaching composition and other laboratory courses rather than articulating the differences that set pedagogy in composition apart from all other courses.

By the late 1930s, another contributor to the Leonard Greenbaum genre of complaint, Oscar Campbell, felt emboldened to take on the load issue, and from an entirely different vantage point. In his famous article, "The Failure of Freshman English," which called for "the abolition of the conventional course in Freshman English," Campbell sees the issue not as the conditions under which writing instructors must labor, but the threat such conditions pose to teachers outside that "queer, unreal world half filled with punctuation marks." His fear was that morale problems in freshman English could spread beyond the confines of composition:

> For the vast majority of those who begin their careers as section hands in Freshman English there is no future in the profession. They cannot hope for even moderate academic promotion. [. . .] I know of large departments of English in which no one has been promoted from an instructorship to an assistant professorship for over ten years. [. . .] This process is natural—yes, inevitable—because the work of a Freshman English instructor does not fit him for the teaching of literature. So at the bottom of almost every large English department lies a kind of morass

> of unhappy, disillusioned men and women which poisons all its fairer regions. (181-82)

Concern for the morale of teachers is a bit of an issue for Campbell, but his main worry is for teachers of literature in large English departments. What will happen to their morale, Campbell wants to know, when "much of the time and energy of professors in such departments is devoted to cajoling and disciplining the Freshman English staff?" (182). Lost in the shuffle, by this point, is any moral dimension to the workload issue. What would be a fair teaching load for a full-time teacher of college composition in the large English department or elsewhere? Given the type of work involved, what would be equitable? Campbell has no interest in such questions, of course; in fact, he makes no mention of teaching loads whatever. The best he can manage is a single reference to "the harried instructor in Freshman English, who labors valiantly to accomplish the impossible, and who meekly submits to serving as the vicarious sacrifice for all the sins of all the other departments in college" (181). If Campbell cared about what heavy loads were doing to composition teachers, he did not say so here. He had other concerns. With Campbell, issues of load in composition were twisted and put to political uses, with the harm composition does redefined in terms of damage to the institution (the department, the literature program) rather than to the individual teacher, the huge cadre of college writing teachers, or the course's standing with the public. For Campbell,

> the most serious of all the objections to this composition course is that it obscures for everyone concerned the extremely important service that English literature, as one of the still living humanities, must render to college students. [. . .] If we allow our colleagues to continue in their conviction that we are mere grammarians, [. . .] what hope is there that anyone will listen to the important message that now, as never before, we must iterate and reiterate. (182)

Campbell's referring to composition teachers as "mere grammarians" says a great deal about how damaging the failure to establish the laboratory model had been for first-year writing. Over a quarter of a century before, Hopkins could invoke "the principle that pupils should learn to write by writing," in declaring composition "ostensibly a laboratory subject." Clearly, though, by the time of Campbell's call for composition's abolition, such an alternative was no longer in the cards. What had happened to the laboratory model for composition and what lessons, administrative and otherwise, might we draw today from its demise?

The Only Course Required of All Students

The industrialization of composition in the decades leading up to the eve of World War II and Campbell's "The Failure of Freshman English" owed a great deal to a relentless, decades-long boom in undergraduate enrollments nationwide. Contemporary historians of composition have made much of the destabilizing surge in enrollments in the post-World War II era, but these increases are nothing in comparison to those of the 1870-1940 period. Consider that, in 1870, 52,000 students were enrolled in U.S. institutions of higher education; a decade later, the figure had risen to 116,000, a stunning 131 percent increase in ten years time. The decade of the 1880s saw its own 35 percent increase, the 1890s a 52 percent boost, the new century's first decade a 49 percent jump, and the years 1910-20 a 68 percent increase. By 1920, no less than 598,000 students were enrolled nationwide. The 1920s decade sent this total soaring above one million thanks to an 84 percent increase for that roaring decade, producing a 1,101,000 total by 1930. The depression of the 1930s slowed the staggering growth rate, but that dark decade still saw its own 36 percent increase, bringing the nationwide total to 1,494,000 by 1940 ("Enrollment"). Confronted with this endless surge, it is easy to see how a shell-shocked composition could wind up in the state Campbell so decried. Still, enrollment increases alone cannot fully explain the sorry delivery system into which composition had evolved.

How did increases at the national level make their presence felt at individual institutions? In *Composition-Rhetoric*, Robert Connors notes that "the average size of the freshman class at Harvard was over two hundred students by 1870, and by 1903 it had grown to more than six hundred." Connors adds that "even in smaller institutions growth was the rule, and by 1900 the enrollment of all of the most important state universities and nearly all of the influential Ivies was above a thousand students" (190-91). Connors relates, as well, something of what these increases meant for individual instructors and programs:

> At Harvard in 1892, Barrett Wendell read daily and fortnightly themes from 170 students—over 24,000 papers each year. At Yale, one professor and one instructor were responsible for 250 composition students; the same was true at Iowa. At Wellesley, one professor and three assistants taught 600 students. At Minnesota, one professor and three assistants taught 800 students in the Department of Rhetoric. (191)

It is not until the aforementioned Hopkins Report appears that we get data on teaching loads of more than anecdotal interest. Data from the Hopkins committee drew upon "surveys [. . .] completed by over six hundred teachers" that "represented around 20 percent of all American colleges." These surveys revealed that "the average number of composition students assigned to a teacher was 105, and that to read all of their students' work, writing teachers would need to spend thirty hours each week on theme-reading alone." These figures stand in sharp contrast to the Hopkins committee's "calculations about upper limits of the students that teachers could effectively teach. Even with the most optimistic view of paper-reading skills, the calculations indicated that 61 writing students per teacher was the upper limit" (192).

Compounding these problems was the rise of a new curriculum built around electives, which had swept away all required courses—all, that is, but first-year writing. Connors notes that "by 1897 the only required course at Harvard for any student was English A, Freshman Composition." As a consequence, "the structure of [. . .] the freshman composition course [. . .] seemed to hark back to the whole-class-based college curriculum" with "a few professors teaching a limited range of courses to entire college classes" (190). Locking the freshman course into the atavistic delivery system of the old whole-class curriculum would prove disastrous for writing instruction, tying it irrevocably to the cloistered world of higher education prior to the Civil War. Richard Ohmann's "Universities and Industrial Culture," in *English in America*, puts into historical perspective the yawning gap opened up between the pre-industrial collegiate system from which composition would struggle to extricate itself and the new industrialized system through which the course would be so cruelly exploited. Of the pre-industrial academy, Ohmann notes that "it is an odd and significant fact that between 1825 and 1875, while the population of the country was rapidly growing and its industry burgeoning, the number of students attending colleges and universities in America remained almost constant." Contrast the explosive increases over the 1870-1940 stretch: Ohmann writes "in the 1870s, at the end of this period of declining importance, enrollment at twenty of the most prestigious colleges rose only 3.5% as against a population growth in the nation of 23%" (282). Elsewhere, Ohmann observes that

> for the fifty years before 1875, universities which were becoming increasingly irrelevant in the American economy, declined in strength and importance. When, for many reasons, universities did begin to produce the kind of education and the kind of new knowledge that society could use, they flourished. This change took place quite rapidly. By 1900, universities were geared for the practical affairs of American society. (290)

In Ohmann's account, English departments became "full participants in the development of the new American university, sharing its growth, its prosperity." Crucially, however, "it was freshman English that university faculties, then as now, wanted from English professors—enough to make it a requirement." Ohmann adds, tellingly, that "this meant that English departments would grow along with the university as long as they staffed freshman English, almost regardless of their success or failure in teaching the subject" (301).

If, as Ohmann suggests, English departments' chief interest in composition would center on the staffing of its innumerable sections, this could not be good news for administrators hoping to explore alternative delivery systems for the course. The story of English departments' active participation in locking composition teachers into impossibly heavy teaching loads is well enough documented that it need not be rehearsed here. According to this by now familiar tale, English departments had plenty of motivation to impose a strict efficiency model on the staffing of an industrialized composition requirement, squeezing as much out of the arrangement as possible. As William Riley Parker notes in his influential account, "Where Do English Departments Come From?" teaching freshman English "quickly entrenched English departments in the college and university structure" (347). Warner Rice sees much the same outcome, observing that "Freshman English courses, being required, bring large enrollments—and numbers mean power" (363). There is, however, another, not so familiar story regarding English departments' taking advantage of composition's status as the only course required of all students. That story holds composition more accountable for its failing to rethink the load issue and its impact on teaching.

Thanks in no small part to Connors's *Composition-Rhetoric*, we know a good deal about how beleaguered composition teachers learned to cut pedagogical corners in order to cope with their heavy teaching loads. Connors helps, as well, in showing how this corner cutting only hastened first-year writing's embrace of grammar and mechanical correctness and its retreat from rhetoric, all but sealing composition's reputation as an intellectually indefensible course. These effects of load on teaching are well known. What is not as well known is how the push to establish composition as a laboratory course only succeeded in compounding problems of load. Connors has shown that the concept of composition as a laboratory course arose in the last quarter of the nineteenth century, at a time when writing instruction was undergoing dramatic changes. He notes that one major change involved "encouragement of student self-expression" and a move "toward more individualized contact between teacher and student." In this regard, Connors cites Frances Lewis's observation, in 1902, that "courses in rhetoric deal largely in practice in self-expression, and the class-room work, once entirely recitation from a text-book, is now often on the laboratory plan." As a consequence, Connors observes, "the rise of 'laboratory work' in composition, while pedagogically productive, meant a completely different set of demands were being placed on teachers." He adds that

> Writing [. . .] was easily seen to demand by its nature an essentially individualized pedagogy. Writing is an interior activity, and although techniques can be used to share writing among students, a primary transaction in any serious composition course came to be seen as being between the student and the teacher. Each student came to be seen as deserving a measurable individual chunk of the teacher's time and energy. [. . .] This inescapable time demand came from the best-known teachers and schools in America, and the related inability of teachers and administrators to grasp its meaning in a changing college environment

led to the nightmare of overwork that composition courses became. (188)

The laboratory course wasn't the only one to emerge in the years following the Civil War. Connors cites Lawrence Veysey's observation, in *The Emergence of the American University*, that "after 1870 three basic types of instruction came to prominence: the laboratory, the lecture, and the seminar." About these newly prominent types of instruction, Connors observes that

> the laboratory was conceived as a specialized scientific instructional form, and the labor-intensive seminar [. . .] was usually reserved for upper-class and graduate students. This left the lecture-sized section as the main choice for most freshman and sophomore courses. (140)

As it turned out, the drive to establish composition as a laboratory course was misguided in at least a couple of ways. In pushing for the lab model, composition teachers assumed that their workloads could be divided up along lines already drawn up for science courses. But would such divisions adequately capture the complexity of instruction in writing? What would become of the manifold tasks not designated for lab work? Would the non-lab portion of teachers' loads require lecturing as in the sciences?

Unresolved questions didn't stop composition teachers from pursuing lab-course status. Connors notes that "some schools were wealthy enough or had prestigious enough faculty members that their writing courses were taught as 'laboratory' courses. John Genung at Amherst was the most obvious leader of this movement." Connors adds that "these first lab-type courses were not much different from regular classes except in their numbers (Henry Frink, the freshman teacher at Amherst, had five assistants for a class of 110 students)." Numbers were crucial, though, so much so "that a movement in favor of composition as 'laboratory work' became very vocal and had by 1900 gained some power" (194).

Another way in which the pursuit of lab-course status proved misguided involves its misreading of higher education's altered instructional landscape. The laboratory course was a product of the emerging university of specialized courses of study and new, scientific knowledge. The last thing it was designed for was to serve as a model for the one course all first-year students had to take. Clearly, the road not taken here was the labor-intensive seminar which, with hindsight, appears only too well suited to learning in composition, where students had come "to be seen as deserving a measurable individual chunk of the teacher's time and energy."

It is easy now, of course, to point out what composition should have done differently in raising load issues so many years ago. Pursuit of lab-course status might have made sense at the time, at least at schools where assigning multiple assistants to individual sections could lighten paper-reading loads. Too many schools lacked such resources, however, so that composition-as-laboratory-course could never gain the ascendancy. In all likelihood, pursuit of the seminar model would have failed as well, but it could have offered a better alternative for reform-minded composition teachers. It is odd that, as Connors notes, "seminar-type writing courses seem never to have been considered" (194). Even if the labor-intensive seminar had been deemed inappropriate for a universally required course, it would have at least had the benefit of providing a potential venue for the more interactive, recursive aspects of learning in composition. Targeting the seminar model could also have helped draw attention to the gap between the range and amounts of work required of successful composition teaching and what little teachers were able to accomplish. Thus, composition could have set out its stall early on as a distinctly different sort of course, with its own unique workload requirements rather than wedging such requirements into a lab-course model. Had it done so, workload definitions might have been enriched and made more complicated over time, rather than left to rigidify in the simplified categories we know today.

More to the point, though, is that the pursuit of laboratory course status exposed a decided lack of inventiveness on composition's part. To this day, this same lack plagues our understanding of load. We have yet to develop the innovative thinking required to link workload realities to serious pursuit of an optimal delivery system. Throughout its history, composition has been entirely too willing to accept categories of delivery better suited to other courses of study—the lab, the lecture, the seminar—rather than venturing forth and creating its own model.

Postwar Consequences

Greenbaum suggests that, if World War II not intervened, Oscar Campbell might have seen his vision of English departments without composition realized. "But the year is 1939," he writes, "the closing year of the Depression, the beginning year of World War II. Other, heavier matters soon press on universities" (178). What Greenbaum might have added, though, is that the twist Campbell gives to the matter of composition teacher morale did survive the war and was put to any number of uses in the postwar years. Fortress Composition's foundation was now securely in place.

If initiatives aimed at bringing about more equitable teaching loads for composition teachers had fallen woefully short of their goals prior to World War II, they stood no better chance in the years after the war. Dramatic enrollment increases in the immediate postwar years made talk of reduced loads or smaller classes unimaginable; if anything, administrative priorities returned again to finding enough qualified teachers to meet the increased demand for entry-level courses. Just how dramatic the increases were during this period is borne out by figures Berlin provides in *Rhetoric and Reality*. "In the 1939-40 school year, enrollment in American colleges and universities was 1,500,000. After shrinking to 800,000 in 1944-45, it jumped to 1,676,000 in 1945-46 and to a peak of 2,444,900 in 1949-50" (96).

It is during this same period, interestingly enough, that English departments had their best chance of freeing themselves of at least a part of their freshman English burden. Communications courses, which had first appeared as part of the general education movement in the 1930s, had progressed to the point where "by 1948, over two hundred colleges and universities had established these courses." Berlin describes such courses as "commonly interdepartmental," combining "writing instruction with lessons in speaking, in reading, and sometimes even in listening" (93). An "important common element," he notes, "was the commitment to teaching" these combined lessons "as a unified set of activities" (96).

To make a long story short, English faculty staved off the threat communications posed by challenging the communications movement's humanist credentials. To reestablish control over first-year courses, English had only to call upon composition's long-standing (but hopelessly underfunded) support for individual self-expression.

Soon enough, as Berlin notes, "English department members began to protest any method of teaching writing that was not based on the study of literature." And Berlin adds this: "If the department was to be saddled with the service course in writing, [. . .] it should at least organize the course around what it knew best—the literary text" (107-8). With individual self-expression recast as self-expression through literary study, the extra load teachers had long carried in order to support attention to individual students' needs could be presented as selfless commitment to the cause of the humanist English department. "In the forties and fifties," as Berlin observes, "literature was seen as serving the individual and acting as a safeguard against collectivist notions that might threaten the ideal of 'rugged individualism on the plane of the spirit' and, finally, on the plane of politics" (111).

Once the dust had settled in the late 1950s, a spate of surveys on load appeared. In these studies, the only definition of load on offer is the old students-per-teacher definition. In the December 1961 issue of *CCC*, "A Study of the Depressed Areas: A Survey of Class Size and Structure Among Freshman Composition Classes Throughout the Country" by William Holmes and Robert McDonnell reported that "we were surprised to find that the medial class size is as high as 25." They expressed surprise, too, that "several reputable schools reported average class sizes from 30 to 40 without indicating any alleviating circumstances such as a 9-hour instructor load, use of teaching or grading assistants or a special large-class program" (246). In 1968, NCTE offered "A Statement of Policy" on "The Workload of a College English Teacher" which concluded with seven recommendations, all but the last defining load in terms of hours ("no more than nine hours should be considered the standard load for college teachers of English"), preparations ("no college English teacher should be obligated to prepare more than three different courses during any academic semester"), or students per teacher ("no English teacher should teach more than 50 composition students"). The last recommendation rises ever so slightly above these most basic definitions of load, but is too vague to mean much. It reads, "Professional, scholarly, and institutional activities should be taken into account in determining teaching loads" (269). With load defined in such primitive terms, is it any wonder that composition failed to rethink its huge institutional apparatus? Is it so surprising that process pedagogies were so easily absorbed into current-traditional practice?

In "Composing English Studies: Toward a Social History of the Discipline," Richard Miller argues for "a vision of composition that places the field's special area of expertise in knowing how to solicit, read, and respond to student work." He proposes that "we reread the institutional history of English studies in light of the solicitation and treatment of student writing." As a first step, Miller suggests beginning with such questions as:

> How, over time, has the student been constructed by teachers of composition [. . .] ? What needs have been attributed to the student and how has the discipline seen fit to respond to those needs? What relationships exist between the kind of writing solicited from students and the theoretical and political commitments of their instructors? (174)

Miller's rereading of English studies' institutional history might address heavy teaching loads in composition as one of the institutional constraints shaping the solicitation and treatment of student writing. It is a history that needs writing, for it could show that an "industrial-strength" delivery system for teaching composition has been in force for some time, though largely invisible. Composition's resistance to reform may be attributable, in part, to our failing to make more visible the effects of this system on our soliciting and treatment of student writing.

I began this essay with a scenario meant to illustrate what can happen when a writing program director tries to bring workload concerns to the attention of higher-level administration. My intent was to show that program directors can be quite naive in imagining that composition's issues with load might carry much if any weight with top-level administrators these days. If anything, such matters appear, today, to be so settled as to be all but impossible to raise anew. Still, much is at stake for writing program directors struggling to re-engage workload issues with the ongoing work of curricular reform. For unless matters of load can be addressed in ways complicated enough to reflect a fuller accounting of the work that goes into teaching composition, first-year writing will continue to labor under constraints imposed by the decades-old industrial model described here.

First-year writing program directors must find ways to make the complications of load consequential and visible, not only for top administrators but for teachers of the course as well. At the very least, such work can help educate instructors in composition's contemporary history, providing them with the perspective needed to assess their work situations more critically. Teachers need to recognize, for instance, that the work of ongoing curricular revision cannot go much further without a thorough review of the impact of recent revisions on the teaching of the course. In this regard, analyses of the re-workings of curricula could show that much new work has been added to the course without, at the same time, any concomitant pruning away of outmoded practices. This development has hurt first-year writing, putting teachers in the position of having to do too many things. Confronted by so many new tasks, they have had to cut back on instruction in writing itself, threatening the integrity of the course. It may be time to conduct a new Hopkins Report, surveying "the cost of English work" in order to help capture the impact of load on teaching in the new century. Such a venture could succeed, too, in producing the data needed to educate higher-level administration in the complexities of today's load issues. We now know, of course, that the Hopkins Report was doomed to fail. Composition had no influence whatever in those days. Times have changed, though, and first-year writing programs are well-positioned now to make claims for what they need to succeed. As it is time, anyway, that program directors raise workload issues yet again, it may well be the moment to find out what clout composition can have today.

Works Cited

Berlin, James. *Rhetoric and Reality: Writing Instruction in American Colleges, 1900-1985.* Carbondale: Southern Illinois UP, 1987.

Campbell, Oscar James. "The Failure of Freshman English." *English Journal, College Edition* 28 (1939): 177-85.

Connors, Robert J. "Rhetoric in the Modern University: The Creation of an Underclass." *Politics of Writing Instruction: Postsecondary.* Ed. Richard Bullock and John Trimbur. Portsmouth, NH: Boynton/Cook, 1991. 55-84.

—. *Composition-Rhetoric: Backgrounds, Pedagogy, and Theory.* Pittsburgh: U of Pittsburgh P, 1997.

Crowley, Sharon. "Around 1971: Current-Traditional Rhetoric and Process Models of Composing." *Composition in the Twentieth Century: Crisis and Change.* Ed. Lynn Bloom, Donald A. Daiker, and Edward M. White. Carbondale: Southern Illinois UP, 1996. 64-74.

"Enrollment in Educational Institutions, by Level and by Control of Institution: 1869-70 to Fall 2006." n.d. *The Digest of Education Statistics 1996* Table 3. http://nces.ed.gov/pubs/d96/D96T003.html (27 Aug. 2003).

Greenbaum, Leonard. "The Tradition of Complaint." *College English* 31 (1969): 174-87.

Holmes, William J., Jr., and Robert F. McDonnell. "A Study of the Depressed Areas: A Survey of Class Size and Structure Among Freshman Composition Classes Throughout the Country." *CCC* 12 (1961): 242-46.

Hopkins, E. M. "Can Good Composition Teaching Be Done Under Present Conditions?" *English Journal* 1 (1912): 1-7.

Miller, Richard. "Composing English Studies: Toward a Social History of the Discipline." *CCC* 45 (1994): 164-79.

Ohmann, Richard. *English in America: A Radical View of the Profession.* New York: Oxford UP, 1976.

Parker, William Riley. "Where Do English Departments Come From?" *College English* 28 (1967): 339-51.

Rice, Warner G. "A Proposal for the Abolition of Freshman English, As It Is Now Commonly Taught, from the College Curriculum." *College English* 21 (1960): 361-67.

Rutland, J. R. "Tendencies in the Administration of Freshman English." *English Journal* 12 (1923): 1-9.

"The Workload of a College English Teacher: A Statement of Policy by the National Council of Teachers of English." *CCC* 19 (1968): 267-70.

Veysey, Lawrence. *Emergence of the American University.* Chicago: U of Chicago P, 1970.

12

Doomed to Repeat It?: A Needed Space for Critique in Historical Recovery

Jeanne Gunner

The project of recovering WPA histories is a significant development in the composition-rhetoric research agenda. It signals a growing awareness of the important role of WPA work in and for the larger field, and it reflects a growing research sophistication within WPA studies, a further step in the long struggle for professionalization. The archival research and resulting historical reconstructions by WPA scholars in this volume introduce formerly unavailable data and formerly unrecognized figures in WPA history. Up to this point, the dearth of archival material has led to a necessary gleaning of early WPA experience from the historical research of scholars such as John Brereton, Robert J. Connors, and James Berlin, whose texts focus on a history of composition studies, not on the writing program or writing program administrator. Thus I am writing at a peculiar moment in this recovery project: while the awareness of the complexity of WPA history is growing, few resources are available, and so I proceed with a more than usual sense of the provisional nature of my argument.

Simply put, my argument is this: historically, administrative needs produced the WPA position, and administrative tasks have defined it, from originary to contemporary times. The discourse of administration preceded the emergence of a body of disciplinary knowledge, and the WPA position thus has discursive roots that tie it to what today we consider the conservative ideologies of writing instruction through the modern era, carried out through administrative practices. The discourse and administrative formation of modern writing programs (which I date using Stephen North's old composition/new Composition categories) recapitulates this history, maintaining the division of administrative work and disciplinary knowledge, and so also maintaining the conservative agenda of writing programs by privileging professionalization over cultural engagement.

The historical evidence for these claims can be at times only interstitial, in that it derives from gaps in the composition histories that for the most part have ignored writing program administrators and administrative work. But I present the argument as one possible interpretive frame for an emerging WPA history because—even if in need of major correction, even if proved substantively wrong—it serves what I hope is a cautionary purpose. As we move forward with the valuable and necessary project of recovering WPA history/ies, we should remain mindful of cultural critiques of the position and its social functions, particularly as Susan Miller, John Trimbur, and Anne Ruggles Gere have articulated them. My concern is to maintain a critical perspective on and a contextualizing awareness of the role writing programs and WPAs have traditionally played in supporting hegemonic cultural practices, in order to ensure that this new historical move does not unintentionally reproduce the repressive practices of our earlier era and the accommodationist positions that have been part of the later period of professionalization. Reconstruction is an opportunity for critique; histories are interested rhetorical forms, and our work should include examination of whose interests are being served by them. Just as Robert Connors warned against the appeal of Decline and Fall narratives among those formulating composition histories, we should take care to resist what might be called Hail and Interpellate narratives: reconstructions that call into official existence WPAs and WPA histories without also invoking critique of the WPA's ideological functions. What I attempt here, then, is a (provisionally) critical argument about the origins of the WPA position, in order to keep in the foreground the kind of political issues that might accompany historical research on the WPA.

The WPA's Discursive Origins

In the major histories of composition studies appearing before 2000, we find very little data on the origins of a WPA-like position, creating an apparent absence of a WPA. Even in the first studies of writing programs, such as Connolly and Vilardi's 1986 work, *New Methods in College Writing Programs*, WPAs exist at best marginally, as background figures occasionally and tangentially referenced. As Barbara L'Eplattenier has argued, however, "[administrative histories] demonstrate that the work of writing program administration has existed as long as there have been institutions offering writing courses" (136). Reviewing a detailed description of one program's placement practices in Warner Taylor's 1929 study, *A National Survey of Conditions in Freshman English*, L'Eplattenier writes,

> Consider, for a moment, the [implicit] administrative tasks. [. . .] Someone had to create a writing prompt, administer the test, develop an evaluation schema, evaluate the responses or train the graders. [. . .] The size and structure of these programs suggests the need for a person who *acted* like a full-time writing program administrator, whether or not he or she was actually *named* WPA or its equivalent. (134)

Lacking self-descriptive WPA histories, we must find the originary WPA refracted through a set of administrative practices, coming into institutional existence as the product of a master administrative discourse. This discourse reflects a set of concerns, perceptions, policies, and values articulated by college administrators who were not necessarily themselves engaged in the teaching of writing. Instead, they were engaged in the cultural work of establishing standards and, as such, were always already more regulatory than reflective.

The implication we might draw is that the WPA is a kind of post-phenomenon, a position that came into existence *after*—after its duties had been identified, after the earliest conversations on the writing curriculum had begun. We can think of it as a later utterance in a chain of statements about literacy, writing, and writing instruction. The influential speakers in these conversations were primarily members of traditional English departments or upper administration. Following Berlin, Brereton, Connors, and other first-generation historians, we can say that the relevant conversation began in the nineteenth century with the perceived literacy crisis, when American prosperity demanded and increasingly depended on ever-growing numbers of professionals being supplied by the university system (Berlin, *Writing Instruction* 59-60), or, alternatively, when a breaching of class lines required some institutional response that would enable class-based differences (Miller, *Textual Carnivals* 47-56), or, in another, more recent formulation, when remediating writing became the means to institutional differentiation among universities, colleges, and high schools (Soliday 25-26). In any case, the inception of Subject A at Harvard established specific administrative responses to specific cultural pressures. As an administrative response, the WPA came into being in an already determined alliance with institutional values and presided over a set of curricular practices that Connors has described as "a sort of twilit underground. [. . .] Composition teaching [and, inferentially, writing program administration were] done, but [. . .] no real scholarship surrounded it [. . .] composition existed as a practice without a coherent theory" ("Writing" 52). Limited, as we always are, by the educational values and disciplinary knowledge of the time, the WPA position consisted to a large extent of what today is called composition's gatekeeping function: administering programs and procedures that helped constitute more and less worthy student groups measured against the privileged form of traditional academic discourse and standardizing a curriculum that reinforced this linguistic privileging. The construction of a hyper-administrative identity was the means by which the WPA position came into being. And the later discourse of WPA professionalization did not challenge the historical privileging of the position's administrative agenda.

What we see in the earliest period of writing program administration, then, is simple hegemonic process. Studies of figures such as Fred Newton Scott and Gertrude Buck certainly show that individual writing program administrators undertook the kind of scholarly research Connors notes as critically short in supply, and that some attempted to develop programs that constituted students as active, individual thinkers and writers. But the "lonely giant" ("Writing" 64), as Connors puts it, could not succeed against the structural forces of the institution:

> Philologists and literary specialists trained their own students to replace them, but rhetoricians did not possess the institutional structures to allow this. As

> the extremely active and respected transitional generations of composition generalists retired or died, they were not replaced. They were, instead, succeeded by the cadre of graduate assistants, low-level instructors, part-timers, and departmental fringe people who became the permanent composition underclass. ("Rhetoric" 65)

As this faculty labor hierarchy evolved, with composition teaching being handed down the ranks, administrative work also became hierarchized, and important matters like budget and hiring decisions, which first resided with the president and then later with the departmental chair, were soon, along with the established curriculum, themselves often handed down to a "course director."

This practice was continued in much the same form through the 1960s. Charles Moran documents one version in his autobiographical essay, "A Life in the Profession":

> [In graduate school] I taught Freshman English, as we all did, to pay the bills. We were told to teach writing and did what we could, but we inevitably bootlegged literature, bringing it into the "writing" class. [. . .] Running the program in the five years I was there were two "instructors": advanced and elderly graduate students who would themselves never get jobs at Brown or at the places we wanted to teach ourselves. From this directorate issued blue-dittoed syllabi and other apparatus that we made our own as best we could. (167)

Moran completed his PhD and moved on to the University of Massachusetts-Amherst; he continues,

> I remember now, though it did not seem remarkable at the time, that the Freshman Program was run by Arthur Williams, an embittered "terminal" Assistant Professor who thought so little of himself that when the Personnel Committee tried to promote him, he refused to be considered, saying that he was not qualified. (169)

Such a director embodies the "immature discipline" phase of our field, when directors "did, or appeared to be trying to do, what was asked of [them] without questioning those expectations" (Janangelo 16). The lowly status and yet *only* status of such WPAs came from their administrative role. Historically, then, the WPA's purpose is to embody administration, to be part of the program's ideological "apparatus."

The foregrounding of administration as an ideological tool that operates through the position is interestingly visible in the case of a leading WPA at the University of Minnesota who, in 1997, was summarily replaced by a colleague, an eighteenth-century literature scholar. Responding to exchanges on the subject on the WPA listserv, the new WPA reported that he was selected as the replacement because he had in the past chaired a review of the program and so "knew something about it"; that, "outside of the Comp specialists," he had "shown more concern and commitment to the program than anyone else"; and that he "care[d] deeply about its viability and so really want[ed] to direct it." His claims to legitimacy—and, clearly, the primary professional credential his institution sought—lay strictly in his "service" orientation. (In a perhaps more opportunistic vein, some English departments appoint as WPA colleagues who are otherwise perceived as unproductive—what we might call the "dead wood" credential, the making of lemonade out of faculty lemons.) Like UCLA's line of acting directors I described in "Decentering the WPA," the Minnesota position is a re-enactment of the original administrative conception of the WPA, a "someone" who takes on the duties of a program, and then, having served the time, moves on to collect some reward. And atavistic though it may seem in our conception of the position, such use of it remains a common current practice because it satisfies the position's ideological purpose.

Stephen North uses Albert Kitzhaber's 1963 CCCC conference presentation on freshman English as a means of dating the end of "old composition" and the rise of "new Composition," a historical division that helps illustrate how the "modern" period of WPA history, the era of professionalization, nevertheless maintained its ties to an administrative ontology. In this period, we see the repetition of the nineteenth-century composition experience: the sense of lost standards; the perceived need for remedial courses; the (re)imposition of the first-year writing course requirement, which in the 1960s had in many places been discontinued; the (re)discovery by "regular" faculty of the writing course's oppressive work load and the time demands of administering a writing program; and the growth of writing programs and WPAs.

What is new—"modern"—is the founding of a professional organization. The Council of Writing Program Administrators was formed, in Ken Bruffee's recollection, in a crowded room at the MLA in 1976 (Bruffee 11). In this telling, the professional organization came out of the discourse of a new literacy crisis, new calls for standards and assessment, an administrative problem and solution, rather than out of the rhetoric-composition research and theory that was distinguishing the new Composition. Thus the national organization for WPAs itself came into existence within the discursive set of "old composition," even though the WPA position as a journeyman appointment on the way to full literary critical work, a model in place since at least 1890, was no longer the only model available (Connors, "Rhetoric" 56). Such stasis in the midst of professionalization (construed as access to the tenure track, among other signs of professional status) was possible because the modern WPA was formulated as an administrator of already established practices, already delimited tasks, even as he or she participated in the knowledge production of the growing field.

In the early modern period, the naming of a writing program director often signified a conservative move to contain innovation, as we see in two program histories. In recounting the history of the University of Michigan's English Composition Board's formation, Patricia Stock places herself among those who were "charged with translating the abstract concept of literacy into specific programs and practices" (85). The ECB, formed in 1978, was one of the first composition programs consciously established as a program; it had no director and existed as a separate entity outside the English department. Reading through Sharon Quiroz's history, it is possible to see its demise as a program and the return of its courses to the department, where it has been placed "under the administration of the Director of Writing [. . .] effectively ending it" (81). The end of Charles Moran's story is similar: at Amherst, when the English department suffered a significant drop in enrollment, it took over the formerly separate composition unit, naming Moran director of the writing program. In a 1980 article by Harry Crosby, we can again see this use of the position to signal the containment of a program that threatened traditional values. Writing about Boston's remedial rhetoric program, he states that the program was organized, administered, and taught by two full professors, two associate professors, and one instructor. Finding the work too demanding, they decided to "help lessen the teaching load by slicing off part of the writing problem. We have employed a writing specialist to work out a program to help especially needy students in grammar, spelling, and punctuation" (86). So we have the modern, professional WPA ensconced in the traditional administrative practices in writing programs whose precedents have been determined and validated by a discourse that is itself a revival of nineteenth-century conservative educational values.

The Cultural Work of the WPA

> [S]o few root metaphors for composition studies have changed in the light of recent theories and research. The discrepancy between new intellectual history, theory, and research in composition and the continuing corrective practices of generations of its professionals has much to do with our failure to work through the symbolic social and political functions of composition courses that these practices still serve. [. . .]
>
> This resistance to cultural work accounts for other resistances in our collective will to renovate our field. [. . .] We still regulate, supervise, place, and exempt composition courses and their students, largely without acknowledging the political connotations of this language. [. . .]
>
> —*Susan Miller*

Miller's words accurately indict writing program administration as historically unable to grapple with political cultural realities. The professionalized WPA has been unable to eradicate the reductive and atheoretical set of practices from which the WPA position developed without erasing itself in the process. The original administrative discourse created an illusory apolitical space whose effect has been the WPA's historical resistance to the political and so to deep examination of the cultural work writing programs perform. WPA discourse began and continues in its mainstream use to operate as (ostensibly) apolitical in a "zone of nowhere-ness" (Bahri), creating a bias against self-critique. In the professional period, such a bias has perhaps been necessary, enmeshed as WPAs have been in fighting for more than contingent status for their positions and work. As Miller argues, "[t]he [modern] director is the strong voice of tradition, but also of hegemonic re-form, who acts and is acted on in ways that help us define what it now commonly means to learn to write" (*Textual Carnivals* 160). We can review a particular administrative phenomenon to see the material consequences that apolitical/uncritical WPA practices enable. The relationship of the professionalizing WPA and the rise and conditions of basic writing programs offers an interesting example of both the genre function of the writing program (see Gunner, "Ideology") and a powerful instance of how increased interest in professionalization helped push language-related political issues off the WPA agenda.

Formal writing programs and basic writing programs proliferated, often in tandem or parallel, in the early 1970s. From then, the conversation on the curriculum of the writing program grew in intensity. This conversation thread centered on the belief that a literacy crisis existed within the traditional discipline of English. The internal sense of crisis then expanded exponentially as concurrent social forces led to greater access to higher education for nontraditional students, expressed ultimately in the form of open admissions in the early 1970s and the literacy crisis later enshrined in the famous *Newsweek* article, "Why Johnny Can't Write," in 1975. With open admissions, "placement" and other sorts of testing became a focus of attention as a means of managing the new administrative deluge created by "under-prepared" students. As a result, an essential aspect of WPA work came into professionally threatening association with lesser "remedial" students (a situation finessed in the representation of such students by Harry Crosby, a WPA Executive Committee member: "The [remedial] rhetoric program at Boston University can best be understood if examined as part of what has been called 'a successful human reclamation project'"(77).

Struggling for professional status, WPAs and writing programs sought normalization by off-loading remedial programs (we "slic[ed] off part of the writing problem [. . .] to help especially needy students") and separating student populations (in effect by class and race), with the result that writing programs clearly became the mainstream field and basic writing the "other." As basic writing theorist Mary Soliday argues, "the needs of students changed less than the opportunity of the faculty during these expansive years [1960-1970] to redefine their goals within an institution" (54). In the same way, the later division of writing programs and basic writing programs during the expansive years of writing programs was likely not an innocent phenomenon resulting from a process of disinterested disciplinary division and classification or improved models of remediation. The separation of WPA work and basic writing was a social and professional act. Basic writing programs were relegated to locations outside the English department: in "academic foundations" programs, tutorial centers, or separate developmental education programs, departments, or colleges (like the University of Minnesota's General College or Boston University's similarly named entity)—perceived "shadow" schools before entrance to the real thing.

Although basic writing programs typically are centers of intensive administrative activity, typically they function without a WPA. There is no clear correlative in basic writing programs to the main writing program's leadership structure—no "Basic Writing WPA," and even today we do not have books on basic writing administration. Among WPA literature, including books and journal articles, there is very little discussion of basic writing; it might be fair to say that the two fields are, at most, tangentially connected, even where basic writing is associated with the larger writing program. With the excision of basic writing, and given a continuing drive for professionalization, the WPA restricted its politics to the internal politics of the profession and moved away from the very public political issues represented by, and now tidily housed in (to use David Bartholomae's image), basic writing. Writing program administrative discourse legitimated such a move, all the while suppressing the questions that the professional discourse of rhetoric-composition research and theory was increasingly foregrounding.

A later instance of this realignment with the "normal" can be seen in the history of the mainstreaming debate, which began at the national Conference on Basic Writing in 1992, where Bartholomae and Peter Dow Adams spoke against the marginalizing effects of basic writing courses and questioned their academic value. Their papers later appeared in the *Journal of Basic Writing*. Rhonda Grego and Nancy Thompson developed a mainstreaming project at the University of South Carolina called the Writing Studio, and the results were published in the *WPA: Writing Program Administration*. They then expanded the discussion, theorizing their work further; this version appeared in *CCC*. This publication history is telling. On the one hand, it can be read as a tale of professional status; *CCC* is the more prestigious location. But of the three discussions of mainstreaming and their publication sites, one is actively political—the *JBW* piece; one is theoretical and political—the *CCC* piece; and one is primarily an administrative description—the *WPA* piece. The *CCC* version of the earlier *WPA* piece takes up Bartholomae's argument that professionalization is a conservative stance, one designed to produce a field that supplies a product to a student-client base that is constructed as/ constituted by needing it. But certain political issues are absent, sliced off, within the *WPA* discourse.

We can further see this amputative move in some foundational taxonomies of WPA work. The Portland Resolution, the WPA's "Guidelines for WPA Positions," sets up two primary categories to map the position: preparation and responsibilities. Preparation is divided into two subcategories: expected knowledge and supplemental preparation. The first includes knowledge of teaching, composition theory and research, professional organizations, and publication; the second—supplemental preparation—begins with a list of seven "business" areas and then notes five "education" areas, with developmental or basic writing mentioned last. The second major category, responsibilities, has eight areas, beginning with scholarship of administration and proceeding through faculty and program development, assessment, registration and scheduling, office management, counseling and advising, and finally articulation, where among the seven items the third one is "coordinating with remedial/developmental programs." "Remedial" and "developmental," especially used in 1992, are outdated terminology, for "basic writing" had much earlier supplanted these derogatory labels. We can see the effort to locate "remedial" writing in a separate place and space, to keep it apart from the writing program, off its agenda, to "coordinate" it, as in the early WPA discourse. If remedial writing is a field associated with race, class, and ethnic issues, it becomes the deviant formation, and, through disassociation, writing programs assume the label of normalcy. We can see this taxonomy repeated in the WPA's "Guidelines for Self-Study to Precede a WPA Evaluation." Again a professionalizing discourse elides social content; again, a single and marginalized reference to basic writing appears, in what is an eleven-page document.

As a WPA, I routinely confront in my daily work the problem created by this conservative discursive heritage re-inscribed within the discourse of professional status. Most of my colleagues assume that writing program administration (even when conceived as tenurable activity) is a set of administrative practices, "old composition," and so can only see my efforts at curricular change—questions about the connection between curriculum and student diversity in particular—as outside the proper business of WPA work. They see my appropriate agenda as attending to hiring, grade disputes, and so on, and these are seen as conflict-free, apolitical activities. Much of the professional discourse I turn to for support is itself apolitical, suppressing social issues of language and power. The WPA itself has no clear social agenda, and so the prevailing construct and practices of the WPA are inevitably and primarily conservative. Topics such as race are absent as substantive issues from WPA work and institutional structures and professional taxonomies. Despite the many "how-to" articles and chapters in the WPA literature, we get few pieces on topics such as how to address multicultural student populations; how to train faculty and TAs in cultural and linguistic diversity; how to consider ethnic and racial difference in assessment practices; how to handle charges of racism in the classroom; how normative whiteness affects writing program design and functioning; what the role of instructor race might be in classroom dynamics. Such issues get redirected or refined as apolitical correctness. Why are certain social issues absent from WPA discourse? Why is it difficult to find these social issues in WPA self-representation, and difficult to raise them in WPA venues? Because our administrative discursive heritage militates against such work, and our much-sought-after professionalization could be threatened by cultural critique of administrative values.

A current sense of this threat is evident in the anxious discourse on the value of WPA courses in graduate composition programs. In a WPA listserv exchange on this subject, a WPA wrote,

> I'm going to sound like a dinosaur here [. . .] . But I am uneasy about the notion of a course devoted to [WPA professional development] issues being included in a PhD curriculum—a curriculum designed to build a candidate's expertise in the theory, research, and practice of rhetoric, composition, linguistics, literacy, and education.

This is not a lone voice but a commonly sounded concern in a continuing, polarizing discussion over the place of WPA issues in the graduate rhetoric-composition curriculum. The unease among those favoring exclusion of such study seems to come from a sense that WPA work is not scholarly; even in its professionalized form, it is separate from research and theory because it is essentially allied with its historical administrative construction.

Reconstruction as Critical Task

> [W]e shall have to study historical records—textbooks, original papers, records of meetings and private conversations, letters, and the like. [. . .]
>
> It is to be admitted that these records do not, by themselves, produce a *unique* solution to our problems. But who has ever assumed that they do? Historical records do not produce a unique solution for historical problems, either, and yet nobody suggests that they be neglected. There is no doubt that the records are *necessary* for a logical study [. . .] . The question is how they should be *used*.
>
> —*Paul Feyerabend*

Knowledge of WPA history is a means to institutional critique, a method of understanding the ways in which writing program administrators and writing programs have historically been implicated in social structures that divide, direct, give access, deny access, replicate inequities, and use language in ways that construct ideologies which have material consequences. Scholars such as James Berlin, Sharon Crowley, Anne Ruggles Gere, Susan Miller, James Slevin, and John Trimbur have helped formulate such issues for the WPA as well as the field of rhetoric-composition as a whole, providing a much-needed set of critical questions forming a means of inquiry into our historical practices and modes of self-representation. Yet many of the proliferating taxonomies of the field in the form of books on WPA work continue to privilege administrative, institutional, and professional politics. The early promise of Janangelo and Hansen's *Resituating Writing: Constructing and Administering Writing Programs* is only recently being picked up in texts such as Rose and Weiser's WPA collections, which help historicize and theorize writing program practices.

Because, as L'Eplattenier argues, "simply having a history creates legitimacy for contemporary work" (136), the emerging historicizing trend is crucial, as is continually contextualizing our history. Hopefully, the narratives that result will be cautious about becoming human reclamation projects which uncritically serve professionalization, and questions of methodology in reconstructing our histories will not be the only intellectual and material challenge we face. Attending to the politics of the historical project might well be a fruitful next step.

Works Cited

Adams, Peter Dow. "Basic Writing Reconsidered." *Journal of Basic Writing* 12.1 (1993): 22-36.

Bahri, Deepika. "Terms of Engagement: Postcolonialism, Transnationalism, and Composition Studies." *JAC: A Journal of Composition Theory* 18 (1998): 29-44.

Bartholomae, David. "The Tidy House: Basic Writing in the American Curriculum." *Journal of Basic Writing* 12.1 (1993): 4-21.

Berlin, James A. *Rhetoric and Reality: Writing Instruction in American Colleges, 1900-1985.* Carbondale: Southern Illinois UP, 1987.

—. *Writing Instruction in Nineteenth-Century American Colleges.* Carbondale: Southern Illinois UP, 1984.

Brereton, John C., ed. *The Origins of Composition Studies in the American College, 1875-1925.* Pittsburgh: U of Pittsburgh P, 1995.

Bruffee, Ken. "Editorial." *WPA: Writing Program Administration* 7.1/2 (1983): 11-12.

Connolly, Paul, and Teresa Vilardi. *New Methods in College Writing Programs.* New York: MLA, 1986.

Connors, Robert J. "Rhetoric in the Modern University: The Creation of an Underclass." *The Politics of Writing Instruction: Postsecondary.* Ed. Richard Bullock and John Trimbur. Portsmouth, NH: Boynton/Cook Heinemann, 1991. 55-84.

—. "Writing the History of Our Discipline." *An Introduction to Composition Studies.* Ed. Erika Lindemann and Gary Tate. New York: Oxford, 1991. 49-71.

Crosby, Harry. "The Rhetoric Program at Boston University's College of Basic Studies." *Basic Writing.* Ed. Lawrence N. Kasden and Daniel R. Hoeber. Urbana, IL: NCTE, 1980. 74-87.

Crowley, Sharon. *Composition in the University.* Pittsburgh: U of Pittsburgh P, 1998.

Feyerabend, Paul. *Against Method.* 3rd edition. New York: Verso, 1993.

Gere, Anne Ruggles. "The Long Revolution in Composition." *Composition in the Twenty-First Century: Crisis and Change.* Ed. Lynn Z. Bloom, Donald A. Daiker, and Edward M. White. Carbondale: Southern Illinois UP, 1996. 119-32.

Grego, Rhonda C., and Nancy S. Thompson. "The Writing Studio Program: Reconfiguring Basic Writing/Freshman Composition." *WPA: Writing Program Administration* 19.1/2 (1995): 66-79.

Gunner, Jeanne. "Decentering the WPA." *WPA: Writing Program Administration* 18.1/2 (1994): 8-15.

—. "Ideology, Theory, and the Genre of Writing Programs." *The Writing Program Administrator as Theorist.* Ed. Shirley K Rose and Irwin Weiser. Portsmouth, NH: Heinemann, 2002. 7-18.

Janangelo, Joseph. "Theorizing Difference and Negotiating Differends: (Un)naming Writing Programs' Many Complexities and Strengths." Ed. Joseph Janangelo and Kristine Hansen. *Resituating Writing: Constructing and Administering Writing Programs.* Portsmouth, NH: Boynton/Cook Heinemann, 1995. 3-22.

Janangelo, Joseph, and Kristine Hansen. *Resituating Writing: Constructing and Administering Writing Programs.* Portsmouth, NH: Boynton/Cook Heinemann, 1995.

Jolliffe, David. "Re: This Just In: Missouri Western job ad." WPA Listserv wpa-l@asuvm.inre.asu.edu 18 December 1998. Accessed 18 December 1998.

L'Eplattenier, Barbara. "Finding Ourselves in the Past: An Argument for Historical Work on WPAs." *The Writing Program Administrator as Researcher.* Ed. Shirley K Rose and Irwin Weiser. Portsmouth, NH: Heinemann, 1999. 131-40.

Miller, Susan. "Composition as a Cultural Artifact: Rethinking History as Theory." *Writing Theory and Critical Theory.* Ed. John Clifford and John Schilb. New York: MLA, 1994. 19-32.

—. *Textual Carnivals: The Politics of Composition.* Carbondale: Southern Illinois UP, 1991.

Moran, Charles. "A Life in the Profession." *An Introduction to Composition Studies.* Ed. Erika Lindemann and Gary Tate. New York: Oxford UP, 1991. 160-82.

North, Stephen M. *The Making of Knowledge in Composition.* Portsmouth, NH: Boynton/Cook Heinemann, 1987.

"The Portland Resolution: Guidelines for Writing Program Administrator Positions." *WPA: Writing Program Administration* 16.1/2 (1992): 88-94.

Quiroz, Sharon. "Collaborating at the ECB: A Reflection." *WPA: Writing Program Administration* 21.2/3 (1998): 81-91.

Rose, Shirley K, and Irwin Weiser, eds. *The Writing Program Administrator as Researcher: Inquiry in Action and Reflection*. Portsmouth: Heinneman, 1999.

Rose, Shirley K, and Irwin Weiser, eds. *The Writing Program Administrator as Theorist: Making Knowledge Work*. Portsmouth: Heinemann, 2002.

Sheils, Merrill. "Why Johnny Can't Write." *Newsweek*. 8 December 1975. 58-63.

Slevin, James. "Depoliticizing and Politicizing Composition Studies." *The Politics of Writing Instruction: Postsecondary*. Ed. Richard Bullock and John Trimbur. Portsmouth: Heinemann, 1991. 1-21.

Soliday, Mary. *The Politics of Remediation: Institutional and Student Needs in Higher Education*. Pittsburgh: U of Pittsburgh P, 2002.

Stock, Patricia L. "A Comprehensive Literacy Program: The English Composition Program." *Forum: Essays on Theory and Practice in the Teaching of Writing*. Ed. Patricia L. Stock. Upper Montclair, NJ: Boynton/Cook, 1983. 85-90.

Trimbur, John. "Writing Instruction and the Politics of Professionalization." *Composition in the Twenty-First Century: Crisis and Change*. Ed. Lynn Z. Bloom, Donald A. Daiker, and Edward M. White. Carbondale: Southern Illinois UP, 1996. 133-45.

Contributing Authors

Suzanne Bordelon is assistant professor in the Department of Rhetoric and Writing Studies at San Diego State University, where she teaches undergraduate and graduate courses in rhetoric and coordinates the department's upper division writing program. She has published in the *Journal of Teaching Writing, Nineteenth-Century Prose,* and *Peitho.* Her work also has been anthologized in *The Changing Tradition: Women in the History of Rhetoric.* Her article is part of a larger project focusing on the work of Gertrude Buck (1871-1922), a teacher and scholar at Vassar College during the Progressive Era.

Deany M. Cheramie is assistant professor of English at Xavier University of Louisiana. She currently directs the composition program and instructs courses in freshman composition and linguistics. She also instructs graduate courses for the division of education in the teaching of writing both for writing across the curriculum and K-12. She has published on the teaching of writing at Historically Black Colleges and Universities and Cajun English and the effects of vernacular on student writing.

Patricia A. Dunn is associate professor of English at Illinois State University, where she teaches graduate and undergraduate courses in composition, writing, and rhetoric. Her publications include two books, the most recent of which is *Talking, Sketching, Moving: Multiple Literacies in the Teaching of Writing* (Boynton/Cook, 2001), and essays in *Rhetoric Review, College Composition and Communication,* and *English Journal.* She is currently a visiting faculty member in the English Department at Stony Brook University, SUNY.

Lynée Lewis Gaillet is associate professor of English at Georgia State University, where she serves as director of lower division studies and teaches a wide range of composition/rhetoric courses. She is the editor of *Scottish Rhetoric and Its Influences* and author of numerous articles and book chapters examining the history of modern writing practices and administration. Her work has appeared in journals such as *Rhetoric Review, Rhetoric Society Quarterly, WPA: Writing Program Administration, Journal of Advanced Composition, Journal of Basic Writing,* and *Composition Studies.*

D'Ann George taught and directed the writing center at Essex Community College and Bridgewater State College. She currently works as a freelance journalist in North Carolina. Her work has been published in the *Writing Lab Newsletter.*

Jeanne Gunner is assistant provost for general education and professor of English and Comparative Literature at Chapman University. Many of her published articles and chapters treat WPA politics and ideology. She is also editor of *College English.*

Amy Heckathorn is assistant professor of Rhetoric and Composition at California State University, Sacramento where she teaches undergraduate and graduate courses on writing, rhetoric, and the teaching of writing. She is currently the Writing Program Administrator.

John Heyda is associate professor of English at Miami University Middletown in Middletown, Ohio, where he teaches composition and film studies courses and serves as coordinator of English. He has published articles in *College Composition and Communication, The Journal of Basic Writing, The Writing Instructor,* and elsewhere. He served as director of composition at Miami University's main campus in Oxford, Ohio, from 1993 to 1995.

Barbara L'Eplattenier is assistant professor in the Department of Rhetoric and Writing at the University of Arkansas—Little Rock, where she teaches in the professional writing track. Her historical research focuses on the rhetoric of Progressive Era women. She has published in *IEEE Transactions on Professional Communication* and *The Writing Program Administrator as Researcher: Inquiry in Action and Reflection.*

Kenneth Lindblom is associate professor of English at Illinois State University, where he teaches graduate and undergraduate courses in rhetoric and composition and co-founded a graduate certificate in the teaching of writing in high school and middle school. He has published essays in *Rhetoric Review, English Journal, Journal of Pragmatics,* and other forums. He is currently a visiting faculty member in the English Department at Stony Brook University, SUNY.

Lisa Mastrangelo is assistant professor of English and coordinator of Women's Studies at the College of St. Elizabeth, where she teaches courses in composition, rhetoric, creative nonfiction, and playwriting. Her research interests include nineteenth-century writing instruction and administration at women's colleges. Her work in this area has been published in *Rhetoric Review*.

Randall Popken is professor of English and director of the writing program at Tarleton State University, where he teaches first-year writing and graduate courses in composition and in discourse theory. His publications have largely been in the areas of genre analysis and discourse acquisition.

Shirley K Rose is associate professor of English at Purdue University, where she recently served as assistant head of the English Department and currently is the director of composition. She mentors teaching assistants in the introductory writing program and teaches graduate courses in writing program administration. She has published essays in *College English, College Composition and Communication, WPA: Writing Program Administration, Journal of Teaching Writing, Rhetoric Review*, and *Journal of Language* and *Learning Across the Disciplines*. With Irwin Weiser, she has edited two collections on the intellectual work of writing program administration: *The WPA as Researcher* and *The WPA as Theorist* (Heinemann).

Jill Terry Rudy is associate professor of English at Brigham Young University. Her dissertation research focused on Stith Thompson and intersections of composition administration and folklore scholarship in his career; she has an article on these issues forthcoming in *College English*. Other research and teaching interests include history of English studies, personal narrative, family folklore, and foodways studies.

Edward M. White is emeritus professor of English at California State University, San Bernardino, and a senior lecturer at the University of Arizona. He is the author of more than fifty articles and book chapters on literature and the teaching of writing, and has written or edited nine books, including the influential *Developing Successful College Writing Programs* and *Teaching and Assessing Writing*.

Acknowledgments and Illustration Credits

Grateful acknowledgment is made to the following for permission to use the following photographs and illustrations:

Illinois State University Archives, Milner Library (Rose Colby)

Special Collections, Vassar College Libraries. Title: Laura J. Wylie and Gertrude Buck. Photo Credit: unknown. Date: unknown (Gertrude Buck and Laura J. Wylie).

University Archives, Spencer Research Library, University of Kansas (Edwin Hopkins).

Bryn Mawr College Library (Regina Crandall).

The Mount Holyoke College Archives and Special Collections (Clara Frances Stevens).

Special Collections, Vassar College Libraries. Title: Portrait of young Laura J. Wylie. Photo Credit: E. L. Baker, Poughkeepsie, NY. Date: 28 December 1900. (Laura J. Wylie).

Grateful acknowledgment is offered to the following for permission to quote from the collections and interviews:

Kenneth Bruffee, Interview (in "Moving Toward a Group Identity: WPA Professionalization from the 1940s to the 1970s" by Amy Heckathorn).

Department English, Purdue University, West Lafayette, IN (in "Representing the Intellectual Work of Writing Program Administration: Professional Narratives of George Wykoff at Purdue 1933-1967" by Shirley K Rose).

Erika Lindemann, Interview (in "Moving Toward a Group Identity: WPA Professionalization from the 1940s to the 1970s" by Amy Heckathorn).

Indiana University Archives, Bloomington, IN (Clark-Thompson interview in "Building a Career by Directing Composition: Harvard, Professionalism, and Stith Thompson at Indiana University" by Jill Terry Rudy).

Illinois State University Archives, Milner Library (in "Cooperative Writing 'Program' Administration at Illinois State Normal University: The Committee on English of 1904-05 and the Influence of Professor J. Rose Colby" by Kenneth Lindblom and Patricia A. Dunn).

Special Collections, Vassar College Libraries (in The "Advance" Toward Democratic Administration: Laura Johnson Wylie and Gertrude Buck of Vassar College" by Suzanne Bordelon).

University Archives, Spencer Research Library, University of Kansas Libraries (in "The WPA as Publishing Scholar: Edwin Hopkins and *The Labor and Cost of the Teaching of English*" by Randall Popken).

Wellesley College Archives, Margaret Clapp Library, Department of English Composition collection, (in "'Is It the Pleasure of This Conference to Have Another?'": Women's Colleges Meeting and Talking about Writing in the Progressive Era" by Lisa Mastrangelo and Barbara L'Eplattenier)

Xavier University Archives and Special Collections, New Orleans (in "Sifting Through Fifty Years of Change: Writing Program Administration at an Historically Black University" by Deany M. Cheramie).

Index

B

Bain, Alexander 183-86
Baker, George Pierce 94
Berlin, James xviii, xxiv, 2, 6-8, 20, 76-77, 86, 126, 141, 153-55, 161, 163, 186, 257-58, 260, 263, 265-66, 275-76
Bizzell, Patricia 176, 186
Blair, Hugh 176
Bonner, Thomas 158, 160, 162-63
Bouise, Oscar 152, 156
Boylston Chair of Rhetoric 74
Brereton, John xvii-xxiv, xxvi, 18, 22, 62, 65, 75, 86, 134, 141, 186, 263, 265, 276
Bruffee, Kenneth 191, 203, 205, 207-08, 210, 212, 214, 269, 276
Bryn Mawr College 9, 23-36, 110, 113-14, 120, 139
Buchanan, Robert 171
Buck, Gertrude xviii, xxi-xxvi, 10, 91-95, 100, 102-105, 108-113, 121-123, 128, 138, 141, 266, 279; democratic approach to administration, 104; English Department at Vassar, 95, 103; Intercollege Conference on English Composition, 131; organicism, 95, 103; sexual orientation, 110; suffrage movement, 94; University of Michigan, 123

Buckley, Linda Ferreira 169, 171, 187

C

Campbell, George 176
Campbell, JoAnn xxiii, xxiv, 94, 105
Campbell, Oscar 249-51, 257, 260
Child, Francis James xxiii, 74, 84, 86
Colby, June Rose xxi, 37, 38, 41-43, 49-61, 64-66, 70; pedagogy, 42, 55, 61; views on writing, 41, 49, 51-53; workload, 56-58
College Composition and Communication 193, 198, 205, 207, 224-26, 238, 258, 273
College English 193, 198, 204, 205, 224, 226, 227, 228, 245
Composition Courses; laboratory model/course, 245, 247, 251, 254; lack of uniformity; Industrial Strength, 245; load, 11, 149, 243-44, 247, 253; pay, 18, 152, 196, 243; process orientation/process-oriented instruction, 242-43; surveys on load, 258; use of themes, 129
Conference on College Composition and Communication 199, 201, 208, 214-215, 217-218,

224-26, 232, 238, 268
Connolly, James,152-153, 156
Connors, Robert, xxiii, xxv, 5, 6, 21, 42, 65, 76, 86, 92, 94, 106, 112, 117, 119, 123, 142, 245, 247, 251-52, 254-56, 260, 263-66, 269, 276
Corbett, Edward P. J. xiii, xix, xx, xxv, 19, 21, 131, 138, 142, 185-86, 216
Council of Writing Program Administrators vii, 191, 208-09, 212, 244, 269
Crandall, Regina xxi, 23, 25-35; demotion, 29; director of Essay Department, 23, 34; pay issues, 26-27, 32; views on composition and literature, 28, 33

D

Davie, George 169, 171-72, 176, 187
Dewey, John 55, 64, 94, 95, 139, 142; *Experience and Education*, 130; influence on Colby, 42; influence on Buck, 94; on Democracy, 95
Dickson, Marcia 174-75, 186-87

E

Entrance Examinations 125

F

Folklore Studies 79, 81
Freshman English News,193, 205, 212, 214

G

Glenn, Cheryl 91, 109-110, 112
Greenbaum, Leonard 245-46, 249, 257, 261
Greenough, Chester N. 31, 75, 76-77

H

Hart, Sophie Chantal 106, 113, 121-23, 134-35, 138; Intercollege Conference on English Composition, 134; student-teacher ratio, 106
Harvard University xxiii, 5, 23-24, 29, 31, 37, 40, 50, 59, 62-63, 73-78, 84, 86-87, 106, 107, 125-126, 129, 139, 143, 182-85, 217, 251-52, 266
Herzberg, Bruce 176, 186
Hesse, Douglas 173, 174, 187
Historically Black Colleges and Universities (HBCUs) 146-47, 155, 161, 163
Hopkins, Edwin xiv, xxi, 5-22, 84, 91, 246-50, 252, 260-61
Horner, Winifred Bryant 21, 169, 171, 185-87

I

Indiana University 71-72, 78-79, 81-83, 86-88

J

Jardine, George; and Alexander Bain, 183; champion of Scottish Education, 172, 176-77; critique of educational systems, 175, 182; moral philosophy, 180; *Outlines of Philosophical Education*, 170, 173, 175-84; the role of composition, 181-82
Jordan, Mary Augusta xxiii, 98, 113, 121-23, 133-35, 138; Vassar from 1870-1880, 98
Journal of Basic Writing 187, 193, 272, 276, 280

K

Kittredge, George Lyman xxiii, 74
Kitzhaber, Albert xiii, 74, 87, 125,

Index   287

142, 186, 188, 197, 199, 213, 268

L

Lindemann, Erika 210, 213, 217, 276-77

M

MacCracken, Henry Noble 102, 105, 111-13, 140, 142-43; on Admissions, 120; on budget cuts, 105; on Laura Johnson Wylie, 102; on Laura Johnson Wylie and Gertrude Buck, 94; on training of Vassar writers, 107
McBay, Shirley 159, 164
McFarland, Betty 158-61, 164
Modern Language Association xxvi, 7, 17, 78, 164, 187, 200-01, 208, 212-14, 216-17, 269, 276-77; Job Information List 194, 201, 213-14
Morris, Elisabeth Woodbridge 93-94, 112, 114
Mount Holyoke College xxiii, xxv, xxvi, 114, 118-19, 121-22, 124-25, 127, 130, 132, 136-43

N

National Catholic Education Association 152

O

Ohmann, Richard, 86, 252-53, 261

P

Purdue University xv, 113, 142, 221-23, 225-26, 229, 231, 236, 238-39, 281

R

Ramsey, Otto 154
Reed, Amy 95, 104-05, 113, 124, 136, 143
Rice, Joseph 158-59, 164,
Royal Commission Reports 177
Russell, David, xxiii, xxvi, 22, 37-41, 47-50, 58, 60, 62, 63, 66, 129, 132-33, 143, 186, 188
Ryan, Mother M. Agatha 150, 152-55
Ryan, Stephen 153, 155-56, 163

S

Sanders, Edwin 159, 164
Savage, Howard 923, 29-35
Scott, Fred Newton xviii, xxi, xxiii, xxvi, 6, 19, 42, 94, 111-112, 114, 123, 139, 140, 186, 266; influence on Buck, 94; relationship to Colby, 42
Sisters of the Blessed Sacrament/ Corporation of the Sisters of the Blessed Sacrament 148, 150-53, 155-56, 161-64
Smith College 118, 120-22, 127-28, 133-34, 138, 140-41
Smith, Adam 176
Snell, Ada F.; departmentalization at Mount Holyoke, 98, 132
Southern Association of Colleges and Schools 157
Sr. M. Frances 150, 153
Sr. M. Helene 155
Sr. M. Josephina 155
Sr. Mary of Nazareth 153-55
St. Andrews University 171
Stevens, Clara Frances xxiii, 119, 121-23, 132-33, 138, 141

T

Taylor, Frederick 7, 22
Taylor, James Monroe 100-01
Taylor, Warner xviii, 265
textbook production 76-77, 137
Thompson, Stith; at Harvard, 73, 75; at Indiana University, 72,

78-79, 81-82; at University of Texas, 75, 77, 83
Tift, Rosa 159, 164
Title III Advanced Institutional Development Program (AIDP) 158, 160, 164

U

University of Glasgow 169-72, 174, 176-79, 183, 187-88
University of Michigan 41-42, 94, 139, 269
University of Texas 75, 77

V

Vassar College xxiv, 91-98, 100-02, 106-09, 111-15, 118, 119-24, 126-28, 136, 139-143, 279
Veysey, Lawrence 255, 261

W

Weiner, Harvey 160, 165
Wellesley College 106, 113, 118-22, 126-28, 131, 133-36, 139-43, 252
WPA: A Newsletter for Writing Program Administrators 206, 212
WPA: Writing Program Administration xiii, 110, 112, 193, 206, 212, 239, 272, 276-77
Writing Program Administration; administrative history of hierarchy, 267; and Basic Writing, 272; and New Composition, 264; and race, 274; History, provisional nature of, 266
Writing Program Administrators; national identity, 269; professional identity, 269; self/individual identification, xviii, 222
Wykoff, George 196, 199, 214, 221-39; and Conference on College Composition and Communication, 224, 232, 238; and National Council of English Teachers, 224, 226, 228, 236; *c.v.*, 223, 225-26, 228-32; Chair of English I, 223, 231; Personnel Record, 223, 228, 233, 235-37; Writing Program Administrator, 223
Wylie, Laura Johnson 91-105, 107-11, 113-15, 140; Bryn Mawr Summer School for Women Workers in Industry, 93, 110, 113-14; democratic Approach to Administration, 95, 99, 108; English Department at Vassar, 93, 102, 107; organicism, 95; presentation to the Vassar Alumnae Association, 95, 111; sexual orientation, 94, 94, 110-111; *Studies in the Evolution of English Criticism*, 93; suffrage movement, 93; Vassar College Chapter of the Settlement Association, 93; Yale, 93

X

Xavier University of Louisiana 145-52, 154-57, 161-65

www.ingramcontent.com/pod-product-compliance
Lightning Source LLC
Chambersburg PA
CBHW021755230426
43669CB00006B/80